# Collaborative
## *practitioners*
# Collaborative
## *schools*

MARLEEN C. PUGACH
*University of Wisconsin, Milwaukee*

LAWRENCE J. JOHNSON
*University of Cincinnati*

Foreword by
STEPHEN LILLY
*California State University, San Marcos*

 **LOVE PUBLISHING COMPANY®**
Denver, Colorado 80222

To our spouses,
Bill Rickards and Sue Johnson,
and to our children,
Lev and Anna Rickards and
Ian and Tara Johnson,
who, each in their own way,
manages to understand that our
commitment to professional collaboration
grows out of a prior commitment
to our rich lives among family
and friends—collaborative communities
if ever they existed.

*MCP*
*LJJ*

Library of Congress Catalog Card Number 94-75177

Copyright © 1995 Love Publishing Company
Printed in the U.S.A.
ISBN 0-89108-234-4

# CONTENTS

**Foreword    vii**
**Preface    xi**


**PART ONE    RECONCEPTUALIZING COLLABORATION    1**

**1    Collaboration and the Complex Work of Teaching    3**

Collaboration in Contemporary
   Educational Practice    6
The Complexities of Collaboration    11
Participating in a Collaborative School    16
A Worthy Challenge    23
Remember...    24
Activities    25


**2    A New Framework for Thinking About Collaboration    27**

An Historical Perspective on
   Professional Collaboration    30
Defining a Multidimensional
   Framework for Collaboration    37
Putting Multidimensional
   Collaboration to Work    43
Remember . . .    43
Activities    44

PART TWO COMMUNICATION: THE
CORNERSTONE OF COLLABORATION **45**

**3** The Foundation for
Good Communication **47**

Communication Cycles  50
Verbal Communication  56
Nonverbal Communication  58
Congruent and Incongruent Messages  60
Communication for Collaboration  62
Remember...  62
Activities  62

**4** Skills to Facilitate
Effective Communication **65**

Offering Support  68
General Openings  70
Reflection  71
Stating the Implied  75
Clarification  76
Silence  79
Placing Events in Context  81
Summarization  82
Practice  83
Remember...  84
Activities  85

**5** Barriers to Effective
Communication **87**

Advice  90
False Reassurances  92
Misdirected Questions  95
Wandering Interaction  96
Interruptions  98
Cliches  99
Minimizing Feelings  101
Quick Fixes  102
Avoiding These Barriers  104
Remember...  104
Activities  105

**6  Working With and
Supporting Groups**  **107**

Types of Groups   110
Group Functioning   112
Responsibilities of Group Members   116
Potential Sources of Group·Conflict   119
Conflict Resolution   123
Working Effectively in Groups   127
Remember...   128
Activities   128

**PART THREE  COLLABORATION IN PRACTICE**  **131**

**7  Collaboration as Specific
Problem Solving**  **133**

Differentiating Classroom-Specific
and Schoolwide Collaborative
Problem Solving   136
The Relationship Between
Classroom-Specific and Schoolwide
Collaborative Problem Solving   141
General Features of Collaborative
Problem Solving   143
General Steps for Problem Solving   144
Structures to Support Classroom-Specific
Collaborative Problem Solving   148
Structures to Support
Schoolwide Collaborative
Problem Solving   158
Interactions Between Schoolwide and
Classroom-Specific Collaboration   163
Achieving a Balance Between
Schoolwide and Classroom-Specific
Problem Solving   167
Remember...   168
Activities   169

**8  Team Teaching as Collaboration**  **171**

Why Team?   175
Principles of Team Teaching   179

Challenges for Teachers Who Team   186
Typical Planning Considerations   189
Setting Up Teams   190
Power of Team Teaching as
   Collaboration   193
Remember...   194
Activities   195

**9** **School-University Collaboration**   **197**

School-University Collaboration
   as a Reform Strategy   199
School-University Collaboration and the
   Continuum of Teacher Development   202
A Day in the Life of a Professional
   Development School   203
The Range of Collaboration in
   School-University Partnerships   207
School-University Collaboration and
   Ongoing Inquiry   209
Guidelines for School-University
   Collaboration   218
Revisiting Collaboration in
   School-University Partnerships   220
Remember...   220
Activities   221

**10** **School-Family Collaboration**   **223**

The Family Defined   226
Family Systems   227
Barriers to Family Participation
   in Schools   236
Developing Family-Oriented Teachers   242
Family Conferences   243
Practical Strategies for
   Communicating with Families   247
Working with Families   249
Remember...   250
Activities   251

**References   253**
**Index   259**

# FOREWORD

*M. Stephen Lilly, Dean, College of Education*
*California State University, San Marcos*

In writing this introduction to a very important new book which will help to redefine relationships between educators and special educators, I have come to the realization (both exciting and depressing) that my first publication in special education hit the presses 24 years ago. In that article, "Special Education: A Teapot in a Tempest," I argued that the "special education paradigm" focused inappropriately on the child as the primary source of problems in teaching and learning, and that special education had evolved into a mechanism for "student sorting" which blames the student for poor learning outcomes and creates self-fulfilling prophecies of limited educational achievement. A year later, in "A Training Based Model for Special Education," I argued further that a system based on student referral, assessment, and labeling, followed by removal of students from mainstream instruction, does not serve students well and is a long-term recipe for educational disaster. While I did not know it at the time, I was arguing in the latter article for schools to become the types of professional learning communities which Marleen Pugach and Larry Johnson want to help create through this book.

I share this historical perspective not to remind readers of the distant past, but to create a bit of a context for analyzing the present and understanding why this is such an important book. We have, indeed, come a long way in special education in the last 25 years, though I suspect that many do not understand or appreciate either the nature or the importance of the journey. I was fundamentally correct in my analysis of the problem in the "Training Based" article, but fundamentally wrong in the solution I suggested. My idea at the time was to stem the rising tide of "referrals" of students for special education testing by providing "consultation" services to classroom teachers, thus enabling them to become increasingly effective in teaching students with learning and behavior problems in their own classrooms.

My error was in assuming that the "problem" was in the regular classroom and curriculum, and the "solution" was in more widespread adoption of the superior paradigm, process, and procedures of special education. Only several years later did I conclude that the more fundamental problem was that the "special education paradigm" had in fact infiltrated all of education, and was the primary influence on teaching and learning in the schools. This was a problem because special education is based almost totally on the process of identifying student-based problems, labeling them, and adjusting instruction accordingly. In the simplest terms possible, the special education paradigm is based on the assumptions that all students cannot learn and that instruction must be parceled out differently to those students capable of effective learning and those who are disabled in the learning process. It is a model based on limitation rather than potential.

The special education paradigm remains largely unchanged in 1994; we still operate systems in which we receive referrals from classroom teachers, test children, name their problems using the outcomes of the tests, and provide truncated educational experiences based on our conclusion about *what's wrong with the student*. If the paradigm remains unchanged in special education, why did I say earlier that we've come a long way in the last 25 years? We've come a long way because this type of thinking about students, teachers, and the learning process is increasingly considered passé at best, and irresponsible at worst, by education leaders, policy makers, and the general education community. We have a lively and healthy education restructuring movement afoot in the United States which seeks to turn traditional paradigms out and replace them with new paradigms based on a belief that all students can learn to use their minds well. Special education has thus far contributed to this paradigm shift in a dubious manner, by providing the purest example of an education system designed to label and sort students, thus marginalizing significant numbers of children in our schools. In other words, we have exemplified the problem more than the solution.

Marleen Pugach and Larry Johnson offer in this book a means for special education to escape the two conceptual traps which place it in substantial peril in an era of school restructuring: (1) the assumption that sorting students and lowering expectations will lead to better education for students; and (2) the assumption that special educators have the answers for classroom teachers "if only they will listen." The authors present a different vision, a vision of a school as a powerful learning community not only for students, but for adults as well (including teachers, administrators, parents, and other school staff). They describe in detail how schools can be more effective professional learning communities, and their description is replete with examples of how teachers can contribute to systemic change in their own schools through effective collaboration and team-based problem solving. The message of this book is one of teacher empowerment, not for its own sake, but toward the end of ensuring successful school experiences for all students.

If you are destined to be, or currently are, a special educator or a classroom teacher, do not miss the "big picture" message of this book. The specific examples of restructuring at the school site which are shared by the authors are actually happening in schools across the country. They are happening as a part of the reformation of schooling, teaching, and learning in this country. These changes challenge the very basis upon which special education has been built in the United States.

What are some of the most important messages in this book? I would suggest the following. If you do not believe that all students can learn, you are incapable of being an effective educator in the 1990s. If you believe that students need to be protected from overly challenging learning experiences, you are incapable of being an effective educator in the 1990s. If you do not believe in the power of professional collaboration, you cannot be an effective educator in the 1990s. For readers who aspire to be special educators, if you do not believe that classroom teachers can teach all students effectively, you are incapable of being an effective special educator in the 1990s. If you believe that special education is special, you cannot be an effective special educator in the 1990s. If you want to be an effective classroom teacher *or* special educator, you must see the school as *your* learning community as well as that of your students, and commit yourself to a career characterized by continuous learning and professional development.

We have argued for decades in special education about issues such as testing, labeling, placement, educational segregation, continua of services, and efficacy of various modes of service delivery to students labeled exceptional. While these continue to be important issues, many educational leaders are baffled about why they are still the subject of contention. The *real* educational issues of this and the next decade relate to student success, standards setting, authentic assessment, teacher empowerment, meaningful parental involvement, peer collaboration, and the building of powerful professional learning communities at the school site. These issues are the subject of this book. If you grasp, own, and act upon the essential messages of the authors as presented in the ensuing pages, you will be an effective educator, which is an essential prerequisite to being an effective special educator.

# PREFACE

The concept of collaboration has taken hold in the field of education with unprecedented impact, and its influence has been felt across nearly every aspect of schooling. In administration it emerges as participatory forms of organizational management. Among classroom teachers it appears in activities such as mentoring, peer coaching, and team teaching, to name a few. In special education it is central to efforts toward inclusive education within general education, a practice predicated on strong relationships among special education and classroom teachers. The fundamental restructuring of the relationship between schools and colleges of education and public schools in the form of professional development schools is another instance of education professionals working more closely than ever before. Finally, the recent embracing of families as full partners in educational practice is a manifestation of collaboration. Typically, though, these efforts to understand and implement collaboration take place separately, diminishing their power to transform schools.

Our own work in collaboration began in the mid-1980s as the field of special education began to intensify its commitment to consultation between special education and general classroom teachers. We were interested in alternative forms of consultation based more on collaboration between classroom teachers as a means of fostering the integration of students with disabilities and less on the traditional consultative relationship between specialists and classroom teachers. Within the field of special education, acknowledging the role of the classroom teacher as a full and knowledgeable partner in the education of students with disabilities took quite a long time but is now generally accepted as an underlying assumption for collaboration to be successful.

This work soon extended to initiating the development of strong collaborative relationships between university faculty in special and general education as part of the larger goal of teacher education reform at the University of Wisconsin-Milwaukee and the University of Cincinnati. Finally it expanded to fostering collaboration between our own respective institutions of higher education and the public schools as part of the move toward urban professional development schools. Time and again we saw parallels in the dynamics of collaboration in these different settings.

In agreeing to write this text, we have tried to tie together these various threads and portray the similarities across collaboration as it occurs in all of its varying contexts in schools rather than to focus on collaboration between special and general education alone. We have attempted to consider these isolated collaborative efforts as part of a larger, integrated trend toward fostering the development of collaborative practitioners in collaborative schools and to go beyond the traditional conception of collaboration as classroom-based problem solving to a wider interpretation that represents the culture and general practice of schools.

The book is divided into three sections. In Part One (Chapters 1 and 2) we present a description of the shift to a collaborative paradigm in the schools and suggest a multidimensional framework that encompasses four basic collaborative functions: facilitative, supportive, informative, and prescriptive. We argue that collaboration is a way of being and not limited to isolated actions; it is a way of redefining how adults interact in schools.

Part Two (Chapters 3, 4, 5, and 6) includes the basic communication skills that form the foundation of any collaborative interaction. Chapter 3 provides a communication model and background information about communication. Chapters 4 and 5 elaborate on ways to facilitate or inhibit communication when engaging in a collaborative dialogue. Chapter 6 addresses group dynamics as it relates to collaboration.

In Part Three (Chapters 7, 8, 9, and 10) we describe how collaboration plays out in practice in four contexts: specific classroom and schoolwide problem solving, team teaching, school-university collaboration, and school-family collaboration. In all of the chapters we provide examples from practice to illustrate the points made within chapters. Each chapter also contains several reflective questions to aid you in relating concepts being discussed to your own situation.

We hope this format provides a reasonable theoretical lens through which to view collaboration, a sound understanding of the communication skills that must be integrated into professional practice for collaboration to work, and a clear picture of what collaboration looks like on a day-to-day basis in schools.

In addition to our own long-standing professional collaboration, over the past several years we both have had the good fortune of working with close colleagues and students who have taught us much about the value of the collaborative enterprise. These people include Caren Wesson, Suzanne Pasch, and Barbara Seidl of the University of Wisconsin-Milwaukee; and Cynthia Warger of Warger, Eavy and Associates. They also include Bob Yinger, Martha Hendricks-Lee, and Margaret LaMontagne at the University of Cincinnati, and Mary Beirne-Smith at the University of Alabama. We are indebted to Steve Lilly, whose early influence on our thinking led us to pursue the ideas we have tried to develop in this book. Finally, we would like to thank all the many students who have challenged us and shaped our thinking as we have joined with them in the process of learning.

In our own efforts at collaboration, we always have worked from the premise that when one is engaged in collaborative work with one's colleagues, there is plenty of opportunity for recognition to go around. This always has proven to be the case. Although at our own institutions of higher education, our collaborative work never has been perceived as an obstacle, it seems to us that, as a general practice, higher education still fails to value collaboration enough. We hope the trend toward collaboration in the schools will begin to have greater impact at the level of higher education as well.

Stan Love, our publisher, shook hands with us at nine o'clock on a dark morning in Anchorage, Alaska, a few years ago and waited patiently for us to complete our end of the bargain. More importantly, he encouraged us to pursue our ideas freely at a time when the field of special education still was uncertain about situating collaboration in a broad, schoolwide context. We also owe a large thanks to Elsie Preston, Selina Wilson, Saundra McCory, and Bonnie M. Kalla, who steadfastly worked with us in the preparation of the manuscript. We would like to acknowledge the contributions of Carolyn Davies, who teaches as part of a collaborative team in Shorewood, Wisconsin, and of the many other teachers from whom we have gained wisdom about building collaborative schools.

# PART ONE

# RECONCEPTUALIZING COLLABORATION

# 1

# COLLABORATION AND THE COMPLEX WORK OF TEACHING

**T**eaching is challenging work. This fact, in all its simplicity, is the reason why professional collaboration finally has come to be recognized and valued as such an important facet of the work adults do in schools. Traditionally, teaching has been thought of as an occupation that requires a lot of interaction with children and youth and very little with other adults. Actually, though, to hear someone say about a teacher, "She's great with the kids, but she has a hard time communicating with grown-ups," is fairly common. Being "good" with children and youth, of course, is one of the cornerstones of teaching. Limiting our conception of teaching to how well we interact with children and youth, however, means being content with a definition of teaching that stops at the classroom door. From this perspective, teaching means going it alone; each classroom is an independent entity with few ties to any other classroom or to the school as a whole. Without professional collaboration, whatever challenges we face as teachers, we face alone within the confines of our classroom's four walls.

In contrast, if we define teaching both as working well with children *and* interacting well with adults, we acknowledge the rich intellectual resource provided by all the adults in schools—teachers, specialists, principals, family members, to name a few—who form the basis of a community of adult learners who can support the complex work schools are expected to perform. With this expanded definition, we also acknowledge the power a school derives from being thought of as a whole community in which each adult who works there is responsible for educating the children and youth who attend and is interested not only in his or her own classroom but also in what goes on in the school at large. Most of all, we recognize that, to be a source of vibrant, intellectual stimulation for all children, no matter what their background, teachers themselves must work in stimulating, supportive, collegial environments. In these environments teachers have the potential to create the collective capacity for initiating and sustaining ongoing improvement in their professional practice so each child they serve receives the highest quality of education possible.

But teaching always has been hard work, so why, only now, does redefining the professional norms of teaching to include collaboration seem so essential? Why is collaboration receiving so much attention? Many developments in the reform-minded educational scene over the past 15 years have converged to encourage educators to rethink the role of adult-adult relationships in schools and to realize the value of professional collaboration and the need to establish it soundly as an expectation for teachers.

## ■ COLLABORATION IN CONTEMPORARY EDUCATIONAL PRACTICE

All of the developments described below are linked to the overarching, fundamental goal of improving the quality of education for students, but they contribute to this goal in different ways. And all of them depend in part on the success of collaboration among adults who work in schools. Let's consider five of these current practices in detail.

### CHANGES IN THE AUTHORITY STRUCTURE OF SCHOOLS

For as long as most of us can remember, schools have been run by principals under the direct guidance and influence of the district office. The reforms of the 1980s, however, introduced the concept of site-based management (SBM) of schools. Site-based management is based on the principle that schools are managed best by those who work at the site itself—the teachers, principal, specialist teachers, secretaries, custodians, and families. This represents a decentralization of authority. Working as a team, representatives of each of these groups are invested with decision-making authority for budgeting, hiring and firing, the instructional program, and school policies. In a site-based managed school, the decision to integrate instruction across subjects or to teach them separately, for example, is a school-based decision. The school is the unit of concern for all those who work in it. Decisions are made with the quality of the school's total educational program in mind. Collegial management of a school site does not mean that everyone works on every task but, instead, that everyone has a stake in every task contributing to the overall success of the educational program. Collaboration is essential to successful implementation of SBM. Without it, consensus on these fundamental decisions could not be reached easily.

## INCREASED TEACHER RESPONSIBILITY FOR THE PROFESSION

Although teaching is considered to be a profession, historically many things about being a teacher are not characteristic of how professionals do their work. For instance, teachers typically have not taken responsibility for evaluating the performance of their peers. Simply because each classroom has been considered an island of its own, teachers have not tended to talk to their peers about what they do, preferring instead, in some cases, to "lock their doors" and be free from external scrutiny. Collaboration implies that this kind of individual power is no longer acceptable, and that what goes on behind the classroom door is, in fact, the responsibility of every adult in the school. Another reason, then, why collaboration has become so valued is that one hallmark of professionalism is having teachers themselves take mutual responsibility for the quality of practice. The goal is to make the profession better as a whole, not just one's own practice of it.

In the last several decades teachers also have not had the authority for developing or interpreting curriculum themselves. Instead, as a rule they were expected to follow the teacher's manual and use the basal texts. Consistent with the principle of site-based management, teachers today are voicing more and more interest in making their own curriculum decisions—those that best fit the needs of the individual students in their building. Along with this kind of curricular responsibility comes the need for teachers to have high levels of curriculum knowledge in each of the subject areas to ensure that these decisions are made responsibly and are based on the most current knowledge.

One of the most important lessons learned from the reforms of the 1980s is that, for teaching to gain the professional respect it deserves, teachers themselves will have to be involved actively in professional activities and take responsibility for what happens to the profession. This shift to greater professionalism means that teachers will no longer stand by and receive directives from principals and district supervisors. It means, instead, that teachers and administrators work together, as colleagues, to make the best decisions for their school and for their profession. An example of this kind of collegial responsibility is the development of mentor teaching programs to support novice teachers in their first, inevitably difficult, year of teaching. Identifying mentors means that as members of a profession, teachers today are willing to take responsibility for supporting new teachers and helping them make the bridge from preservice to practicing teaching. Taking on this responsibility means exerting influence on the stability of the teaching profession as a whole.

Finally, teachers themselves can participate actively in studying their own teaching and sharing their inquiry with their colleagues. In this way, collaboration serves to support teachers as they generate an understanding of their own professional practice.

## GROWING DIVERSITY OF STUDENT POPULATION

As the social fabric of society has changed, children and youth bring more challenges to teachers than ever before. These changes characterize urban, suburban, and rural schools alike. Children from diverse backgrounds with diverse family structures, cultures, languages, customs, interests, and socioeconomic levels can be found in every classroom in America. Their levels of preparation for traditional school tasks vary greatly.

In this increasingly complex world of students, teachers undoubtedly will need support from other adults for a variety of reasons:

- from parents, families, and other teachers to understand the different ethnic and cultural backgrounds from which their students may come
- from social service agency personnel to find assistance for students whose home lives may be troubled
- from teachers who specialize in bilingual education/English as a second language.

Most important in the context of the increased diversity of the student population is that teachers will need to support each other to meet the challenges their students pose.

These are not just challenges regarding instruction. Teachers do not always represent the ethnic and racial groups of their students, nor are they always from the same socioeconomic groups as their students. One of the biggest challenges for teachers of diverse student populations is the need to reflect on how comfortable they feel working with their heterogeneous classes. Do teachers see their students' diversity as a deficit, or are they able to recognize the assets children bring by virtue of their different life experiences? Is a child who speaks another language considered to be a problem, or does the teacher recognize the resource that language represents? Are teachers interested in these differences and challenges as sources of potential growth for the whole class, or do they consistently see these differences as inconveniences? These are difficult questions, some of the most difficult ones teachers face, but in the context of today's schools, they bear serious attention on the part of every school staff. Teachers need to know that, as they struggle with the personal reflection necessary to confront their own stereotypes and concerns about students who are different from themselves, their professional peers are equally willing to engage in this kind of self-inquiry.

As teachers face the instructional changes inherent in teaching diverse groups of students, the value of a collaborative working environment, one in which support can be expected and found readily, becomes paramount. In the absence of collaboration, it will be far more difficult to assure that all students not only are accepted in the schools but also are actively supported in accessing the full array of educational experiences.

## INCREASED INTEGRATION OF STUDENTS WITH DISABILITIES

One specific aspect of the increased diversity of the student population is the trend toward greater and greater integration of students with disabilities into schools and classrooms nationwide. Some students currently labeled as having disabilities, notably those with mild academic problems, may have difficulties that are more similar to than different from their peers, requiring collaboration to change the general instructional program so it better accommodates all of the students (Johnson & Bauer, 1992). Others have enduring disabilities—such as physical or cognitive impairments—which may require that classroom teachers, or groups of classroom teachers, and special education personnel work collaboratively on a continuous basis.

This latter kind of collaboration also includes collaboration with related services personnel—for example, specialists who may provide physical therapy or mobility training.

Professional collaboration between special education and classroom teachers is not new. It has taken place to varying extents since mainstreaming came into common practice in the mid-1970s. In the past 10 years, however, the expectation for integration has increased enormously, and new forms of collaboration have been developed and implemented, many of them successfully. These collaborative activities include:

- one-to-one consultation between special education and classroom teachers
- small teams of teachers working together
- team teaching, or co-teaching, in which special education and classroom teachers or groups of classroom teachers form permanent teaching teams to allow more complete and ongoing forms of integration

Some of these interactions have more formal structures than others, but each can be successful only to the extent that the adults who share responsibility for the students—be they students with disabilities or not—work well together, support each other, and learn from each other.

## MORE COMPLEX FORMS OF INSTRUCTION

A final, and fundamental, development that requires collaboration is the changing nature of instruction itself. Contemporary researchers who study teaching and learning have made a convincing case for more complex, active forms of instruction, which demand much greater and more varied skill on the part of teachers. Most notable is the finding that children learn most effectively when they are involved actively in constructing their own knowledge (for a summary of constructivist learning, see Levine, 1992)—that is, actively working with new knowledge to fit it into their existing cognitive frameworks. In contrast, teaching traditionally has relied on the lecture method, as documented in Goodlad's (1984) study of schools. At the elementary school level, the overuse of workbooks and skill-driven curriculums has been found wanting, as these approaches rarely provide students with the opportunity to engage in high-level problem solving. In addition, convincing evidence of the power of cooperative learning (Slavin, 1991) has accumulated. Also, experiments with interdisciplinary approaches to curriculum are being tried with success, especially at the middle school level (Beane, 1990).

Teaching according to principles of constructivism, utilizing organizational structures such as cooperative learning, and introducing interdisciplinary thematic units means that teachers no longer can rely on lectures and repetitive drill work if they expect to prepare their students effectively for the 21st century. No longer can teachers assume that merely by lecturing or by providing individual drill-and-practice worksheets will the students gain the capacity to go on learning as adults. Rather, teachers are expected to provide meaningful, challenging, and complex tasks, plan for interactive group activities, and become involved in developing curricula that better match what is known about teaching and learning. This applies to all students, not only those we traditionally think of as "more capable."

If these changes in teaching practice are to come about, teachers in general and special education alike will have to support each other in taking risks as they attempt to change what they traditionally have done. Research has shown us that in a collegial, collaborative school environment, risk taking and experimentation are far more likely to occur than in a school where the status quo prevails (Little, 1982; Rosenholtz, 1989).

## ◾ THE COMPLEXITIES OF COLLABORATION

We can see that a wide range of reasons accounts for why collaboration among the adults within a school is coming to be seen as a necessary part of the way teachers do their work. Whether it is simply for personal support in a time of changing expectations, for maximizing the kind of results that accrue when teachers work with specialists on a given student's problems, for working together to implement new approaches to teaching and to develop specific interventions to enable students with disabilities to be educated with their general education peers, or for generating new knowledge derived from classroom practice, collaboration is acknowledged to have been one of the most glaring, persistently absent characteristics of teachers' work—and the one most in need of being implemented.

Another way to think about how schools might be different if a collaborative professional ethic were to dominate is that they would become "communities of learners" in which all participants would contribute to their own and each others' growth. If we think of teachers as members of a community of learners rather than as isolated individuals performing a narrow set of instructional duties, we shift our thinking to how teachers can both learn from and contribute to the learning of their peers on many counts, be they schoolwide issues or solving the problems of a specific child with a specific set of needs. Each collaborative interaction, although it may occur for multiple reasons in multiple contexts, contributes to the building of a collaborative school. "The thing that distinguishes collaborative communities from most other communities is the desire to construct new meanings about the world through interaction with others" (Schrage, 1990, p. 48). In schools, these kinds of interdependent intellectual and personal communities also serve as important models for students as they try to make sense of their place in the world.

How will this shift to a collaborative norm of professional interaction occur? If it is so crucial to improving schooling, how do we get there? What will schools look like where collaboration is deeply ingrained? How will we know when a school has become a collaborative work environment? How will the old norms of isolation be shed? Because collaboration quickly has become a buzzword among educators, we should take the time to think critically about what collaboration actually means in a school and what it actually is and is not.

To get a sense of the dimensions of collaboration, let's look at how the teachers and staff interact in one elementary school. As you read, be thinking about how well they work together and whether their interactions constitute professional collaboration. Jot down your thoughts about collaboration at Elm Elementary. What are the teachers' strengths as collaborative professionals? Their weaknesses?

Elm Elementary School is located in the inner city of a large, metropolitan school district. The student population is entirely African-American, the majority of whom are from low socioeconomic backgrounds. Most of the students live in the neighborhood, which is considered among the rougher neighborhoods in the city. Student achievement levels at the school are consistently low, and the teachers talk about this as a source of frustration. They seem to care a great deal about their students and want them to do well. The school takes a traditional approach to curriculum and instruction but tries various new programs each year in an attempt to improve the situation.

At faculty meetings a lot of friendly conversation goes on before things come to order. During the meetings everyone listens attentively to the specific suggestions made. Outside of faculty meetings few formal professional interactions occur. Grade-level meetings, for example, are rare. Depending on individual teachers' levels of interest, classes occasionally work together for certain activities.

The teachers like to work in this building. They report that it is a friendly place. Many of the teachers socialize together on Friday afternoons, play volleyball together on weekends, and celebrate one another's birthdays joyfully. Students from the local university also report that the school is a good site for field experiences and student-teaching placements. They are quickly accepted and made to feel part of the school. This feeling of acceptance extends to the paraprofessionals who work in the building, as well as to the parents. Guests and visitors are welcomed wholeheartedly. Beginning teachers are paired with experienced buddies and easily fit into the social structure of the staff.

In describing the school staff, the phrase "We're all family here" is heard commonly. In the teachers' lounge the conversation is friendly, with little negative talk about the students. A feeling of camaraderie is evident. Teachers willingly share ideas that have worked in their classrooms. On staff development days there is almost always a shared potluck meal. The administration pitches in actively, and the principal often is the *one serving the staff at these festive occasions. When a staff member or one of his or her family members is sick, the staff members rally around to support their colleague.*

---

## THE ROLE OF PERSONAL SUPPORT

Few of us would want to work in a school where, at the least, adults were not congenial toward each other. All things being equal, most of us would opt for congeniality as opposed to either hostility or benign isolation. The way adults treat each other at work goes a long way toward creating a certain atmosphere, or ethos, in a school building. This atmosphere extends not only to the adults but also to the students themselves, who usually are quick to pick up on how teachers are treating their peers.

Creating a cordial, personally supportive environment is an important goal for all workplaces. The work of teachers, in particular, produces so much stress, by virtue of the long stretches of time working with a group of children each day, that personal support is vital. In schools populated by children who live in conditions of poverty like those attending Elm Elementary, teachers also deal with the stress of their students' lives. Without personal support the day-to-day experience of teaching likely would be much more difficult. Personal support allows the teachers at Elm to deal with these challenges and promotes the personal caring they show toward their students.

## SHARING INFORMATION AND IDEAS

In addition to the congenial atmosphere and the personal support teachers provide each other at Elm Elementary, they share their ideas and talk about what is working for them in their classrooms. In contrast to much talk in teachers' lounges, these teachers are respectful of their students and help their colleagues by offering suggestions about specific instances of successful lessons, tips for managing classes well, ideas for field trips, and so on. This kind of sharing allows teachers to gain a new bank of ideas to add to their existing repertoires.

Within each teacher's private world of practice in the classroom, sharing ideas with colleagues indicates mutual caring, much like the mutual caring in the personal realm that is evident at Elm. Teachers listen to one another's ideas and are grateful that ideas are not hoarded, as is the case among teachers in some schools. This cooperative professional atmosphere is noted with admiration especially by student teachers, beginning teachers, and substitute teachers who work in the building.

## IS BEING "NICE" ENOUGH?

Despite the warm, personal environment at Elm Elementary and the sharing of ideas that have worked, achievement levels of the students have not improved over the years. Although the teachers seem to work well together, their goals are independent of those of their colleagues. They have no sense of mutual commitment to a common purpose.

This shared commitment to a schoolwide goal is precisely what distinguishes collaboration from simple cooperation. Collaborating with other teachers is not just a matter of being cooperative, of being nice to your colleagues. Being nice is important for creating a pleasant atmosphere, but it can easily exist independent of focused, mutually agreed-upon educational goals. Barth (1990) has offered a helpful distinction, reminding us not to confuse collegiality with congeniality.

Likewise, sharing good ideas and information can exist independent of teachers' sharing a common goal. The kind of sharing that goes on at Elm Elementary is really a kind of information swapping. The result is meant to embellish the capacity of each teacher. Giving advice is limited in its ability to lead to sustained, improved teaching practice. Although it may provide a short-term solution to a given problem, it does not effectively address the underlying changes that may have to be made to improve the quality of instruction for the teacher who is seeking advice (Aldinger, Warger, & Eavy, 1991; Pugach & Johnson, 1988b). When advice is given in the absence of a schoolwide goal, the receiver is not under any obligation to use it; the only context in which it might appear is in the individual classroom. Further, sometimes when teachers give advice, they really are saying, "You ought to do it my way." At Elm Elementary, advice is given freely, but this does not seem to have contributed to better education for its students. Giving advice results in a collective awareness of individual actions (Schrage, 1990), but, because each teacher can go about his or her business independently, a school characterized by well intended advice giving and exchanges of ideas cannot be said to be truly collaborative.

A distinction also should be made between communicating well and collaborating. The skills you will learn from Chapters 3, 4, 5, and 6 of this book are skills of good communication, and communicating well is a critical part of collaboration. But being a good communicator without sharing a common goal with your colleagues is also possible. People who collaborate share a vision of where they want to go, of the purpose for which they are communicating (Schrage, 1990). That goal transcends individual interests, but the creative energies of the individuals committed to the collaboration are what makes reaching the collective goal possible. Collaboration is a more challenging goal than good communication. You have to negotiate what the common goal is, be able to articulate it, and keep the vision in mind. Communicating well allows you to achieve the vision. Without prior agreement regarding the common goal, however, each participant may have a different reason for communicating.

Despite the pleasant atmosphere the staff of Elm Elementary has created, it is cooperative, but not collaborative. No common goal is driving the work of this staff. Although staff members are empathetic toward each other and their students, they are not improving the conditions of learning in their school—even though they may be making progress as individual teachers. If the promise of collaboration as an instrument of school reform is to be realized, the question, "Collaborative for what purpose?" must be foremost in our minds.

## ■ PARTICIPATING IN A COLLABORATIVE SCHOOL

Now that we have a clearer idea of exactly what collaboration is, let's turn to what kind of people make good collaborative professionals and what collaboration actually may look like in a school. Then you can begin to reflect on your strengths as a collaborative professional and where you may need to grow to take on this role effectively.

### QUALITIES OF COLLABORATIVE PROFESSIONALS

1. People who are effective at collaboration recognize that the goal is complex and requires a joint effort to achieve that goal. Improving the educational process for diverse groups of children and youth is an extraordinarily complex goal, and

the process of change is not always efficient. A critical part of recognizing the complexity of collaboration in the schools is acknowledging that many of the current problems in schools are anchored in either blatant or subtle inequities in the way schools treat ethnic, racial, or language-minority students or students with disabilities. Teachers could make many responses to the new complexity of teaching. One response is to say merely that they are doing the best they can in their classrooms. A more optimistic, realistic, and promising professional response is to acknowledge that, if everyone pulls together, schools can more readily become challenging, motivating places for children and adults alike.

2. People who are effective at collaboration acknowledge and honor the creativity generated by working together with others. Working together not only makes the task more manageable, but collaborative interactions also lead to results that are more creative than what any single individual could have designed alone. Collaborative efforts work because they add value to the solution (Schrage, 1990).

Accepting this characteristic of collaboration further signifies that one is willing to share with all participants the recognition for subsequent accomplishments. Valuing the creativity generated by the group means taking pride in the group's accomplishments toward the goal. This doesn't mean forgetting the natural human need for individual recognition but, rather, that the needs of individuals do not surface as obstacles to group achievement.

3. People who are effective at collaboration enjoy the social nature of joint problem solving. Collaborative interactions are not always easy. Just because people are committed to a common goal does not mean they always get along on the way (Schrage, 1990). In any case, collaboration does not occur when people do not work well together or plainly do not enjoy being around other adults. Part of the responsibility of working well together is the ability to respect other participants in the collaboration, even if you don't always agree with them. When collaborative interactions first begin, *trust* among the participants has to be established. With trust, disagreements take place within a context of respect for others.

4. People who are effective at collaboration value the growth they experience as a result of participating in the collaboration. Collaboration would not be attractive as a way of dealing with complex problems if some benefit did not accrue to the individual. Of course, the major benefit is reaching the common goal the participants set out. Professionals who collaborate, however, also value the intellectual growth that takes place as a result of working with others. Collaboration is intellectually stimulating. It fosters intellectual challenge and promotes intellectual growth.

5. People who are effective at collaboration are reflective about their own professional practice. People who invest the time and energy in collaborative efforts are not satisfied with the same routine of teaching day in and day out. Instead, they challenge themselves to grow and improve their practice at the same time that they contribute to the improved practice of the whole. Teachers cannot contribute to the goal of better education in schools without being aware of the quality of their own individual practice. This is what being a reflective teacher means. Without understanding the effects of your own decisions and actions in the classroom, changing them for the better is difficult.

Thoughtful, reflective teachers do not change their practice with each successive educational bandwagon that comes along. They deliberate with their colleagues about the merits and pitfalls of new methods and implement them only when the benefits are clear and consistent with accepted principles of teaching and learning. Collaboration in schools means change both within individual classrooms and in schoolwide practices in accordance with the common goals identified by the staff at a school site.

John Dewey (1933), the noted progressive educator, defined reflective teaching in terms of three specific qualities. First, reflective teachers are *open-minded*. They are accepting of all the students they teach and are flexible about how to work with them. Second, they are *wholehearted*. By this, Dewey meant that they are genuinely enthusiastic about their work, take a serious interest in it, and are aware of new developments that can assist them in their teaching. Finally, reflective teachers are *intellectually responsible*. By this, Dewey meant that teachers should be aware that their instructional decisions have consequences for the students they teach and teachers should take responsibility for those consequences. Together these three qualities encourage teachers to improve their own teaching as a means to reaching the common vision.

Stop for a moment to review these five basic qualities. They should add another broad dimension to your conception of teaching as a profession. Have you already drawn on these qualities in your experiences in school? In other situations? Which can you confidently say you have, and for which do you need additional experiences? Are you comfortable accepting collaboration as an integral part of your professional responsibilities?

## ESTABLISHING COLLABORATIVE CULTURES

Another important distinction that should be made with respect to collaboration is differentiating between creating a collaborative *culture* and implementing various collaborative *structures*, or specific models, for working together. This distinction has been made by Hargreaves and Dawe (1990), who reminded us that a vast array of collaborative structures—for example, mentor teachers or peer coaching—have been developed over the past several years, but that implementing them does not necessarily mean the staff in a particular school is developing a collaborative culture or workplace. They defined collaborative cultures as "evolutionary relationships of openness, trust and support among teachers where they define and develop their own purposes as a community" (p. 227). When a school culture becomes collaborative rather than isolated, it promotes the professional growth of all of its teachers and staff members.

But what is the relationship between the goal of establishing a collaborative school culture and all of the specific collaborative structures that have sprung up in schools? For example, does instituting

peer coaching in a building foster the development of a collaborative culture? What about problem-solving teams to facilitate the integration of students with disabilities? Team teaching? The point
Hargreaves and Dawe made in distinguishing between cultures and
structures is that thinking a school is becoming collaborative simply
by mandating a joint activity such as peer coaching is easy. In reality, the district or building administrator might have supported the
idea of adopting the structure without devoting sufficient time and
attention to the overall school context in which collaboration is supposed to occur. When this happens, collaborative structures such as
peer coaching or consultation can too easily become examples of
"contrived collegiality" (p. 230). These contrived structures do not
take the place of the challenging work of creating mutual trust among
teachers. When they are simply mandated, they are not based on the
identification and acceptance of common goals.

Collaboration is something people come to accept. It cannot be
imposed. Some people seek out collaboration naturally because it fits
with the way they feel comfortable working. They already value the
joint creativity it unleashes and work willingly with others toward the
common purpose of building schools that support the education of all
students. Others come to appreciate its benefits only after they see it
working. What is important to understand is that creating a collaborative culture in schools is an evolutionary process.

Identifying a common goal establishes the purpose for the collaboration, but building trust among participants who have not engaged in this kind of work before—even if they are committed to the
common goal—takes time and hard work. Therefore, one should not
"write off" potential participants just because they do not seem to
be interested at first. Rather than working only with those who volunteer, collaboration should be seen as a *progressively inclusive* effort. It may start with staunch supporters, but those involved in initiating collaborative efforts in schools have to be committed to keeping the door open to those who initially may choose not to participate. More than just keeping an open mind, a continuous process of
inviting expanded participation is important.

What should be clear from this discussion is that forcing people
to collaborate by mandating artificial structures for interaction and
expecting a truly collaborative outcome is not likely to work. Those
who are interested in building effective, broad-based collaborative
cultures have to be sensitive to the tendency for administrators, spe-

cialists, or teachers themselves to be so taken with a certain model of collaboration that they push for its implementation in a contrived manner, perhaps missing the larger purpose.

## THE PLACE OF COLLABORATIVE STRUCTURES IN FOSTERING COLLABORATIVE CULTURES

We would not want to leave you with the impression that a school must have already developed into a collaborative culture before introducing any specific structures. Creating professional, collaborative schools is a developmental process. Considering the centuries during which teaching has been an isolated profession, no one can expect the shift to collaboration to be achieved easily or quickly. Change takes time, and those who hope to change the profession of teaching need to accept the pace of change as well as continue to push for it. What is the specific role, if any, for the vast array of collaborative structures that exist in the eventual development of schoolwide collaborative cultures?

Let's imagine that a group of five teachers at Elm Elementary is interested in shifting away from basal reading texts to literature as the basis for reading and writing instruction. The principal doesn't mind, and a small budget is available for purchasing the necessary books, many of which reflect the cultural experiences of the school's students. These teachers have identified their common goal—the basis of their collaboration—and have decided to meet weekly to share their progress and provide mutual help as they all embark on this new instructional venture. They also have agreed that at least once a month they will use their preparation time to come in and observe each other's reading and writing instruction, to get ideas and to give suggestions. Further, they have agreed to read an article related to literature-based instruction once a month and to meet after school to discuss it as a means of bringing new information to the group.

At the same time, the special education teachers, who serve mostly third, fourth, and fifth graders, have met with the principal to talk about the possibility of trying team teaching on a limited basis. They heard about this from other schools but are apprehensive about it. They talk with two classroom teachers who also want to see students with disabilities included on a more permanent basis and who are frustrated with the limitations imposed on special education teachers through pull-out programs of remediation. The classroom teachers are somewhat hesitant to change the way they organize their instruction, and all of the teachers are unsure about what team teaching will be like, but they agree to try. As they review their schedules, they realize that, with some juggling of specialists' schedules, they can have at least one 45-minute period of common time per week for joint planning. They decide to begin on a limited basis at the start of the second semester. Their common goal is twofold: integrating students with disabilities and improving the capacity of the regular classroom teachers, through teaming, to reach more children who are having problems in school. They have found out that the district has a small support group made up of special education and classroom teachers who are teaming in various schools. The group meets each month to share ideas and help with problem solving.

These two scenarios represent two separate collaborative efforts that take their direction from two different kinds of collaborative structures that have emerged over the past decade. The first is a peer support structure. By deciding to observe each other, the teachers are agreeing to break out of their classroom isolation and are taking steps toward peer coaching as a support mechanism for instructional change. In the second scenario, the teachers are implementing one of the many variations of increased integration between special and regular education—namely, collaborative team teaching.

Neither effort involves the whole school, but each constitutes a small collaborative team and follows the basic principles of collaboration. Common goals are clear, commitment to those goals has been established beforehand, enough mutual trust is present at least to begin the effort. The structures have not been imposed top-down, although in the case of the special education collaboration, the special education teachers did have to seek out classroom teachers who might be willing to work with them. They were all nervous about the change. By agreeing to attempt this together, however, they implicitly agreed to support each other.

These separate collegial activities give the participants an opportunity to work with a specific collaborative structure. In the second group the teachers also were to be part of a larger network of professional collaboration in their district. Each instance of collaboration can work to sustain the interest of that group of teachers in a building and can add incrementally to the eventual establishment of a collaborative ethos in the school (Fullan & Stiegelbauer, 1991). If one of the foremost goals of collaboration is to professionalize teaching, these smaller efforts can contribute substantially to the professionalization of the larger group, which in turn can provide leadership for subsequent schoolwide collaborative efforts. The networking of teachers who come together to support various professional interests is an important developmental activity in building collaborative schools.

In addition to providing experience in collaboration for small groups of teachers, these more limited collaborations based on well-defined structures play a second crucial role in contributing to a schoolwide ethos of collaboration: They create new models for professional interaction for other teachers in the building who may never before have conceptualized what real collaboration among teachers might look like. If you've always gone about your work in relative isolation, if you've thought that sharing good ideas was enough in terms of professional interaction among teachers, if you've never worked toward a clearly defined mutual goal, chances are that you don't have a sense of what collaboration might be like. By having some teachers create new models for working together, others begin to get new mental images of how things can be different. If these smaller instances of collaboration meet with success, the threat of collaborative work may diminish for others in the future. That is why the success of these initial collaborations is important in this time of transition from isolated to collegial professional relationships.

Efforts to transform schools into collaborative workplaces likely will occur on many levels, and the transition will not look the same in each school or each district. Some schools may begin by identifying schoolwide goals. Others may initiate individual collaborative efforts—like those described here—as the catalysts for change. In either case, work in one mode should not preclude work in the other. Multiple collaborative activities can take place simultaneously.

## ■ A Worthy Challenge

Is making the shift to collaboration as a professional norm worth the effort? The position we take is a resounding "Yes!" This stance is not based on an abstract vision of collaboration. Rather, it emerges from both authors' experiences for the past several years as members of intensive collaborations for the purpose of reforming teacher education for urban schools. Driven by this goal, each institution's work was energized by the collective efforts of its faculty members. The professional and personal satisfaction that results from being part of a successful team that begins to see the payoff for its collective work is extraordinary. Whether you are beginning your career as an educational professional or thinking about renewing your commitment to it, collaboration provides the piece that has been missing for so long for those who work in schools—the collegial community of professionals who work together to support the complex work of teaching.

The challenge is not whether we do or do not collaborate. It is, instead, whether as professionals we have the collective will to meet the needs of the students in our schools in a way that is both feasible and satisfying. This is the common goal for which collaboration is needed. The needs of too many students are unmet in today's school. Most often these are students whose race, ethnicity, language, or disability sets them apart. The unrelated efforts of individual teachers, no matter how heroic, will not be enough to meet this challenge. We know more than ever before about the most effective approaches to curriculum and instruction; we can be confident of the untapped potential of children who live in poverty, who do not speak English yet, or who have disabilities; and we have learned a great deal about the value of cooperative organizational structures for students. These developments no doubt will advance our potential to improve education a great deal. Nevertheless, to unleash the creative energies of teachers, to kindle the intellectual challenge for teachers as a means of renewing the educational system for all children, collaboration is indeed a worthy goal.

## ■ REMEMBER...

1. Teaching is more than just working well with your students. It means working well with your adult colleagues and the adult family members of those students.
2. Several developments in education have converged to make collaboration an essential part of a teacher's work: changes in authority structures, more teacher responsibility, greater diversity of the student population, inclusion of students with disabilities, and increased complexity of instruction.

3. Collaboration provides a way for adults who work in schools to form a "community of learners" who can grow professionally and improve the school.
4. Collaboration is more than just sharing ideas. It means working together to identify and reach mutually agreed-upon, schoolwide goals so education can be responsive to the diverse student population schools serve.
5. Collaboration grows out of trust between professionals. It cannot be constructed artificially.

## ■ ACTIVITIES

- Think of a time when you worked with a group of your peers. Briefly describe the situation and decide whether your interactions were collaborative. Why or why not?
- Think of a school in which you have worked, either for field experience (if you are a prospective teacher) or where you have taught. How would you describe it in terms of its being a collaborative workplace? Identify specific examples or nonexamples that support your viewpoint. What changes would have to occur for the school to become collaborative?
- Rate yourself on the five qualities of a collaborative professional discussed in this chapter. What activities could you name to assist people in developing these qualities as preparation for teaching?
- Split up into small groups and prepare a mini-debate on the proposal, "A teacher's job is to help children learn, not to help other adults learn."

# 2

# A New Framework for Thinking About Collaboration

**B**roadly defined, collaboration occurs when all members of a school's staff are working together and supporting each other to provide the highest quality of curriculum and instruction for the diverse students they serve. How this happens specifically, what skills support collaborative practice in schools, and the context in which those skills are embedded in action in real schools, all constitute the purpose of this book. As its authors, we have to think about what collaboration is from our own individual experiences with and ideas about what it should be. Our own biases regarding collaboration should be evident from the framework we have adopted. But before we go any further in defining our own specific conception of collaboration—the conception that drives this book—we would like you to consider what you think collaboration is and identify some of the biases you may bring to the discussion.

Take a few minutes and see what comes to mind when you think about collaboration among those who work in schools. Do you think about it in terms of helping? Of giving advice? Of providing answers to others? Of teaching a colleague who knows less than you do? See how many different aspects of collaboration you consider, and keep them in mind as we present our views on what collaboration is and is not.

## ■ AN HISTORICAL PERSPECTIVE ON PROFESSIONAL COLLABORATION

To understand the role of collaboration in the schools, we have to understand the prevailing norms of professional interaction and how collaboration has been dealt with in the past. Where has collaboration been practiced? With what degree of success? How are the norms associated with professional interaction changing? The following historical look at collaboration will serve as a backdrop against which we will introduce a guiding framework for thinking about collaboration throughout the book.

### FROM ISOLATION TO INTERACTION

Although the word *collaboration* is common educational parlance today, teaching has been historically a highly isolated, rather than a collaborative, profession. In his landmark study of teacher socialization, Lortie (1975) identified "the persistence of separation and low task interdependence" (p. 15) in "egg-crate" schools as the distinguishing organizational factor of schooling. As long as teachers were not interdependent, what each did in his or her own classroom did not affect colleagues' work. With the exception of a brief and limited foray into team teaching during the latter 1960s and early 1970s (Cohen, 1981), which never caught on nationwide, teaching has been marked by the absence of collaboration. Not until the major reform efforts beginning in the 1980s did collaboration begin to be seen as one of the critical goals of educational reform.

The history of collaboration has been a bit different, however, in the fields of special education and school psychology. In the early 1970s consultation began to be seen as a logical extension of the service delivery continuum for special education students. Up to this point, resource rooms offering pull-out services had been the option that afforded the greatest degree of interaction with general education. Although consultation long had been a feature of the services offered by school psychologists, its appearance in special education heralded the recognition that some features of the general education environment caused problems for students labeled as having disabilities. The purpose of shifting to a consultation model was to encourage special education teachers to provide training to general classroom teachers (Lilly, 1971). Therefore, consultation was an indirect service to students; special education teachers instead worked with classroom teachers directly, and the results of that work were thought to benefit students with disabilities.

The appearance of the consultation model meant a marked increase in interaction between special and general education teachers. What soon became obvious, though, was that more often than not these interactions were not actually collaborative. The early practice of consultation was based on the hierarchical notion that special education teachers and school psychologists had the answers to the problems classroom teachers were describing. Those solutions often reflected behavioral methods used in special education—for example, the heavy use of extrinsic reinforcement, which was often seen as the most credible approach to solving the kinds of problems teachers were encountering. Special educators and school psychologists, then, were seen (and often saw themselves) as experts who brought a new set of solutions that, if followed, would make general education more like special education and, thus, clear the way for students with disabilities to be successful.

This model, which became known as the *expert model of consultation*, was characterized by a one-way channel of communication in which the consultant provided the expertise to develop an intervention plan and the classroom teacher used it. Input from general education teachers typically was not sought because, as a group, they were not seen as possessing expertise. No other option seemed to exist, primarily because of the role specialists played in the school staff hierarchy, with classroom teachers being on its lower end.

Throughout the late 1970s and 1980s, it became apparent that classroom teachers were not readily implementing the suggestions of their special education and school psychology colleagues, and more and more special educators and school psychologists recognized the need for greater parity among specialists and general classroom teachers if consultation were to be effective (Idol, Paolucci-Whitcomb, & Nevin, 1986; Johnson, Pugach, & Hammitte, 1988; Pugach & Johnson, 1988a). This change was needed to promote ownership on the part of classroom teachers for whatever interventions were designed.

*Collaboration* began to be used to describe the need for greater parity among participants in professional interactions. This eventually evolved into the term *collaborative consultation*, which became the new, acceptable model of professional interaction, one in which specialists refrained from prescribing solutions hierarchically and, instead, worked as equal partners with classroom teachers. Providing direct prescriptions to classroom teachers began to be seen increasingly as inappropriate precisely because it did not seem to fit the basic tenets of collaboration—namely, that equals with different kinds of expertise come together to solve problems, and that their joint efforts are more powerful than the efforts of either one in isolation.

Stop for a minute and consider the various strengths that classroom teachers bring to a collaborative school. Special education teachers? Administrators? Make a list of strengths for each. How does each kind of expertise complement the others?

One other important idea introduced during this time of transition was that special education teachers might not always have to be present to solve the classroom problems general education teachers might be experiencing with special education students. For many of those problems, classroom teachers themselves might have enough collective expertise to do the job (Chalfant, Pysh, & Moultrie, 1979; Pugach & Johnson, 1988a). This became an important consideration because, with the expectation that special education teachers would work with more and more students—those labeled as having disabilities and those without disabilities, models of service delivery that required the participation of special educators in every problem-solving interaction were both inefficient and illogical. To make good on the belief that classroom teachers did in truth have expertise to bring to bear on classroom problems, part of the collaboration trend had to acknowledge that expertise overtly. At the same time, others continued to argue for a much more direct, prescriptive approach by special educators and school psychologists (Fuchs, Fuchs, & Bahr, 1990). The majority, however, accepted what came to be called a collaborative form of consultation, in which highly prescriptive forms of problem solving were considered to be generally inappropriate.

This period of argumentation dominated the last half of the 1980s. Today, the terms consultation and collaboration often are used interchangeably to describe the broad class of activities in which specialists work with classroom teachers to provide assistance. The preference, however, has shifted decidedly away from the term consultation, as it evokes the expert model. What typifies the relationship between special and general education today is a desire for collaborative interactions in which special education teachers and school psychologists refrain from providing expert advice for fear of being overly prescriptive and in which specialists and teachers work together to meet the needs not only of children who are formally labeled but also of all children in need of assistance.

The recognition of problems with conventional consultation was not the only thing that contributed to the shift in how relationships among specialists and classroom teachers came to be defined. In 1986 the then Secretary of the Office of Special Education and Rehabilitative Services made a landmark statement that since has come to be known as the *regular education initiative* (REI) (Will, 1986). This statement described problems with the prevailing special education delivery system and promoted much greater interaction between special education and classroom teachers. In this document Will supported the need to identify new, dynamic models of special education that would better serve not only those labeled as having disabilities but also children who generally were regarded as being at risk for school failure, usually children in minority groups. This document signaled another level of support for the changes that were being advocated in the form and substance of a consultative model of special education service delivery.

## AN INCLUSIVE APPROACH TO COLLABORATION

Many recent textbooks that explore the issue of professional relationships between special and general education teachers pay considerable attention to clarifying what consultation and collaborative consultation are and are not (e.g., Dettmer, Thurston, & Dyck, 1993; Friend & Cook, 1992). In our view, arguments over the terms *consultation, collaboration*, and *collaborative consultation* probably have been more of a hindrance than a help in acknowledging the full range of collaborative interactions that have to occur in any school if we are to serve the diverse student populations for which we are responsible. As an historical development in changing the way special education services are delivered, the arguments probably were inevitable and helped to clarify the direction in which the field might finally go.

These historical developments in defining collaboration illustrate that, in reality, the relationship between teachers and specialists cannot be limited exclusively to one kind of interaction or another. Collaboration is not a unidimensional activity but, rather, exists along a continuum spanning the range from teachers' developing solutions together to specialists' prescribing solutions in the infrequent instances when unique expertise is needed. Further, every collaborative interaction does not require a formal, step-by-step approach to problem solving. Collaboration is not synonymous with structured problem solving, although, to be sure, problem solving is common in collaboration.

The promise of collaboration for those who work in schools lies first in creating work environments in which an ethic of care (Noddings, 1992) exists among colleagues for the purpose of educating children and youth and dominates professional interactions. That ethic of care has to extend to developing common schoolwide goals for learning, for curriculum, and for instruction. One way of demonstrating this sense of caring is for adults to work together for the children they serve. Interactions that fall under the general practice of collaboration ought to emanate from a philosophical framework in which each professional in a school is valued as having skills and expertise to contribute to the collaborative process. But rather than worry about whether one is permitted to give advice, to prescribe, or to assist in problem solving, professionals need to feel comfortable moving among the various forms of collaboration as needed.

Different situations require different kinds of collegial interactions, and all of the professionals in a school should be prepared for a multidimensional range of collaborative interactions throughout their work. When teachers collaborate, they are called upon at various times to support their colleagues, to help colleagues recognize their own problem-solving capacities, to provide information on a variety of issues, and sometimes even to suggest a specific path for a colleague to take. If collaboration is defined in this multidimensional manner, the specific character of the situation is what determines which kind of collaboration will best fit any given interaction. Until you've begun talking together, you are not likely to be able to predict which kind of approach may be required.

The literature on collaboration emerging from general school reform contains little discussion of whether it is preferable to provide a colleague with a direct solution for a particular problem or to work together to develop a solution. Instead, talk focuses on developing a school based on supporting continuous improvement for *everyone's* practice: teachers, administrators, teacher education students, specialists, and the students themselves. The assumption is that all teachers and staff members need to grow and everyone is a potential source of expertise on some subject needed to foster schoolwide improvement. There are no preconceived prohibitions for what kinds of interactions are appropriate. By taking a schoolwide perspective, collaboration can be defined more broadly. Within this definition the roles professionals play when they interact are not seen as absolute but, rather, are acceptable as long as they support the schoolwide goal of building effective relationships among the adults who work there. Therefore, to prepare professionals for a single collaborative role seems to miss the point. People need to know how to shift from role to role depending on the situation they are addressing. Even within a given situation, they might shift from role to role.

---

*What does a broad school or districtwide perspective on change look like? In Calexico, California, a school district in which about 80% of the students are limited in their capacity to speak English (Schmidt, 1993), the district decided that individual programs in supplemental bilingual education simply were not working. Instead, each school uses a broad array of strategies across all grades to get the job of education done, and to "give access to all of the students, regardless of their background" (p. 7). Rather than making bilingual education or English as a Second Language classes solely the responsibility of a specialty teacher, all teachers work toward the same goal, beginning with whatever language strength the children bring and work from that point. So, for example, in an elementary school that utilizes whole language, children are encouraged to write in the language that is strongest for them. Children of different language abilities are placed in the same classes to foster peer teaching. All teachers are encouraged to extend their certification to include bilingual education.*

*The vision for full integration of bilingual education across the curriculum is represented in a statement all administrators must sign, committing them to respect the culture and language of their students. The responsibility for reaching students who formerly were isolated in bilingual education programs has expanded to include collaboration among everyone who works in the district. Although getting to this point took a lot of time and effort, the achievement scores of the students currently are on the rise (Schmidt, 1993).*

Once the focus of professional interactions shifts to developing a schoolwide norm of responsible mutual interaction, "consultation" seems inappropriate as a term to describe how teachers and other school staff members work together in schools. This terminology introduces a number of difficulties, chiefly because of the emphasis it seems to place on a hierarchical approach to problem solving. Further complicating the choice of terminology is that education suffers from overspecialization, which can devalue the special expertise of the classroom teacher. Use of the term *consultation* seems to have led special educators and school psychologists in the wrong direction, emphasizing, as it does, individual interactions exclusively and not schoolwide goals regarding how professionals work together. Even the term *collaborative consultation*, while clearly promoting parity among participants, fails to capture the wider intentions of schoolwide collaboration and still places collaboration in the framework of special education/school psychology, from which the term arose.

In a school setting, where classroom teachers, specialists, and administrators all bring a unique form of expertise to problem situations, the general term *collaboration* seems to be a more accurate description of the dynamics that take place (or should take place) among all the stakeholders involved in a child's education. In the context of a multidimensional framework, the broader term *collaboration* can include a wide range of interactions, including situations in which a more direct approach is required. In this book we have elected to adopt a framework based on the term *collaboration* alone, primarily to honor the broad-based nature of professional interactions in schools and to stress the need for the goals of special educators or school psychologists with respect to collaboration to be nested within the larger educational community in which they work.

## ▓ Defining a Multidimensional Framework for Collaboration

As we have indicated thus far, collaborative schools are places where people are committed to working together for school improvement. Beyond that, how specifically shall we define "working together?" In what different ways do adults actually interact in schools in the broad context of collaboration we described in the previous chapter? How do the various kinds of interactions relate to each other, if at all? As we noted, suggestions from the general education reform literature are very general with respect to collaboration—it is held as an overriding goal for all professionals—while the literature from special education/school psychology has moved toward a more unidimensional interpretation of collaboration, favoring the joint solution of problems involving specialists and general education teachers.

A multidimensional framework for collaboration instead includes a broad range of professional interactions that take place among a collaborative staff in schools. Within this framework, when interacting with their peers, professionals draw on and shift between four basic roles, all of which represent dimensions of collaboration. The ultimate purpose of all of these aspects of collaboration is to improve the practice of teaching so a more diverse range of students can be successfully served. The four roles that form the underlying framework for schoolwide collaboration are (Johnson & Pugach, 1992):

1. The supportive role.
2. The facilitative role.
3. The informative role.
4. The prescriptive role.

Within a multidimensional framework these fundamental roles make up the continuum of collaborative relationships. Between any two individuals in a school, the nature of their relationship will change depending on the situation in which they are collaborating. Further, the roles often overlap, and during a single meeting a teacher might draw on more than one of the dimensions of collaboration.

By creating a multidimensional framework, we are stressing that it is not only all right to engage in each of these forms of interaction, but that it is actually natural in the course of a school year to do so. Fundamental to this multidimensional framework is the principle that all education professionals who work in schools potentially act in any of these four roles depending on the situation. No one role is reserved for a certain person by virtue of his or her title. And if any one of these dimensions is missing, the full potential of collaboration is not likely to be realized.

## THE SUPPORTIVE DIMENSION OF COLLABORATION

To maintain a healthy work environment in schools—which are apt to be complex and often hectic places—one of the most important and fundamental dimensions of collaboration is support. The support function is defined conventionally: caring and being there for your colleagues to share in times of need and in times of joy. Support takes many forms in a school that is striving to become a caring community of learners.

First, basic interpersonal support is needed because, in schools as in all workplaces, many people work together and go through life experiences and life cycles together. Interpersonal support is present when staffs celebrate events together, such as births or marriages or graduations. It is needed when staff members go through difficulties such as family deaths or divorces. This kind of support may occur in groups, or it may occur between individuals. Interpersonal support represents a basic level of caring between staff members. This is the dimension of collaboration we saw in Chapter 1 in our hypothetical sketch of Elm Elementary School. As we argued, however, interpersonal support alone is not enough to propel a school to work toward a common goal.

Another form of interpersonal support is recognition for work well done. In many schools a curious, often unspoken ethic mitigates too much public recognition when, for example, a teacher has been cited for some kind of award or has participated in a professional presentation outside of school. Collaborative schools ought to be places where achievements such as these are celebrated, primarily because they usually are evidence of professional growth and effort, precisely the kind of practices to which all education professionals should aspire.

These kinds of personal supports are necessary, but not sufficient, for a collaborative school. A professional support function must be present as well. Everyone who has taught school knows that teachers have more challenging classes in some years than in others. Likewise, teachers may have one or two especially challenging students from time to time. In a collaborative school colleagues must support one another in these situations to help them get through tough situations. Specifically, this may mean asking your colleague how things are going, agreeing to be a guest worker with a targeted child in your own classroom from time to time, or stopping by the classroom when you have a few free minutes to provide a bit of relief.

Another form of professional support comes when a teacher or groups of teachers are trying out new methods of instruction or new conceptions of curriculum. For example, if a school is shifting to a fully hands-on/minds-on integrated approach to teaching science, support is needed for people to share their instructional successes and to provide a place for teachers to air the problems they are facing as they struggle with these new approaches. This means devoting time to talking purposefully with one another about what has worked, what mutual problems can be identified, and what strategies might best overcome the problems. Support for instructional or curricular innovation also might include participating in peer coaching as a means of providing specific feedback. The history of special education consultation suggests that most often these conversations take place one-to-one but that only one of the partners, the classroom teacher, typically is in the position of facing problems as he or she attempts to implement a technique suggested by a special education colleague. We are suggesting that those conversations should have a much larger context across colleagues in a school.

Still another form of professional support comes when teachers become mentors to beginning teachers. Sometimes these relationships are established formally and are structured such that a beginning teacher is expected only to work closely with her mentor. In a collaborative school, however, beginning teachers could seek out multiple sources of assistance, from those with whom they feel most comfortable in mentoring relationships (Cole, 1991).

Giving this kind of support comes easily and intuitively to some professionals. Others have to learn how to provide it. Although it may seem like a fairly simple aspect of collaboration, providing support is a challenging role because a person has to give it in genuine ways. The support function is not enough, though. Different situations demand that professionals draw upon other dimensions of collaboration as well.

## THE FACILITATIVE DIMENSION OF COLLABORATION

Colleagues take on the role of facilitators when they help their peers develop the capacity to solve problems, engage in tasks, or deal independently with professional challenges. As such, the facilitative dimension of collaboration is related to the concept of *scaffolded instruction* (Palincsar, 1986), in which those with greater knowledge and skill support those who cannot yet function independently in that particular realm. The facilitative dimension of collaboration is a growth dimension. It "nudges" teachers who may not realize they have the capacity to move forward. It is the dimension of collaboration that provides just enough modeling or demonstration to enable a peer to master a new approach, to come up with a new solution, and to gain confidence in his or her own skills.

One example of this facilitative dimension of collaboration is demonstration. When peers demonstrate a specific methodology for a colleague, they are providing the opportunity for a colleague to see a new methodology in action and to model it. A second example is peer coaching, in which a person gives feedback to another after observing that person attempting to implement a new methodology. This feedback enables the other person to better understand how to improve the next lesson. Third, in peer collaboration (Johnson & Pugach, 1991) teachers who want assistance with a classroom-based problem work with colleagues who help them utilize all of the information and expertise they already have to develop and implement practical, creative solutions.

The facilitative role differs substantially from advice giving or support in that it specifically focuses on helping peers develop their own skills to a greater extent than before. Suppose one of your colleagues is attempting to implement cooperative learning and is experimenting with how to structure her classes according to its principles. You are well trained in cooperative learning techniques and have much to offer. You might agree to demonstrate a cooperative learning lesson during one of your planning periods, or you might agree to review a videotape of your colleague's first try at using cooperative learning in the classroom. You also might agree to co-teach a lesson, taking the lead while your colleague is working closely with you. To be sure, an element of support is there when one is playing a facilitative role, but acquiring the new teaching skill, strategy, or methodology is what distinguishes this dimension of professional collaboration.

## THE INFORMATION-GIVING DIMENSION OF COLLABORATION

Within a collaborative school teachers and other staff members share information to help each other with challenging situations. When sharing information, the goal is to provide direct assistance to one's colleagues so they are better equipped to deal with problems on an ongoing basis. Sharing information can take many forms as a dimension of collaboration. It simply might be a situation in which one colleague relates knowledge of appropriate resources (for example, instructional materials or professional literature) pertinent to a situation. It might consist of describing what has worked in one's own classroom.

Sharing information can be thought of as a relatively directive form of collaboration. The colleague who receives the information does not necessarily have to utilize the information shared. The informing dimension of collaboration is a good example of acknowledging that others have invaluable expertise. That expertise should not be foisted upon one's colleagues (a problem discussed in greater detail in Chapter 5) but, instead, should be tapped only when some kind of external knowledge or resource clearly is needed or should be made in the form of suggestions a teacher may or may not use.

Perhaps one of the most important facets of information sharing is putting colleagues in touch with other professionals who might be able to assist them, or networking. As a form of collaboration, networking provides for identifying human resources—both within the school and without—who can assist with specific problems. Fundamentally this means knowing who has what expertise within a school or community. Networking may come more easily to some teachers and school staff than others. Including colleagues in your networking activities and making sure they feel comfortable contacting people they may not have met contribute to the potential for networking. For more intensive, less frequent problems such as low-incidence disabilities or a serious mental health problem, a teacher might initiate a formal referral for assistance. In this situation the collaborative colleague helps the peer access the appropriate assistance, whether it is within the school system or through an outside agency.

## THE PRESCRIPTIVE DIMENSION OF COLLABORATION

The fourth and final dimension of collaboration, and the most directive one, is the dimension of prescribing a path of action to a colleague. In the traditional hierarchical model of consultation that dominated the 1970s and the early 1980s, prescriptive approaches were seen as the best way to ensure that special education methodology was transferred readily to general education classrooms. The predominance of this approach signaled a long period during which classroom teachers were viewed primarily as recipients of these prescriptions for practice, and not as having expertise themselves. As a result, teachers often did not implement the prescriptions they received. The reason most often cited for this outcome was the absence of real ownership for the prescription on the teacher's part.

Moving away from prescription as a dominant collaborative activity, however, does not mean it should never take place. In a multidimensional approach to collaboration, a specific methodology or practice might be "just right" for the situation you are encountering with a colleague. How do you know when to be prescriptive? Given the negative experience with prescriptive approaches in the past, one rule of thumb is that other dimensions of collaboration are more likely to encourage teachers to take ownership for the changes they are trying to implement. When teachers are supported in their efforts to change what they are doing to accommodate the range of students they teach more appropriately, when their colleagues facilitate their use of new methodologies, and when they can network with others who may be attempting the same changes, the likelihood of making the change seems to be greater than when someone simply tells them what to do. The rule of thumb, then, is to be always attentive to the way teachers do change their teaching practice—namely, through day-to-day implementation and feedback.

If, however, a colleague has been trying in good faith to make the changes needed to become more accommodating of the student population and requests directive assistance, prescription may be in order. Prescription also may be needed when a teacher is struggling with a new methodology and really needs assistance to get back on track after a setback. In the latter instance, one might move back and forth between prescription and facilitation to provide the most complete collaboration possible.

## ■ PUTTING MULTIDIMENSIONAL COLLABORATION TO WORK

Although these four dimensions of collaboration have been presented separately, in practice those who work in schools alternate among these four approaches rather than select one, use it in a pure form, and ignore the other three. They have been described separately here to point out their contrasting elements.

Collaboration essentially is based on building healthy working relationships among adults for the purpose of helping children and youth in schools. Building these relationships means that all adults who work in a school must engage in continuous collaboration for a variety of purposes related to this goal. Not everyone takes part in all forms of collaboration all of the time, but each of the four dimensions is essential if collaboration is to transcend the simple goal of making school a nice place for the adults who work there. The kind of support collaboration offers must be accompanied by a clear set of schoolwide goals that make investing in these multiple activities worthwhile.

## ■ REMEMBER . . .

1. Collaboration is a multidimensional activity that encompasses supporting, facilitating, informing, and prescribing.
2. The four dimensions of collaboration usually are not used in their pure forms. Teachers move back and forth among them in any collaborative interaction.
3. Collaboration traditionally has not been part of the job of teaching.
4. Within special education and school psychology the tradition of consultation has shifted from an expert model to a more collaborative model.
5. Collaboration among school professionals is based on the philosophy that all professionals have something important to contribute to the collaborative process.

## ■ ACTIVITIES

- Reconsider the thoughts you had on collaboration when you began to read this chapter. Jot them down. Divide into small groups and discuss your original thoughts, compare them with your peers' ideas, and see how your thinking has shifted, if at all. Are the shifts important? Why?
- Prepare a brief presentation on the benefits of a multidimensional approach to collaboration.
- Describe a collaborative interaction you have observed or participated in. Was the interaction successful? Which of the four dimensions of collaboration came into play?
- In each of four small groups, discuss one of the four dimensions of collaboration and create examples in writing. After 10 to 15 minutes of brainstorming, post, read, and then discuss the examples. Which rely on one of the four dimensions of collaboration exclusively and which rely on a combination?

# PART TWO

# COMMUNICATION: THE CORNERSTONE OF COLLABORATION

# THE FOUNDATION FOR GOOD COMMUNICATION

In the previous two chapters we provided a framework for thinking about collaboration in a more inclusive manner. Essentially we argued that collaboration is a way of being and is not limited to isolated actions. Before we can continue with this line of thought, we must understand that, to collaborate effectively, certain foundational skills must be acquired. Perhaps the most important skill of effective collaborators is the ability to communicate ideas effectively. Communication is the foundation of all interactions between humans. Without the ability to communicate, our lives would be barren. Effective communication enables us to exchange experiences and establish a sense of unity with others (Hames & Joseph, 1986). The sharing and sense of unity are what define us as people. In this chapter and in the following three chapters, a communication model will be presented, verbal and nonverbal aspects will be explored, continuous feedback will be discussed, practices that facilitate or inhibit communication will be illustrated, and group processing as it relates to collaboration will be delineated.

Before you read on, consider the last time you had a conversation with someone with whom you felt you were not connecting. What aspects of this conversation led you to believe you weren't connecting? How could you have changed the way you participated in the conversation to feel more connected? When you read the next section, reflect on this conversation and ask yourself if part of the problem was incomplete communication cycles.

## ■ COMMUNICATION CYCLES

Communication is a deceptively simple process made up of four components: a sender, a channel, an environment, and a receiver. Figure 3.1 illustrates a model of these components. A communication cycle is initiated when the sender sends a message by some kind of channel through an environment to a receiver of that message. In human relationships the channels for messages typically are auditory or visual. A verbal message consists of words, whereas a nonverbal message consists of things such as gestures, facial expressions, and even pitch or tone of voice. Senders simultaneously send both verbal and nonverbal messages through the environment to the receiver. The receiver picks up the message through a combination of visual and auditory means and gains meaning by interpreting the combined visual and auditory message. The receiver then becomes a sender and provides direct or indirect feedback to the original sender (who now becomes a receiver), which helps the original sender understand that the original message was understood. This cycle continues throughout the interaction, and through continuous feedback participants in the interaction communicate.

**FIGURE 3.1**

**COMMUNICATION CYCLE**

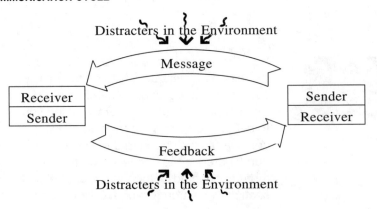

Unfortunately, when they send a message to their colleagues, people often believe they are communicating regardless of their colleagues' understanding of the message. This common mistake often leads to problems. Communication is a cyclical process that occurs only when all individuals participating in the process understand the message. For communication to occur, sending a message is not enough. In other words, the message must be understood accurately by the receiver. Two individuals can engage in an interaction that actually involves little communication.

---

*Raul is an eighth-grade science teacher who has been working very hard to incorporate Jason into his class. Jason receives special education services because of his behavior. Although he is bright, Jason often is belligerent and, at times, aggressive, which inhibits his learning. During science class Jason had a blow-up and ran out of the room. Raul decided to call Ms. Jackson, Jason's mother, about Jason's behavior in class, and the following interaction took place:*

*Raul:* I'm sorry to have to bother you at home, but you asked that I call you if Jason had any problems in class.

*Ms. Jackson:* Don't be silly. I'm glad you called. I've been having trouble with Jason's behavior myself lately.

*Raul:* Today in class Jason got upset with one of the students and shoved him, knocking over some expensive equipment.

*Ms. Jackson:* I'm upset with Jason, too. Last night he yelled at his sister during dinner for no reason. I just don't know what to do with him when he gets like that.

*Raul:* This isn't the first time something like this has happened, and if we can't get this under control, we may have to reassess his placement in my class.

*Ms. Jackson:* I know just what you mean. He yells at his sister or me all the time, and I don't know why he gets angry so easily.

> *Raul:* I appreciate your willingness to
> talk to me about my concern with Jason's be-
> havior in class. Maybe we can get together to
> develop some kind of plan.
>
> *Ms. Jackson:* No problem. Any time you want to talk, just give
> me a call.

---

On the surface this seems to be a positive interaction, but in reality the two parties are not communicating. Raul is talking about Jason's behavior in school, and Ms. Jackson is talking about his behavior at home. They are engaged in a parallel conversation with little understanding of each other's messages. As a result, they are talking but not communicating. The effectiveness of communication between individuals is determined by the degree to which both the sender and the receiver have the same understanding of the message being sent.

Continuous feedback provides the means for individuals to share information and to modify messages or to provide clarification when a message is misunderstood. Continuous feedback is a process through which individuals constantly receive feedback about how their messages are being received. For example, when we speak, we hear ourselves talking. As a result, we hear what we're saying and, more important, how we're saying it. We can determine if our verbal and visual message is consistent with our intentions. We must judge whether the tone and intonation of the message we are sending match our intended message. In addition to hearing ourselves, we pick up subtle reactions from the receiver, such as nods, a raised eyebrow, a frown, and so on. All of these actions by the receiver indicate that our message is being received in the way we intended. A frown, a look of disgust, or a smile, too, can be an indicator that we need to change our message in some way or that our message is not being understood.

The feedback we receive is both direct and indirect. When receivers demonstrate by their actions that they have understood the message, the feedback is characterized as direct.

---

*Terry is a school psychologist, and Jim is a classroom teacher. They have scheduled a meeting with Mr. Jones to talk about a home management plan. They run into each other in the hall, and the following interaction occurs:*

*Terry: Jim, do you know what time we will meet with Mr. Jones?"*

*Jim: On Tuesday at four o'clock.*

---

In this example, Jim's verbal response or direct feedback to Terry clearly indicates that he understands the message being sent. As shown in the next example, direct feedback also can be provided nonverbally.

---

*Tara is excited about Ian's birthday and is sitting at the breakfast table talking to her mother about his present. All of a sudden her mom squints her eyes and gives Tara a stern look. Tara immediately stops talking. Just at that moment Ian comes into the room.*

---

Tara's mother sent a nonverbal message—a stern look—indicating that Tara should stop talking. Tara's actions provided direct feedback that she understood the message.

Indirect feedback, in contrast, occurs when the receiver indicates that he or she is aware that a message has been sent but he or she doesn't understand the message.

---

*While they were sitting in the teachers' lounge at lunch, the following interaction takes place between two third-grade teachers.*

*Tom: Sue, would you please pass the ketchup?*

*Sue: (Looking at Tom, puzzled) Huh?*

---

Sue's question to Tom provides indirect feedback that she does not understand his message and that she needs clarification. Even though her response is brief, she indicates clearly that she doesn't understand what he said. Indirect feedback also can occur without a great deal of verbal exchanges.

*Tom: Sue, would you please pass the ketchup?*
*Sue: (Looking at Tom, puzzled) Huh?*
*Tom: I said, please pass the ketchup.*
*Sue: (Hands him the mustard.)*

This time Sue's actions clearly indicate that she is aware a message had been sent. Equally clear, however, is that she does not understand the message. Obviously, Tom and Sue do not have the same understanding of the message, and Tom is going to have to send his message in a different way to complete the communication cycle. When someone is having trouble understanding your message, a good strategy is to change how you are sending the message slightly.

*Kate and Shauna are both second-grade teachers, and their classes join together for certain activities. In preparation for an upcoming meeting with Molly's parents, Kate and Shauna are talking about some of Molly's strengths.*

*Kate: One aspect we should emphasize is Molly's ability to share with the other kids during reading.*

*Shauna: You think Molly shares well? I always thought she was a little possessive with her things.*

*Kate: No, that's not what I mean. I was referring to her ability to share during reading.*

*Shauna: Now I'm really confused. If you don't mean sharing her things, what kind of sharing do you mean?*

*Kate: I'm referring to the way she shares! You know how she shares from the stories she reads!*

The problem in this interaction is that when Kate realizes Shauna is confused, she repeats essentially the same phrase that caused the confusion ("her ability to share") in an attempt to clarify the misunderstanding. As one might expect, repeating the phrase that caused the confusion usually just intensifies the receiver's confusion. Rather than clarifying the miscommunication, the two people may become frustrated, further inhibiting communication. A better strategy is to send the message using different words or emphasis.

> *Kate:* One aspect we should emphasize is Molly's ability to share with the other kids during reading.
> *Shauna:* You think Molly shares well? I always thought she was a little possessive with her things.
> *Kate:* No, that's not what I mean. I was referring to her ability to relay key ideas from stories.
> *Shauna:* Oh, yes! She can be very insightful.

This is a more efficient interaction that avoids needless confusion. Another technique is to ask the sender to say the statement or question in another way because the receiver is having trouble understanding the intent of the message. This is a powerful technique that can help clarify a confusing message quickly. Let's return to the first example and see how Shauna could have used this technique to help Kate provide a clear message.

> *Kate:* One aspect we should emphasize is Molly's ability to share with the other kids during reading.
> *Shauna:* You think Molly shares well? I always thought she was a little possessive with her things.
> *Kate:* No, that's not what I mean. I was referring to her ability to share during reading.
> *Shauna:* Now I'm really confused. If you don't mean sharing her things, I don't understand what you mean. Can you say it another way?
> *Kate:* I think we should emphasize how Molly is able to relate her interpretations of stories and ideas to her peers.

Asking colleagues to repeat their messages in another way forces them to think through the essential ideas of the message and other words that will convey this message. In this way the receiver hears the message with different words than those that were misunderstood. As a result, the confusion can be bypassed and the communication cycle can be closed.

Finally, the messages we send pass through an environment. Often, this environment is noisy and includes other messages that can compete and interfere with the receiver's understanding of the message. Not only can environmental distracters influence a message, but the framework of the environment can also have an effect. For example, if two teachers are talking in the lounge about one of the teachers' children and a third teacher also is sitting in that lounge, the way messages are sent and received are likely to be different than if the two were alone. Carrying this further, the same message spoken in a classroom with other children around takes on a third form.

Distracters in the environment can be intense or mild. The intensity of the distracter is proportional to its inhibiting impact on the communication. Noise, for instance, is an obvious distracter. All of us have experienced the futility of trying to talk over a loud band. Many other distracters are more subtle, such as accents, voice tone, other conversations in the room, other activities in the room, the temperature or room comfort, and even the appearance of the room.

The way in which the sender constructs and sends the message can serve as a distracter, too. If the speaker uses sentences of great length, the complexity of the structure can confuse the listener and prevent him or her from interpreting the meaning accurately. If the sender speaks too quickly or interprets the same word or words differently than the receiver does, confusion can be the result. Finally, if words are used in an inappropriate context, they can inhibit the listener's understanding. In a similar way, being unaware of body language and how it can inhibit or enhance the message being sent is problematic.

## ■ VERBAL COMMUNICATION

Verbal communication is transmitted through an arbitrary set of codes that we call *language*. These arbitrary sets of codes are agreed upon by people who use those codes. Language is made up of four components: phonology, syntax, semantics, and pragmatics (Lane & Molyneaux, 1992).

## PHONOLOGY

Phonology refers to the variety of individual sounds that compose our language. The word *pet*, for example, is made up of three sounds or phonemes: the consonant *p*, the vowel sound *e,* and the consonant *t*. Based on regional dialects and different accents, these sounds can be slightly different. As long as the sounds have sufficient similarity, however, the sender and the receiver recognize them as the same, and the word is recognizable. At times, though, dialects can inhibit our ability to communicate.

## SYNTAX

The rules of the language for how words go together are referred to as syntax. The rules are arbitrary and, again, they are agreed upon by users of the language. These rules include parts of speech, grammar, and sentence structure. Each language has its own set of syntactical rules that allow for a wide variety of meanings. When we make grammar errors or use long, complex sentence structures, we can inhibit our ability to communicate our ideas.

## SEMANTICS

The meaning of words and their connection to the arbitrary set of symbols and sounds that make up words is called semantics. To communicate effectively, the sender and the receiver must have a common understanding of the words being used. Words have both a *denotation* definition, which can be thought of as the dictionary definition, and a *connotation* definition, which is the implied meaning of the word from context. How the word is used in a sentence, the body language of the person using the word, and the sentences that precede and follow the word are all indicators of the intended meaning of the word.

Semantics is an area of particular concern to individuals who are trying to collaborate with their colleagues. We must have a common understanding of the words we use. Education is full of jargon. We talk about linkages, networking, and integration, to name a few. Typically, all of us have a slightly different meaning for these words. We cannot assume that we all have the same understanding as each other. Rather, we must check each other's understanding to be sure we are on the same wavelength.

## PRAGMATICS

How language is used in different environments and contexts is referred to as pragmatics. We all have expectations for communication in certain environments. For example, when a group of people is watching a football game, hooting, hollering, and screaming are appropriate. Watching a tennis match, however, requires a whole different set of expectations.

Inappropriate interaction for the environment sends a confused message. Someone screaming at a tennis match to show support for a player will bring the ire of the referee, the players, and other audience members. An individual quietly and calmly watching an exciting football game may be thought to be disengaged and uncaring about the outcome. These same kinds of roles can affect the way we interact in collaborative relationships. Saying something unexpected to your colleague can impede communication and understanding.

## ■ NONVERBAL COMMUNICATION

Nonverbal communication is extremely powerful. Often the nonverbal messages we send are a more accurate representation of our actual intent than what we actually say. We all know people who frown, sigh, and then say they are fine—when their whole body and orientation indicate they are not at all fine. Although nonverbal messages can be confusing, nonverbal language often is what gives us a real understanding of the intended message. Like verbal communication, nonverbal communication is made up of several components. These have been defined in different ways, but we have organized them into three components: physical, temporal, and surroundings.

### PHYSICAL

The speaker's age, physical condition, and vocal inflection add to our understanding of the message. For example, when a teacher says to students, "Would you please be quiet?" they usually understand that this is not a question but a command. In a similar fashion, the way in which we respond to our colleagues can send a message quite different from what we intended. The distance between individuals in the interaction also impacts the interaction. We can define distance zones that characterize different kinds of interactions. Generally, the more informal and intimate the interaction, the smaller the zone. When we violate someone's distance zone, we make them uncomfortable and can communicate lack of respect toward their own needs.

The physical posture we display when interacting provides an important message to the receiver. Eye contact and an open stance while leaning forward slightly communicate to individuals that you are attending to them. Looking at your watch, not making eye contact, sitting away from the individual, and other disengaging behavior can communicate that you are not interested in what the person is saying.

## TEMPORAL

Temporal factors relate to the amount of time we are willing to spend with a speaker. Time is an interesting factor, and how we spend it with one another can communicate powerful expectations. If people always are left waiting for you to come to meetings, you are communicating that your time is more valuable than their time. Similarly, the amount of time scheduled for an interaction is an indication of the importance placed on that interaction. The shorter the time, the less important is the interaction. This is an important message to keep in mind when scheduling meetings with teachers or parents. For example, because of time constraints, schools frequently schedule meetings with parents at 15-minute intervals, which may communicate to parents, despite school rhetoric that parental input is important, that these meetings are unimportant to the professionals at the school. When scheduling important meetings, members must be on time and plenty of time must be allotted for the meeting.

## SURROUNDINGS

The setting in which the interaction occurs and the clothes and appearance we bring to an interaction are important. A meeting in a classroom with bolted-down desks and attached seats makes open communication between participants difficult. On the other hand, desks that can be moved to form a circle will facilitate communication. Further, uncomfortable surroundings can inhibit communication because individuals become distracted by their discomfort. A room with poor acoustics or plagued by noise can have a similar negative impact on communication.

Clothes, too, can indicate difference in status. An individual who dresses down can communicate a different status than someone who wears formal dress, which may imply that he or she is in authority.

 Before you read the next section, think about the last time you had an emotion you wanted to keep secret. Were you able to keep it secret? Did some people see through your facade, or were you able to fool everyone? If people found out about your secret, what part of your behavior gave you away?

## ■ CONGRUENT AND INCONGRUENT MESSAGES

Our messages are rarely single-channeled (Molyneaux & Lane, 1982). Most messages come across in multiple ways. While we are talking, we also are sending a whole series of nonverbal messages. A multidimensional message can improve understanding if the various dimensions are congruent—if the facial expressions, the body, the verbal and nonverbal messages are essentially communicating the same idea. Conversely, when the verbal and nonverbal messages are communicating different ideas, the overall message can be confusing.

> *Jack walks into the office to check his mailbox and has the following interaction with June, the school secretary.*
> *Jack: Hey, June! How was your weekend?*
> *June: (With a deep frown and a slight sigh) Great.*

Although her verbal message indicates that her weekend was great, her nonverbal message clearly reveals that her weekend was anything but great. Incongruent messages can confuse the receiver because the receiver then must decide which of the messages is the most accurate. On the other hand, if June had responded to Jack's question with a congruent message, he would have little doubt about the message being sent.

---

*Jack:* Hey, June! How was your weekend?
*June:* (A big smile comes across her face and her eyes light up) Great!

---

This message is much clearer because the verbal and the non-verbal content is consistent. When the verbal and nonverbal messages being sent are consistent, the combined message is congruent. When the verbal message and the nonverbal message disagree, the combined message is incongruent.

Congruent messages are much clearer and more easily understood than incongruent messages because one does not have to sort out the differences between verbal and nonverbal messages and then make decisions as to which is most accurate. Conversely, incongruent messages are made up of different verbal and nonverbal messages that can be confusing and are ripe for misinterpretation.

Typically, our nonverbal behavior supplements and augments what we say verbally. When nonverbal and verbal messages are congruent, the nonverbal enhances and facilitates understanding. When the verbal and nonverbal messages are incongruent or different, the nonverbal message typically provides greater insight. As a result, if a speaker is sending an incongruent message, one should look to the nonverbal message to gain the understanding. Nonverbal aspects of our behavior are under less conscious control than the verbal aspects. Sometimes we are unaware of the nonverbal message we are sending. Therefore, astute listeners listen not only with their ears but also with their eyes. Pointing out the inconsistency to the person sending the message and asking for some clarification may be helpful.

As a word of caution, when individuals from different cultures are interacting, they may see nonverbal aspects of behavior that are not used in their own culture. Therefore, "typical" interpretations of nonverbal aspects of behavior made by individuals engaging in cross-cultural communication can be misleading. One must be extremely sensitive to cultural differences and should not make assumptions about expected behavior.

## ■ COMMUNICATION FOR COLLABORATION

Communication is the foundation upon which effective collaboration is built. Good communication skills are a prerequisite for collaboration. If we cannot communicate effectively with our colleagues and others, a collaborative relationship is not possible. Communication seems a simple process, one that we often take for granted, but in reality it is a complex interplay of interactions. At the most basic level it involves a sender, a message, and a receiver. In Chapters 4 and 5 we provide specific suggestions regarding skills to facilitate communication and overcome obstacles that can inhibit communication.

## ■ REMEMBER...

1. Communication is a cyclical process that involves a sender, a message, and a receiver.
2. For the cycle to be complete, a sender must send a message and a receiver must provide feedback to the sender, indicating that the message was understood accurately. Feedback can be direct or indirect.
3. Messages are transmitted through verbal and nonverbal means.
4. The environment or setting can introduce distracters that impede the understanding of messages and the communication process.
5. When verbal and nonverbal messages are different, the message is incongruent. When messages are mixed, the nonverbal message generally is most reflective of the true message.

## ■ ACTIVITIES

■ Using a brief case study of a child, engage in the following activity with four or more people: One person reads the case study and whispers it from memory to another member. Each member, in turn, whispers the key components of the case study to another member of the group. The last member of the group relates the case study aloud, and then the first member reads the case study. Discuss differences between the key components in the original case study and those related by the last member. Discuss factors that contributed to the differences. In particular, focus on the role that lack of feedback played in the outcome of this activity.

■ Keep a list of all of the incongruent messages you receive during the next week. Discuss these lists as a group, and generate an overall list. Describe the situation and the clues that suggest the communication was incongruent.

■ Select five or more pictures from magazines or other sources that depict clear emotions. Write down the emotion being expressed. After all group members show their pictures, discuss the emotions depicted in each of the pictures. Discuss differences and similarities in interpreting these emotions. Describe aspects of the pictures that led to the interpretations.

# SKILLS TO FACILITATE EFFECTIVE COMMUNICATION

**L**istening skills are important particularly when engaging in a collaborative relationship with your peers. These are the skills that will help you clarify and understand the messages being sent to you. When you are first learning these skills, they likely will seem artificial. As you use these active listening skills, however, they will become more comfortable to you and will become incorporated into your repertoire of communication. They can be learned only through practice. Through this practice you will develop your own style of communication and natural ways to utilize active listening to enhance your understanding of others.

In this chapter we identify active listening skills that can help you understand the messages a speaker sends to you. Developing good listening skills is a primary step toward collaborating with colleagues and families. You must have a good understanding of the intent. The skills to be covered in this chapter include: offering support, general openings, reflection, stating the implied, clarification, silence, placing the event in context, and summarization. The chapter concludes with some suggestions about ways to develop your own communication style so you can include these skills as part of your natural style of communication.

Think about an individual you consider to be a good listener. Visualize the last time you had a conversation with this individual. What aspects of this individual's behavior contributes to his or her skills as a listener? Is it the way this listener positions his or her body and makes eye contact? Is it how that person responds to what you are saying? Is it a combination of nonverbal and verbal language? As you read this chapter, reflect on the actions of the individual you have selected as a good listener and see if you can identify any of the following practices he or she has incorporated into his or her repertoire of interacting.

## ■ OFFERING SUPPORT

Offering support means indicating to a colleague that you are there to listen and try to help that person work through a concern. Letting a colleague know you are ready to help and will make time for him or her is an important message in itself and indicates that you are supportive. Clear expectations, however, must be established in regard to place and time.

You must communicate clearly when you have an appropriate place to talk. The teachers' lounge, with a lot of teachers around the table, may not be the best place to discuss a student's problem; nor is the hallway an appropriate place for this discussion, when other children might be around.

Time to talk is equally important. Sometimes people begin a collaborative dialogue when they clearly do not have enough time to finish the dialogue. Letting your colleague know you have an engagement in a few minutes and suggesting a time when both would be available is better. If you have classroom responsibilities and only 10 minutes before the children return, you don't want to engage in a collaborative problem-solving session. If you find yourself in this situation, you might listen a while and, before things get too far, say, "I think this is important, and I'm glad you came to talk to me, but I have students coming in a few minutes. When can you and I get together and talk about this more?" In this way, you indicate to your colleague that you care and that you do have time. The colleague can recognize easily why this isn't the best time. If, on the other hand, you try to rush and complete the conversation before the bell rings, your colleague may interpret the interaction to mean that you don't care and are not willing to spend the time.

---

> *You have to go to an IEP meeting in 15 minutes. The school psychologist, Sandy, whom you have been working with to develop a management plan for Jack, stops by to tell you about an idea that she has. You and Sandy talk for about 5 minutes. You recognize that this is a rather complex intervention and some careful discussion is needed to identify possible pitfalls. Rather than rushing Sandy or supporting her by telling her that it sounds like a great idea before you have had a chance to think through all the options, you should find a way to (a) indicate your interest, (b) explain why now is not a good time for a discussion, and (c) settle on a better time to meet. You might say:*
>
> *Jim:* Sandy, on the surface this sounds like a great idea, but I want to make sure you've got the time to do this and Evelyn can help you implement the study. I have an IEP meeting in ten minutes, though. I can meet you in the morning and bring in coffee and doughnuts, and we can think this through when we're both fresh.
>
> *Sandy:* Sure. Sounds great. Make sure you get French crullers. You know those are my favorite.

---

In this scenario Sandy is asking Jim for his opinion about what she is planning to do. Jim might have given quick, and perhaps careless, feedback. If the plan didn't work, careless feedback could have hindered their relationship later on. To be honest about limitations on your time is more appropriate than to rush the situation. Equally important is for Jim to show up the next day. If he doesn't, he will communicate to Sandy that he really doesn't care or have the time for her. We must recognize that we cannot be available 24 hours a day to help others sort through problems. We must be honest when we don't have the time to interact.

## ■ GENERAL OPENINGS

When you first engage in collaborative dialogue, you should not get too specific too soon. Statements such as, "what's up?" "would you like to talk?" "how are things going?"—all are broad statements that allow a colleague the opportunity to begin focusing on the issue confronting him or her and to begin defining problems. Subtle differences in the way you start the communication can create either a sense of openness or a sense of enclosure.

---

*Ms. Thomas is a first-year teacher and just completed her first month of school. She has a difficult and challenging class and is trying to work on management skills. You have been asked to be a mentor for Ms. Thomas. It's lunchtime, and you decide to stop by Ms. Thomas's room to see if she would like to have lunch with you. As you enter her room you notice that she is staring out the window and appears to have been crying. Consider the following four opening statements:*

*Response 1: June, why are you so upset?*

*Response 2: Oh, June, you're worrying about your students' acting up. Don't worry, we all have trouble our first year. It'll get a lot better.*

*Response 3: (Seeing that June is upset, you decide to "put on a good face" and pretend like you did not notice that June seems upset.) "Hey, June, let's get some grub."*

*Response 4: Hi, June. How are things going?*

---

*Response 1* is far too specific and can make Ms. Thomas defensive. Ms. Thomas may not want to discuss the fact that she seems upset. It may upset her even more that her being upset was so obvious to you. Being so direct with her might make her uncomfortable and not enable you to gain a greater understanding about what is wrong. Without understanding why she is upset, you are likely to make her withdraw rather than open up. This is an inappropriate opening statement.

*Response 2* makes a critical assumption that may or may not be true. The assumption is that Ms. Thomas is upset because the students are acting up. Although this may be a plausible assumption, many other factors could be contributing to why Ms. Thomas is upset. The assumption could be unwarranted and derail the communication. In addition, it provides false reassurance that things will get better when, in reality, things don't always get better by themselves. Sometimes we have to work on changing activities. False reassurances can hinder the process.

*Response 3* could be a successful response depending on what follows this opening. There are times when it is better not to address a problem or a concern, thus providing your colleague with some "space." This kind of an approach may also provide an opportunity for your colleague to make the first move and indicate that there is a concern about which she would like to talk. It is important to remember, however, that your colleague most likely is aware that you sense that something is wrong but have chosen not to acknowledge your concern. If this becomes an interactional pattern, it is doubtful that you and your colleague will become effective collaborators.

*Response 4* is the best of the four. It is broad enough to provide an avenue for Ms. Thomas to begin talking. It doesn't provide any false reassurances, nor does it directly point to the emotions Ms. Thomas may be uncomfortable addressing. This response allows Ms. Thomas to set the stage for the discussion and gain greater understanding.

## ■ REFLECTION

Reflection is a technique in which the receiver restates key information the sender has sent, for the purpose of gaining greater clarity in the message. This enhances the receiver's understanding of the message and allows the sender to reflect on the receiver's interpretation and modify that message to be consistent with the sender's intended message. The key information must be paraphrased and communicated back to the sender. In this way the sender gets a clearer understanding of the problem and the message that he or she is sending to the receiver about the problem. This is a critical dynamic because reflection not only clarifies the message for the receiver but also provides an opportunity for the sender to reflect on the problem and better understand critical factors related to it.

Typically, individuals beginning to use active listening skills have little trouble incorporating reflection into their repertoire. Incorporating reflection in a natural way, however, is difficult and requires practice. To take two or three key phrases from the previous statement and restate them to your colleagues is easy, but this often results in a stilted form of conversation. Although reflection is a powerful tool, it should be used sparingly because it can create a sense of phoniness when overused.

---

*Cory and Tom are close friends and have taught fifth grade for the past 4 years. They do a lot of planning together and often share ideas and frustrations. Tom is grading papers after school one day when Cory walks in, obviously upset over something.*

*Cory:* I'm so upset. My lesson fell flat on its face.

*Tom:* You're upset.

*Cory:* Yes. I thought this would be a great lesson.

*Tom:* You thought you'd planned well.

*Cory:* Yes. I spent a lot of time on this lesson. I'm not sure what happened.

---

In the example Tom is using reflection for a dual purpose. First, he is helping Cory gain a greater understanding of her intended message and the problem that is bothering her. At the same time, Tom is identifying key words within each sentence and feeding those back to Cory to make sure his interpretation is the same as her intended message. The first reflection is a direct paraphrase of words Cory said. It provided the opportunity for Cory to go into more depth as to why she was upset. In the second reflection Cory restates the implied meaning of her statement and carries the conversation further.

---

*Indrani and Binh are first-grade teachers serving on the district-wide curriculum committee to pick a new reading series. They have agreed to meet to discus some unique con-*

cerns of the primary grades. Before they can get down to business, however, Indrani clearly is upset and Binh tries to help her find out why.

Indrani: I've had it with these kids! Every time I go back to the reading group, the kids act out and don't do the work. I don't care how hard I try, they're always disruptive.

Binh: You're upset with the children.

Indrani: Yes. I'm upset with the children. They don't listen to me. They act out, and they don't value the time I spend preparing for these lessons.

Binh: The children don't value the time you spend.

Indrani: Yes! I told you I'm upset with them. These kids just don't listen.

---

In this example Binh is paraphrasing only a surface level of the conversation and not the key intent. The first reflection, although not particularly deep, could have been appropriate if Binh had followed with a reflection that moved Indrani's understanding of the problem further. Both of the reflections, however, focus on the message that Indrani is upset. That message is clear, and the second reflection serves only to exasperate Indrani. Even though Binh has good intentions, he probably makes the situation worse. Focusing on factors that contributed to Indrani's being upset would have been more helpful.

---

José and Chelsea are third- and fourth-grade teachers, respectively. They often combine their classes and team-teach. José has asked Chelsea if she will meet with him to discuss some problems he is having with Danielle.

José: I don't know what to do with Danielle. She seems so bored in class. No matter what I give her to do, it just doesn't seem like she's interested in what's going on.

Chelsea: She seems bored?

José: Yes. The other day I did a story on dinosaurs. All kids like dinosaurs. It seems like she just doesn't get into it. I'm not sure what else to do. I don't think

> *she's ever going to learn anything.*
>
> Chelsea: *Danielle can't learn?*
>
> José: *Well, it sure seems that way. I spend extra time with her. I give her feedback. I try to reinforce her. I just don't know what to do.*
>
> Chelsea: *You spend extra time?*
>
> José: *Yes. At the end of each lesson, I call her up to my desk and go over the information that she is supposed to learn on her own. But it just doesn't seem to help.*

The first time Chelsea reflects on José's messages, she is just indicating generally that she's interested in listening, but she hasn't really helped José clarify his statement. In the second example Chelsea picks a specific aspect of what he said to follow up. By picking a specific phrase, Chelsea is beginning to focus the conversation. José then goes on to indicate his frustration with the situation. Chelsea could have chosen to follow up on José's frustration by saying, "You seem frustrated." This would have been an equally good response and might have helped José to focus on his frustration. Chelsea, however, chooses to focus on the child and reflect José's frustration by saying, "Danielle can't learn?" This gives José an opening to discuss what he'd already tried with Danielle to get her to learn. When Chelsea focuses on the brief phrase, "You spend extra time," José then goes into greater detail. Chelsea has moved José successfully from indicating some general frustration to talking about strategies he has tried and why they may or may not have been effective. This is a good use of reflection to help José narrow down what he is trying to communicate to Chelsea and begin to reflect on things he has tried.

After reading the descriptions of listening practices and the corresponding examples, think about your own interaction style. Are any of these practices in your current repertoire of interacting? Do some practices seem more natural than others? Do you think these practices would be effective if they were applied artificially? What steps can you take to incorporate some of these practices into your repertoire of interacting?

## ■ STATING THE IMPLIED

One method to move the conversation along is a technique called *stating the implied*. This technique is particularly effective when used with reflection because it can help make the conversation feel more natural. Rather than stating exactly what has been said, the receiver verbalizes what he or she understands is the underlying message being sent. This provides the sender with an opportunity to concur or to further refine the message. Although reflection and verbalization of the implied are similar skills, they have key differences.

---

*It's before school on a brisk November day, and Rebecca decides to go into the teachers' lounge to get a cup of coffee before the students come. When she enters, she sees Carlos sitting at a table by himself, obviously looking disappointed. Rebecca fills her coffee and goes over to sit by Carlos. They engage in the following conversation:*

Rebecca: *Hey, Carlos, what's up?*

Carlos: *Oh, not much.*

Rebecca: *Come on, you don't seem like yourself. What's the deal?*

Carlos: *Oh, I don't know. Sometimes I wonder if teaching is all it's cut out to be.*

Rebecca: *Teaching all it's cut out to be? That seems a little dramatic.*

Carlos: *Maybe it's just Monday blues or...I don't know.*

Rebecca: *This seems like a little more than Monday blues to me. I haven't seen you this down since the last time you bet on Phoenix to go to the Super Bowl.*

Carlos: *Well, it's Ian. I thought I'd really made progress. He seemed to be getting his work done. He seemed to be getting his assignments in and really changing his whole attitude about school.*

> *Rebecca:* *So you're concerned about Ian.*
> *Carlos:* *Well, yes, I'm concerned, but...no, I've been really discouraged. I thought with all the hard work we do, he'd get a passing grade in social studies. But I just talked to his social studies teacher, and he's not getting a passing grade.*

---

To Rebecca, Carlos clearly is upset. Rather than reflecting Carlos's words, Rebecca verbalizes the messages she is receiving from Carlos's body language and gives Carlos the chance to clarify if this secondary message is accurate. When Carlos indicates that "maybe it's just Monday blues" Rebecca could have used reflection and said, "So you think it's just Monday blues?" but this would have been inefficient, and Rebecca's choice to verbalize the implied moves the conversation quickly to the source of the concern.

What also should be clear from this example is that Carlos and Rebecca have a friendship and a rapport that allows her to probe into his feeling in the way she does. Verbalizing implied messages can be quite threatening when the individuals involved have not established rapport. Having established rapport, however, when Rebecca verbalizes the messages she is receiving through nonverbal channels, she is able to get Carlos to talk about his real concern, the amount of time he had put in working with Ian and Ian's apparent setback in social studies. Reflection probably would not have had the same outcome.

## ■ CLARIFICATION

When engaged in a collaborative dialogue, at times you will have to seek clarification to gain greater understanding of the information being sent to you. When you become confused about what you are being told, you must stop your partner and ask for clarification. Although admitting you are confused may be difficult for you or you may not want to indicate to your partner that you had not been listening, you have to put those feelings aside and seek clarification. If you allow your partner to continue when you are confused about the message, the confusion will escalate.

How do people become confused? *First*, the manner in which your partner is sending the message can lead to confusion. People who are upset or concerned tend to flit between several different thoughts and send messages that contain parts of each of these thoughts. When this happens, you have to slow down your colleague, ask some key questions, and, in the process, help the person begin to sort out what's really important about the situation.

*Second*, you may need to seek clarification because of your own lack of attention. All of us are human and, after listening to a person for a while, you may find that you have begun to think about your own problems or other issues not related to what the individual is saying. All of a sudden you may realize that you aren't really sure what was said in the last couple of minutes. Trying to bluff through this situation is a mistake. Although you may be concerned that you will be communicating to your partner that you were not listening, that is far better than pretending you were listening. By your responses, your partner will become aware that you had not been listening to what was said.

Therefore, being honest and expressing that you lost track of the conversation, asking for repetition or identifying the last clear thing you remembered, and asking for the rest of the content, is a far better strategy than bluffing. Furthermore, if you do try to bluff through the situation, you are likely to become more confused and will be less able to help your partner.

---

*LaTonya, a third-grade teacher, comes storming into Isaac's classroom after the students have left. LaTonya obviously is extremely upset, and the following dialogue is exchanged:*

Isaac: *Wow! You look angry. What's got your goat?*

LaTonya: *Hot isn't the name for it! I thought Sue was going to the resource room today, but she sat in my class all day long.*

Isaac: *Oh?*

LaTonya: *I'm so mad at that principal. Did you know that yesterday he changed the morning bell and didn't even tell us third-grade teachers?*

Isaac: *So you're upset with the principal?*

> *LaTonya:* Ever since he's come here, I don't know what's go-
> ing on. You know, I really liked Mr. Jones and wish
> he hadn't left. He was the kind of principal who al-
> ways seemed to let us know what was going on.

In this interaction LaTonya clearly is upset. Isaac appropriately starts with a broad opening statement that allows LaTonya to indicate why she is upset. Early in the conversation, however, LaTonya brings in the principal and talks about being upset about the bell schedule. This is confusing, and the conversation does not indicate why the principal is important to LaTonya's concern about Sue going to the resource room. This is where Isaac makes his mistake. Rather than following up and seeking clarification, Isaac uses reflection and asks LaTonya if she is upset with the principal. In the subsequent conversation, LaTonya's response to Isaac's original reflection further carries the conversation away from LaTonya's original concern, which was that Sue was to go into the resource room today. This would have been a critical point for Isaac to ask for clarification, to ask what the principal and bell scheduling have to do with being concerned about Sue's going into the resource room. Let's consider the following scenario, in which clarification is sought.

> *Isaac:* Wow! You look angry. What's got your goat?
> *LaTonya:* Angry! You have no idea how angry I am. I thought
> Sue was supposed to go the resource room today,
> but she was in my class all day long. I'm so mad at
> the principal. Do you know that yesterday he
> changed the second morning bell without telling any
> of us third-grade teachers?
> *Isaac:* Wait a minute. I'm just a little confused. How does
> the principal not letting you know about the bells
> relate to Sue?
> *LaTonya:* Well, I'll tell you. It's just another example of the
> information he doesn't tell us. As I understand it,
> Sue can't go into the resource room until next week
> because her mother is indicating some concern, but
> no one told me this until I went to the special educa-
> tion teacher.

By seeking clarification, it becomes clear as to why the principal was brought into this situation. In fact, the real locus of the problem seems not be that Sue did not go to the resource room. Rather, it may be the lack of communication between LaTonya and the principal. Now that the real problem has been revealed, Isaac can help LaTonya come up with some possible solutions.

## ■ SILENCE

One of the most powerful tools you have as a collaborative colleague is the appropriate use of silence to indicate that you need more information from your colleague. Unfortunately, silence is a technique that frequently is overlooked. Humans seem to have an urgent need to fill in the gap when others are silent. A certain amount of uneasiness sets in when you are in a group and nobody is saying anything or when you are sitting with someone who is not saying anything. Ironically, only when people are extremely comfortable with each other, such as husbands and wives or those in other kinds of intense relationships, are they able to be silent together.

As a collaborative practitioner, you can use silence to your advantage. If you avoid falling into the trap of being uncomfortable and speaking just because no one else is speaking, the silence can create a sense of uneasiness on your colleague's part that, when combined with the appropriate body language, will indicate that you need more information. Your colleague likely will oblige.

Another reason why silence is such an important technique is that you don't have to worry about sounding phony. Many of the techniques we have discussed so far, such as reflection and seeking clarification, can sound stilted and unnatural unless you are an accomplished reflective listener. Another benefit of incorporating silence into your collaborative interactional style is that it provides you and your colleague a moment to think and reflect upon what is being said. From this reflection the most salient aspects of the conversation often are selected and help the interaction go forward.

---

*You go to pick up your mail in the main office, and you overhear two fifth-grade teachers talking about Maggie, a sixth-grade science teacher. It seems that when she wasn't paying attention, one of her students poked his pen through all of her slides from Egypt. Some of the negatives were damaged in the processing of the slides, and Maggie isn't sure if these slides are replaceable. The two teachers are talking about how upset Maggie is and how she is sitting in the room alone, staring out of the window. You decide to go down and talk with Maggie. You walk over to her, pull up a chair next to her, and say:*

> Derek: *I just heard what happened. You must be furious.*
> *(At this point Derek sits quietly and allows a moment or two for Maggie to respond.)*
> Maggie: *I don't think furious is the right word.*
> Derek: *You're not furious?*
> Maggie: *I think I'm really hurt. I don't know why Roger would try to hurt me.*

---

Derek uses silence appropriately. He is a good friend of Maggie's, and he knows how important these slides of Egypt were to her. By allowing the silence, Derek indicates that he is there for Maggie and that he is ready to listen if she has something to say. By giving Maggie space and time, she is able to think through her feelings on the issue and take time to reflect on her feelings. Eventually, Maggie is able to articulate that she is hurt. The time provided is important. Had Derek been uncomfortable with the silence and added a lot more information, Maggie probably would not have made this revelation and the conversation might have gone a different way.

---

*Maggie acknowledges that Derek has come in. Derek pulls up a chair and sits down.*

> Derek: *You must be really angry.*
> Maggie: *(Continues to stare out of the window.)*
> Derek: *(After a few moments) I would have killed him if he had done the same thing to my stuff. I don't know how you kept your temper.*
> Maggie: *I don't know. I just didn't think I should yell at him. I didn't know the right thing to do.*

> *Derek:* When I brought my pottery in from Mexico last year and Anne dropped it on the floor, I know everybody said it was a mistake, but I'll tell you, I wasn't so sure it was a mistake, and I let her parents know what I really thought.
>
> *Maggie:* I'm not sure what I'm going to do.

In this example, Derek is uncomfortable with the silence and, in an attempt to show he is there and to empathize by relating a similar event in his life, he talks about his own situation and how he dealt with the problem. He does not really help Maggie come to grips with the key events about this situation and how she feels about it. As was apparent in the first situation, the feeling that Maggie has is not anger but, rather, a feeling of hurt. Derek's response to a similar situation had been anger, and he assumes wrongly that Maggie is having a similar reaction. This mistaken assumption guides Derek's subsequent questions and inhibits Maggie's understanding of her own feelings.

Used appropriately, silence can be a natural means to integrate active listening skills into your style of communication. As a word of caution, though, using silence advantageously is a difficult skill that requires some sophistication. As we will discuss in the next chapter, the inappropriate use of silence can inhibit communication.

## ■ PLACING EVENTS IN CONTEXT

As a conversation develops, the need to create a context to place events in time or sequence becomes increasingly important. This skill is used when the collaborative dialogue involves some rather substantial or complex information. It places events into their proper order and helps identify events that are unrelated to the issue under examination.

> *Jessie stops by Shenice's class one morning and asks Shenice if she has a moment to talk. They are both seventh-grade teachers and have the luxury of not having a homeroom,*

*so they have a little time before the first class begins. Shenice and Jessie begin talking about what's happening in Jessie's classroom. After a while, it becomes clear that Shenice is still having problems with Damon.*

Shenice: *I just can't figure it out. No matter what happens, Damon is throwing spit wads, yelling, or doing something annoying.*

Jessie: *What were you doing the last time Damon threw a spit wad?*

Shenice: *Yesterday he started throwing spit wads when they were putting their homework problems up on the board.*

Jessie: *Where were you when he was throwing spit wads?*

Shenice: *Well, I usually go over and sit on the side.*

Jessie: *How far away from Damon were you when this happened?*

---

Although Damon's disruptive behavior during the math period clearly is what is causing Shenice's concern, knowing the specifics related to this concern is difficult at first. Jessie begins placing the event into some kind of time and sequence. This strategy reveals that the disruptive behavior occurred when Shenice selected people to put their math problems on the board and after she had moved to the side of the room to monitor the problems. In this way, Jessie facilitates Shenice's understanding of when and where the problem occurred.

## ■ SUMMARIZATION

Every collaborative interaction should end with a summary of what has taken place during the interaction and the actions that people are to take as a result of the interaction. The summary is important for two reasons:

1. It gives both individuals in the relationship a chance to hear the key points and to agree on what was said or to disagree and revise the content of the interaction and make some clarifications regarding key events.

2. It makes public the action that everybody is to take, thus avoiding misunderstandings about agreements or next steps.

---

*Selina has been working with Saundra on ways to help Maria complete her independent seatwork. The two agree that Saundra is going to spend an extra couple of minutes with Maria alone, making sure she understands what she is supposed to do and going over the directions. Selina ends the conversation like this:*

*Selina:* Sounds like you've worked out a good plan. As I understand it, every day you are going to mark in your plan book whether you spent five minutes talking with Maria about the directions. You're going to determine the effectiveness based on whether Maria gets her work done or not, so what you'll be looking for is incomplete work or complete work.

*Saundra:* Yes, that's what we talked about. I'm going to spend five minutes with Maria, and I'll mark in my book every day whether I did it or not, and I think this is going to be easy. It'll be really easy to talk to Maria about her completing these activities.

*Selina:* Sounds great. Let's get together in a couple of weeks and see how it's going.

---

Selina summarizes the key actions that Saundra is going to take as a result of their consultative relationship. Afterward, Saundra confirms that Selina's understanding is the same, and they set a time to get together and discuss this further.

## ▋ PRACTICE

The communication skills discussed in this chapter require practice to become part of your repertoire of collaborative interaction skills. You are going to have to work on these skills and try to develop your own style in using them. When conversations sound stilted and contrived, it inhibits collaborative interactions. The more you work on the skills to make them part of your repertoire, the more natural they will become and the more effective you will be as a collaborative colleague. Identifying practices that you now use only partially and those that already seem comfortable to you will help you as you try to incorporate these skills into your own communication style. By consciously practicing with your friends and family, the skills gradually will become part of your repertoire.

You do not need to learn all of these practices, nor is any one of them in isolation the most effective. Rather, a combination of practices will become your style of interacting. People who combine these practices in a natural manner are characterized as being good listeners.

## ■ REMEMBER...

1. Don't try to get into the meat of a conversation too quickly. Start with some general statements, and ease into important information.
2. Offering support is the key first step. You must make clear to someone that you are ready and willing to listen, and you can provide the parameters around when this should occur. When you are offering yourself to a colleague, you should follow through on your commitments and set realistic timeframes and reactions.
3. Reflection is a skill in which you restate key phases of your colleague's statement into a question. This allows your colleagues to hear what you're hearing as if you were an audio mirror, and gives them a chance to further refine and develop their thoughts.
4. Stating the implied is important because the implied message often is the most important message.
5. If, for some reason, you become confused or your concentration wanes, you should seek clarification to get yourself back into the conversation.
6. Silence is a powerful tool that, if incorporated appropriately, should help you develop a natural interaction style.
7. As conversations move forward, you must place information into a context that orders it into the proper time and sequence.

8. The information gained from an interaction should be summarized so the parties to the conversation are clear as to key information and actions to be taken as a result of the interaction.

## ■ ACTIVITIES

- Participate in role-play situations that depict a teacher interacting with: (a) a parent, (b) a specialist, and (c) an administrator. Work in pairs, and have the role-plays videotaped. One person in the pair should role-play a teacher, and the other should be interacting with the teacher. When the videotapes are played, the individual playing the teacher is to describe everything he or she did to facilitate communication and then ask the viewers to elaborate or expand on the *positive* aspects of the interaction. (Our experience with this activity indicates that the viewers tend to focus on the negative aspects of this interaction.)
- To expand the above activity: Pairs of students engage in two role-playing activities. The first role-play should be done prior to studying the information on communication and skills that facilitate or inhibit communication. The second role-play is done after that information has been presented. Participants meet in small groups or as a class to discuss differences between the first role-play and the second one.
- Over the next week, keep a list of incidents in which someone used one or more of the communication skills addressed in this chapter. Discuss these lists in class, and generate a combined list. What impact did this activity have on you?

# 5

# Barriers to Effective Communication

n Chapters 3 and 4 we talked about techniques to enhance your ability to listen and communicate with your colleagues. These are extremely important skills that, if practiced and incorporated into your standard style of interaction, will enable you to be effective in collaborative interactions. Unfortunately, we all sometimes engage in an interactional style that diminishes our ability to listen and thereby communicate. Usually this results from poor habits that we unknowingly have adopted over time. Without an understanding of communication as a cycle involving both a receiver and a sender, we might assume that we communicated successfully merely because we sent the message. Without feedback from the receiver indicating that the message sent was understood accurately, this is a faulty assumption. The communication cycle must be completed before we communicate.

To communicate effectively, we must also recognize barriers to communication and eliminate them systematically from our interaction style. Recognizing these barriers and becoming aware of how easily they can become a part of your interactional style is the first step toward eliminating them from your style of communication.

 As you read through the common barriers to communication, think about conversations in which you or your colleague have run into one of these barriers. In retrospect, do you believe you and your colleague ever really completed the communication? Were you or your colleague able

to recover and eventually communicate? If so, how did you do this? Did the interchange result in anger, frustration, or other negative emotions?

## ■ ADVICE

Perhaps the most common error that someone can make in a collaborative relationship is to give advice too quickly. We walk a fine line when trying to help our colleagues. Often they are seeking a suggestion or alternative strategy to help solve a problem. Making a suggestion that a colleague may choose to implement, however, is quite different from giving a colleague advice where the advice giver implies that he or she has the correct and only answer. If it is pressed too strongly, giving advice can negate the professionalism of our colleague by dictating a specific course of action. Compounding this problem is the fact that, when we give advice too strongly, we are making suggestions that come from our own repertoire of effective strategies but may not be within our colleague's repertoire. Finally, giving advice may create dependence; we may be treating our colleagues not as equal professionals but instead as individuals who do not have the capacity to act on their own—even if the resulting intervention has been successful.

Advice giving that results in such professional disenfranchisement should be avoided. Suggesting alternatives to consider, however, is different and is something we should want to do. Our colleagues, though, always should be the ones to decide what they wish to implement in their own classrooms.

*Amelia is an eighth-grade English teacher, and the school is embarking on a full inclusion model. Amelia's class has been targeted to incorporate some of the children who have been in the self-contained special education classroom. These children have mild to moderate disabilities, and Amelia is trying to figure out a way to differentiate instructions and incorporate all of these children. She goes to Keiko, the resource room teacher, and they begin discussing some possibilities.*

Amelia: *I really care about these kids, and I'm excited about the opportunities, but at the same time I'm scared and wonder if I can really handle such differences in abilities.*

Keiko: *Sounds like you're concerned about the wide range of abilities you're going to have in your classroom.*

Amelia: *I am. I've never had such a range of differences before, and I don't know how to construct a lesson so both groups of kids will survive.*

Keiko: *If I were you, I'd get away from the idea that all these kids are going to be involved equally in the classroom and recognize that the best you're going to do is to socially integrate these kids in some cases.*

Amelia: *So you don't think I should try to develop lessons to incorporate all of the kids?*

Keiko: *No. I wouldn't try that. I'd recognize some of their limitations, and with half of the kids in the classroom, that's the best you're going to do. You might want to have two sets of lessons that all the kids can work on individually and then work on some group topics where you can include all the students.*

Amelia: *Huh! You have some interesting ideas. Maybe I'll try that. Would you mind helping me with my first lesson?*

---

On the surface this looks like a helpful interaction. Keiko began by facilitating Amelia's reflection and elaboration of her concern. The fatal flaw in this interaction is that Keiko quickly gave Amelia advice and told her to recognize that some of the children are never going to be completely integrated into her classroom and that she should regard social integration as sufficient. Keiko's suggestions may set lower expectations on Amelia's part and limit the possibilities for these children. Other strategies, such as cooperative learning, might be considered. Here is an alternative interaction.

> *Ameila:* I really care about these kids, and I'm excited about the opportunities, but at the same time I'm scared and wonder if I can really handle such differences in abilities.
>
> *Keiko:* Sounds like you're concerned about the wide range of abilities you're going to have in your classroom.
>
> *Ameila:* That's probably it. There are so many kids and such differences between the kids, I'm just not sure how things are going to work out.
>
> *Keiko:* Are you concerned about everything? Or are you most concerned about some specific parts of the classroom or your routine?
>
> *Ameila:* Well, now that you've mentioned it, I guess I'm most concerned about having the kids work independently. I don't know how I'm going to incorporate these kids into my reading groups, and I worry that it will take too much of my time.
>
> *Keiko:* Let's focus on your reading groups. Maybe there's a way to incorporate these kids that you haven't thought about.

In this example Amelia and Keiko have a similar interaction, but Keiko avoids the enticing lure to offer advice and instead encourages reflection and seeks clarification to gain a greater understanding of Amelia's concerns. Once the concerns begin to be identified, Keiko helps facilitate Amelia's thinking by beginning to explore possible ways to modify her approach to reading.

## ■ FALSE REASSURANCES

Perhaps one of the most well intentioned errors that results in the most serious consequences is giving false reassurances. This occurs when you indicate to a colleague that everything is going to work out and there is nothing to worry about or that you are sure the problem is going to be solved. In an attempt to ease your colleague's concern, you dismiss the problem. Providing false reassurances also puts you in a difficult spot because, although we all would like every problem to be resolved, some problems do not have an easy solution. In addition, if we assure a person that it's all going to work out, this could minimize the motivation to work toward a successful resolution. Finally, if the person thinks that perhaps the problem wasn't so intense after all, he or she may feel uncomfortable talking about the problem, inhibiting further communication.

---

*Esteban is a brand new eighth-grade science teacher. The school feels fortunate to get Esteban. He comes highly recommended and brings a strong science background to the school. During the first couple of weeks of the year, the principal notices that Esteban seems distant and preoccupied. She decides that perhaps it's time to sit down with him and talk about what might be happening in his class.*

*Mrs. Jones:* Hi, Esteban. I thought I'd stop by this morning and see how things are going for you as the new teacher. You may not be aware, but I make it a practice to stop in and see what's up.

*Esteban:* Oh, that's a good idea. I'm really glad you stopped by.

*Mrs. Jones:* Well, Esteban, what's up? Seems like you've got some neat activities planned for the kids.

*Esteban:* Well, I guess. But I don't know. I guess they are neat activities. I don't know if the kids will like them.

*Mrs. Jones:* You sound unsure. Is something going on that's causing you some concern?

*Esteban:* Well, not really. Everything seems to be fine. It's just...

*Mrs. Jones:* Esteban, I know you say everything is just fine, but I can't help but hear some doubt.

*Esteban:* Well, I guess you're right. It just seems that I spend so much time planning for each of these lessons. I work sometimes three and four hours after school. I'm going to get married soon, and I'm having a hard time trying to balance my per-

> *sonal life and school. And even though I spend a lot of time preparing, it seems I'm just not getting it right. Sometimes the lesson seems to go over the kids' heads. Other times the lesson seems too simple. Sometimes I have too much time, and sometimes I don't have enough.*
>
> Mrs. Jones: *Oh, is that all? Esteban, you're just going to have to come to grips with your first year of teaching. You came highly recommended. I'm sure you're going to be a great teacher! It's your first year, and I wouldn't worry. It's not really a big deal.*

In this example the principal did an excellent job of using broad opening statements and getting to the discussion quickly of what apparently was wrong with Esteban. The principal followed with some good reflective statements to help Esteban clarify his feelings and then to express his concern. At that point the conversation broke down. The principal minimized his feelings as if they were not important, and she gave him false reassurances that he was not to worry, that everything would work out fine.

The danger in this interaction is twofold. *First*, because Mrs. Jones's comments minimized Esteban's feelings, he is led to believe that his problem is trivial and that in a similar situation others would not worry. As a result, he may think he is unable to deal with the most trivial of problems. If other issues become a problem for Esteban, he probably will not bring them forward because, in this case, what he thought was a problem seemed trivial to someone he respected. He would not likely want to be told a second time that his concerns are unimportant. *Second*, this problem may not work itself out and may continue to be a problem for Esteban. He might have real difficulty organizing his time to provide effective lessons and create a balance between his personal and professional lives. His problem may be compounded because he has been led to believe that it is something that typically works itself out. If it doesn't, he will begin to question not only why he is having a problem but also why the problem isn't working itself out.

## ■ MISDIRECTED QUESTIONS

In a collaborative relationship one of your most important roles is to ask questions and to help the individual reflect upon what's happening in his or her situation to gain greater understanding. Questions are the primary means of directing these conversations and developing mutual understanding. If, however, too many questions are being asked or these questions lack a consistent direction, they will inhibit the conversation. These questions will lead your colleague to focus on various aspects of the communication without ever clearly developing a meaningful dialogue about the situation. This is another reason why reflective listening must become a natural part of your conversation. On the one hand, you must ask questions to guide your colleagues and facilitate their and your understanding. On the other hand, too many questions or irrelevant questions prevent your colleague from developing a clear line of thought and inhibit the communication process.

---

Shakeel is a elementary school gym teacher who has been trying to find a way to incorporate Terry into gym classes. Terry seems angry all of the time. He is tall and has a strong sense of coordination, and Shakeel thinks athletics may present an opportunity for Terry. Molly is Terry's homeroom teacher. One day Shakeel stops by Molly's class with a couple of cups of coffee. The following interaction occurs:

Shakeel: Hey, Molly, I thought I'd bring you some coffee and ask for a piece of your wisdom....That is, if you've got the time.

Molly: For coffee, your time is my time.

Shakeel: I'm struggling with Terry in class, and I'm not quite sure what I should try to help him be less angry and so interested in fighting.

Molly: So you're concerned about Terry.

Shakeel: Yes, he seems...

Molly: So you're worried about his attention span.

Shakeel: No, I'm not worried about Terry's attention span.

Molly: Does he come in late for class?

Shakeel: Well, yes. Sometimes he comes in late for class.

> *Molly:* You're not worried about him being late for class?
> *Shakeel:* Yes, I'm worried about him being late for class, but there are other problems.
> *Molly:* There are other problems?
> *Shakeel:* Yes. There are other problems. I'm worried about how Terry gets along with other students.
> *Molly:* Is Terry absent a lot?

---

This dialogue exemplifies many of the problems with misdirected questioning. First, questions are asked in a rapid-fire pace that does not give Shakeel an opportunity to think. At one point Shakeel actually is interrupted before he can complete his thought. When too many questions are asked too fast, your colleague likely will start responding to the questions and will not have time to reflect on what is happening in the classroom or the concerns that led the colleague to seek your help.

Another problem with this example is that the questions were not particularly focused and lacked any consistent line of thought. For example, raising questions about Terry's tardiness may have been relevant, but to keep dwelling on his tardiness when Shakeel seemed concerned about other issues, too, was inhibiting. The emphasis on Terry's tardiness and then on his potential absences may have brought Shakeel so far off track that he would not be able to get to the larger problem concerning him.

Asking too many questions often becomes a problem when someone is uncomfortable with reflective listening or is concentrating on potential questions rather than listening. Any time you are trying to help a colleague gain understanding about what is happening in the classroom and you are doing most of the talking, something is wrong. If you pay attention and listen, questions will flow naturally. The important trends within the conversation will become apparent, and you will have a naturally flowing conversation as opposed to a choppy interaction confused with a lot of questions.

## ■ WANDERING INTERACTION

Similar to the previous barrier is an interaction that wanders and does not follow a logical progression. If we are interacting with a colleague and our attention begins to wander, we change the subject unknowingly and the interaction will wander. This abruptly inhibits the communication and clearly indicates that we have not been listening and perhaps that we do not care about what is being said. When you find your attention wandering, you should bring it to the attention of your colleague immediately and seek clarification of the subject at hand. The more engaged and skilled we become as listeners, the easier it is to avoid this pitfall.

---

*Concha is a primary level special education teacher, and Mary is a first-grade teacher. In her classroom Mary has Todd, classified as having mild mental retardation. Todd spends a half hour with Concha in the resource room and the remainder of his day in the regular classroom. Mary has been troubled by Todd's feelings of inadequacy when he is involved in any academics in the classroom. She has asked Concha to come in and help her sort through some issues.*

*Concha:* *Mary, I'm glad we have this chance to get together and talk about Todd. I know you're concerned about how Todd is feeling in comparison with the other kids.*

*Mary:* *Yes. Todd's a good kid. I really like him, and the kids like him, but it hurts me when we're working on math facts or any other academically oriented activity. Even though I try to get Todd involved in meaningful ways, he just doesn't understand things at the same level as the other kids, and he knows it.*

*Concha:* *You know, I really think Todd is a good kid, too. Do you know that the other day one of the fifth-grade boys was teasing a first-grade girl and Todd stepped in and stopped those kids?*

*Mary:* *Really! I've seen Todd take risks in other ways and go out of his way to help kids. That's why I'm so concerned about his feelings when we're working on academic activities.*

*Concha:* *You know, speaking of risk taking, I think risk taking is something Todd needs to do more of, and he should be encouraged to take a risk at any opportunity that presents itself.*

---

In this example Mary is trying to talk about ways to help Todd feel more comfortable in her classroom when the ability levels of Todd and the other kids clearly are different. She is concerned about his feelings and self-esteem. Concha, though, changes the subject and at the end gives some advice that isn't even related to the problem that concerns Mary. Changing the subject like this is problematic. First, it breaks Mary's conversation about Todd and inhibits her ability to reflect on the situation and gain greater understanding. Second, it suggests to Mary that she is not being listened to and may even suggest to her that Concha is not interested in her problem. This situation is likely to discourage Mary from seeking Concha's help in the future. Finally, this kind of a conversation is frustrating, which is another reason Mary may not be interested in talking with Concha again.

## ■ INTERRUPTIONS

When we are engaging in a collaborative interaction that is leading toward greater understanding, interruptions can disrupt the flow of the conversation and hinder our colleague's ability to understand the situation more fully. Interruption is linked closely to changing the subject. Frequently, we interrupt when we have lost our train of thought. It also can occur when time becomes an issue and we interrupt in an attempt to get to the heart of the problem too quickly. That is why setting realistic time parameters for collaborative interactions is so important.

---

*Tom and Jack are seventh and eighth-grade science teachers, respectively. They carpool together and consider this an important time to talk about what happens in the classroom. Jack is uncharacteristically quiet during the drive to school today.*

    *Tom:* *You seem a little quiet today. Did you get enough sleep last night?*

    *Jack:* *Yeah, I got enough sleep. It's just that...*

    *Tom:* *So you got enough sleep and didn't watch movies like you usually do, huh?*

> *Jack:* No, I didn't watch movies last night, but I'm really con-
> cerned about Jill.
> *Tom:* Jill?
> *Jack:* Yeah. I'm really concerned about Jill. She...
> *Tom:* How could you be concerned about Jill? She seems to
> have everything together.
> *Jack:* I know she seems to have it all together but...
> *Tom:* Seems to have it together? How could you say she
> seems to have it together? I've never seen a student
> her age so sure of her future and how to get there.

In this situation Jack is having a hard time getting his thoughts heard. The interruptions are frustrating and do not lead to greater understanding. To the contrary, they communicate to Jack that Tom is not listening, nor does Tom seem to care about the problem Jack is facing. The interruptions not only inhibit this interaction but also can discourage Jack from bringing other concerns to Tom for discussion in the future.

## ■ CLICHES

Responding to a colleague's problem with a cliche is a sure-fire way to inhibit the communication. Cliches diminish the feelings of the person with whom you are interacting. They often are used without thought and are part of regional speech patterns. In virtually no situation is a cliche an appropriate response. If you hear yourself using a cliche, you should backtrack immediately and clarify your response.

> *Morty comes storming out of his classroom and bumps
> into Tom in the hallway. Morty is obviously upset. Tom
> carpools with Morty and is an old high school buddy.*
> *Tom:* Hey, what's the matter with you, pal? You look really
> upset.
> *Morty:* I've had it with these kids. No matter how hard I work,
> they don't seem to care about anything. Last period

> *three of the kids were fooling around and broke my last*
> *box of microslides. I've got to go to the supply room*
> *and get more. I've had it.*
> Tom: *Hey, Morty, don't make a mountain out of a mole hill.*
> *Kids will be kids.*

At this point, Morty probably is ready to hit Tom, and Tom has done nothing to help diffuse the situation. If anything, Morty probably is now angry at his friend as well as frustrated about what happened in the classroom. Two cliches minimized Morty's feelings and made the situation worse by increasing his anger and frustration. Now let's take the conversation a little further.

> Tom: *Hey, what's the matter with you, pal? You look really*
> *upset.*
> Morty: *I've had it with these kids. No matter how hard I work,*
> *they don't seem to care about anything. Last period*
> *three of the kids were fooling around and broke my last*
> *box of microslides. I've got to go to the supply room*
> *and get more. I've had it.*
> Tom: *Hey, Morty, don't make a mountain out of a mole hill.*
> *Kids will be kids.*
> Morty: *Don't give me that garbage! You have no idea of how I*
> *feel.*
> Tom: *You're right. That was stupid to say. Tell you what. I'll*
> *get the slides for you, and why don't you get a cup of*
> *coffee.*
> Morty: *Thanks. I could use a cup of coffee.*
> Tom: *If you'd like, maybe we can talk about it on the way*
> *home.*

As the conversation progressed, Tom was able to recover from his error and successfully diffuse the situation. More important, he offered his help to Morty in an appropriate way and laid the groundwork for helping Morty sort out his concerns and develop a solution.

As you read these common barriers, have you recognized any of which you or a colleague have been guilty? Did you see any barriers that may be recurring in your own conversational style? If so, what steps can you take to eliminate or avoid these barriers? When you are with a colleague and he or she puts up one of these barriers, what can you do to help get the conversation back on track?

## ■ MINIMIZING FEELINGS

We have talked about a number of ways that minimize the feelings of someone with whom you are interacting. False reassurances, changing the subject, and cliches are examples of ways in which people minimize feelings and inhibit colleagues from interacting further with you. Feelings can be minimized in other, more subtle ways, too. Consider the following.

---

*Merle has always taught third grade. This year she was transferred to a kindergarten class and is having difficulty trying to organize the free flow of kindergarten and maintain some sense of order. John, the school principal, recognizes that Merle is having problems and stops by one morning with doughnuts and coffee.*

John: *I thought you might like a couple of doughnuts and coffee on the three-month anniversary of our hiring you.*

Merle: *That's really nice, John. I appreciate the coffee and doughnuts.*

John: *How are things going?*

Merle: *I don't know. I get here at seven o'clock every morning to make sure I have everything set up for the kids, and I stay until four-thirty or five every day, going over everything I've done, reviewing the students' work, and planning for the next day. But I'm still not hitting it. I*

> *think I have lessons that either are too short and not*
> *challenging enough or are way over the heads of these*
> *kids.*
> John: *Merle, I wouldn't take it so seriously. Any teacher who*
> *shifts grades has trouble adjusting to a new age group.*

In this example John begins by doing some positive things. Bringing coffee and doughnuts is a real show of support and a clear offering of himself to the teacher. He uses broad opening statements to begin the interaction and is being attentive as Merle explains her concerns. As soon as John tells her not to worry because this is a problem all teachers face, however, he devalues her as an individual and makes her feel as if her concerns are not important. Merle probably will not continue to share concerns or problems with John, because she may be reluctant to be devalued a second time. If people think they have a problem, they do have a problem, no matter how trivial the problem may seem to us. As effective collaborative colleagues, our role is not to make judgments regarding the worth or value of a problem. Rather, it is to help colleagues gain a greater understanding of the problem so they can identify a solution.

## ■ Quick Fixes

Moving too quickly to fix a problem poses a barrier similar to giving advice. Actually, these two barriers often occur at the same time. People often make assumptions about problems when they do not spend the time with colleagues to really help them explore what is happening in the classroom and what may be causing concern. By not spending adequate time to consider all the factors related to a problem, you and your colleague may end up working on a symptom of the problem instead of the actual problem. When this happens, you and your colleague are unlikely to change whatever was causing the problem that led to your interaction in the first place. Furthermore, spending time and effort working on something that is not the true problem can frustrate your colleague and lead him or her to conclude that collaboration is an inadequate way to solve problems.

> *Vanessa is a first grader who has not had similar oppor-*
> *tunities of other children in her new school in that she hasn't*
> *been in preschool or kindergarten. Nonetheless, she is a bright*
> *little first grader who has just moved into the area. Because*
> *she is new to the school and hasn't attended school before,*
> *Kerry has asked Will to come and observe. The following con-*
> *versation takes place after Will has observed Kerry's class*
> *several times.*
>
> > *Will:* *Do you have some time when we can talk? I have*
> > *some ideas I want to bounce off you.*
> >
> > *Kerry:* *Great. This is a good time for me. The kids won't be*
> > *here for another thirty minutes.*
> >
> > *Will:* *In my opinion, we have a little girl who has some cog-*
> > *nitive delays. I think we ought to refer her to special*
> > *education for a full diagnostic.*
> >
> > *Kerry:* *That's strange. She seems to be really insightful when*
> > *I talk to her.*
> >
> > *Will:* *That may be, but don't you notice all the difficulty she*
> > *has describing the pictures in the stories you read?*
> > *She doesn't seem to know the most common of pic-*
> > *tures. I also believe she has no idea of any letters.*
> > *Anything the least bit abstract is beyond her compre-*
> > *hension.*

In this case, Will makes an assumption without adequate reflection. As a result he begins to develop a plan for something that is
not a problem. Upon testing, it turns out that Vanessa's real problem
is that she needs glasses. Vanessa has not had good medical care
during her early years, and no one ever thought to test her vision.
Jumping to conclusions so quickly could seriously hurt Vanessa. In
the process of getting her tested, negative biases could have been
formed and expectations for her performance could have been seriously damaged. Kerry provided some information in conflict with
Will's observations, but Will did not listen. He was more interested
in making a case to support his position. Had Will used good listening skills, he and Kerry could have explored her observations and
may have reached a different, more realistic conclusion about Vanessa's
problems.

## ■ AVOIDING THESE BARRIERS

Barriers to communication often arise when people are attempting to communicate, and their use can result in miscommunication. You should learn to recognize these barriers and discipline yourself to remove them from your interactional style. In this way, your effectiveness as a collaborative colleague will be enhanced.

## ■ REMEMBER...

1. The kind of advice giving that encourages dependency and disenfranchises a colleague professionally is different from making suggestions that your colleague may or may not choose to implement.
2. Giving a colleague false reassurances minimizes the importance of the problem and can compound it if things don't work out as you predict.
3. Too many or unfocused questions inhibit the development of a consistent train of thought and understanding.
4. Wandering and changing topics in a dialogue communicates that you are not listening and shifts the attention of your colleague away from the problem being discussed.
5. Interrupting is frustrating and will thwart a colleague's ability to express concerns and explore the problem.
6. Using a cliche as a response trivializes the conversation and impedes further discussion.
7. Responding to colleagues in ways that minimize their feelings can make them feel inadequate as professionals. As a result, problems are less likely to be solved, and these colleagues probably will be less inclined to discuss other concerns or problems in the future.
8. Jumping to a quick fix based on underdeveloped reflections can result in working on symptoms of the problem rather than getting at the root of the problem.

## █ ACTIVITIES

- Expand the role-playing activity described in chapter 4 to include barriers to effective communication. After discussing strengths or positive aspects of the interaction, suggest ways to enhance the interaction.
- Engage in the role-playing twice: (a) prior to reading the information on communication skills, and (b) again after the information on communication skills has been presented. This can be done either in small groups or as a whole class (depending on the size of the class). Discuss differences between the first role-play and the final role-play.
- Over the next week, keep a list of incidents in which someone put up a barrier to communication. Exchange the lists in class, and generate a general class list. How did this activity affect your perception of your own communication style?

# 6

# WORKING WITH
# AND
# SUPPORTING GROUPS

The topic of the previous three chapters was the communication process and factors that facilitate or inhibit effective communication. Most of the examples were of interactions between two individuals, as a way of illustrating clearly the communication facilitator or inhibitor. Many of the concepts presented in Chapters 3, 4, and 5 apply to group interactions as well. The group is a common unit of interaction within schools, and communication within the context of a group of more than two has unique qualities. When more than two individuals interact, a set of dynamics comes into play that further complicates the communication process. In this chapter we describe those dynamics and provide examples to illustrate key concepts.

As you read through this chapter, think about the discussions you have had in class. What kind of group was operating? Has the class functioned like different types of groups during different activities (breaks, discussions, projects, etc.)? When you are part of different types of groups, can you identify differences in communication styles, formality, proximal distance between group members, body language?

## ■ TYPES OF GROUPS

Human society interacts in an endless number of groups. The typical teacher is a member of a faculty, a family, possibly a student group, a club, and so on. The defining characteristic of a group is that it contains more than two individuals working toward a unified purpose (Hames & Joseph, 1986). Combs, Avila, and Purkey (1971) described the basic types of groups as: conversational, instructional, decision-making, problem-solving, and discovery.

### CONVERSATIONAL GROUPS

Informal groups in which individuals exchange information in a casual manner fit the conversational category. Conversational groups usually lack an articulated purpose, other than to exchange information, and they are characterized by extensive participation by group members. These groups also tend to be composed of individuals who have good interpersonal compatibility and have joined the group voluntarily. Conversational groups meet during lunch, at coffee klatches, and at any other time individuals come together to interact informally.

### INSTRUCTIONAL GROUPS

Instructional groups come together formally to learn new information or skills. Instructional groups almost always have a leader or facilitator who orchestrates group activities. Although instructional groups can be participatory—in which all members relate information and contribute to others' learning—they also can be unidimensional in that certain types of information flow in one direction. Generally, the leader or facilitator presents new ideas or techniques and members generate questions and concerns. Membership in these groups can be voluntary or mandatory. Inservices, faculty meetings, and other forms of staff development are examples of instructional groups in the educational milieu.

### DECISION-MAKING GROUPS

Like instructional groups, decision-making groups tend to be formal in nature. Although in rare instances the group has no clear leader or facilitator, an individual usually orchestrates group discussion. This type of group is participatory and is characterized by a collection of information from a variety of sources related to the decision to be made. Sometimes all members of the group make the decision jointly, such as in a library selection committee or a group that determines a student's eligibility for special education. Other groups make recommendations to decision makers, such as a school board or local school administrators. Examples of an advisory group are a textbook selection committee and a search committee.

## PROBLEM-SOLVING GROUPS

The problem-solving group often is considered to be a specific form of a decision-making group. The important difference is that the primary purpose is to solve a problem. As a result, not only does this group make a decision regarding the problem to be solved, but it also continues to work to develop a plan to solve the problem. Like decision-making groups, problem-solving groups tend to be formal in nature and a leader or facilitator usually orchestrates the problem solving. Teacher assistance teams, building support teams, and intervention assistance teams are examples of problem-solving groups. These groups tend to take two forms, each of which can be mandatory or voluntary. Sometimes they are structured so problems are brought to the group and the group makes suggestions on ways the problem can be solved. In the other cases, groups are formed as a means of support; all members of the group bring problems and participate in developing plans to solve the problems.

## DISCOVERY GROUPS

As with most of the groups discussed so far, discovery groups are formal in nature. The main purpose of this type of group is for members to engage to gain greater self-awareness or understanding. The group tends to have a highly skilled leader with expertise in therapeutic communication. Within schools these groups are voluntary. Examples are stress management groups and other self-help groups.

Although professionals within the school are likely to find themselves in all five types of groups, three—instructional, problem-solving, and discovery—are those in which school problems typically are addressed in a formal way.

Have you ever wondered why you feel comfortable in some groups and uncomfortable in other groups? What factors led you to feel this way? Was it the size of the group, group members, where the group met, what the group discussed, how you were feeling, or some other issue that contributed to your level of comfort? If you have been a part of a group over a long period, how did the dynamics change over time, and what factors contributed to these changes?

## ■ GROUP FUNCTIONING

Good communication among group members is essential for its success. Without open and honest lines of communication, the group will not be able to maximize its effectiveness because norms, roles, and goals of the group cannot be defined appropriately. The group facilitator and group members alike should encourage effective communication skills as discussed in Chapter 3. Later in this section we will delineate responsibilities of various group members as a means of establishing an effective group. First, however, we will describe general components of effective groups, responsibilities of group members, sources of group conflict, and techniques to address group conflict.

### GROUP DYNAMICS

Group dynamics determines whether the group will be effective and positive. Improper group dynamics can deter productivity and impede the group from achieving its objectives. The three components of group dynamics are: structure, process, and function (Hames & Joseph, 1986). Structure relates to the framework of the group. Process refers to the developmental growth pattern of groups. Function incorporates the tasks a group undertakes to achieve its purpose.

### Group Structure

Group structure refers to the overall building blocks of the group, those components or elements that provide the framework within which the group operates. The structure is not static and can change. The facilitator has to be aware of how the components of the structure can affect group dynamics and the group's ability to be effective. Components of group structure are its size, composition, physical environment, and format (Hames & Joseph, 1986).

*Size.* In organizing a group, one of the most important decisions a facilitator can make is the size of the group. Groups that are too large inhibit communication and the free flow of ideas. On the other hand, small groups can narrow the possibilities for discussion because of the limited number of individuals involved. Although the literature is inconsistent with regard to optimal size of a group, some consensus emerges. Generally, groups smaller than four people place undue burdens on group members and can inhibit the group's effectiveness. Groups larger than 10 tend to inhibit the free sharing of ideas and place greater demands on the leadership abilities of the group facilitator. Groups between six and 10 members tend to have more member participation, higher levels of member satisfaction, and more intense member relationships, and they establish member consensus more readily.

*Composition.* Positive characteristics of individual group members include: (a) the ability to resolve conflicts, (b) the ability to communicate clearly, (c) stability and openness, and (d) the willingness to take risks (Abelson & Woodman, 1983). Each group member brings individual competencies that can contribute to the group's success as a unit, yet individual members may not appreciate or recognize the skills of their colleagues.

*Physical Environment.* An often overlooked concern in the group is the environment in which it will be functioning. The environment, or setting, can facilitate or inhibit group member participation. Size of the room, lighting, atmosphere, comfort, location, and acoustics are all important. Think of the times you have been in large conference rooms for a small group meeting and had trouble hearing those around you. If you cannot hear what is going on, it is difficult to be a participating group member. By the same token, if the room is uncomfortable because of temperature control or seating, group members may be attending to their discomfort instead of the purpose of the group. Seating arrangements can facilitate group participation when people face one another and can see each other. Having a table large enough to allow people enough space to spread out and take notes also facilitates discussion.

*Format.* The manner in which a group conducts its business is called the format. Format exists along a continuum, from highly structured groups that rely on Robert's Rules of Order to informal social gatherings with few rules. Well organized groups are apt to be more efficient in accomplishing their tasks. More informal groups are usually less efficient but provide greater opportunity for all members to participate and share. A delicate balance must be maintained between the rigidity of the group and the permissiveness of an unstructured format. The structure must be formal enough to propel the group toward accomplishing its task, but this must be balanced with an inclusive or participatory style in which members are encouraged to relate information in a more permissive manner.

**Group Process**

Like individuals, groups proceed through a relatively predictable sequence as they attempt to accomplish their objectives. Tuckman and Jensen (1977) described a model of group functioning that has five stages of development: forming, storming, norming, performing, and adjourning.

*Forming.* In the forming phase a general orientation to the group takes place. Relationships are begun and established at a superficial level. The initial purpose for the group is discussed. The complete structure of group activities is not yet determined, and networks of communication are just beginning to be established. During this stage group members are trying to gain an understanding of the group's purpose, leadership of the group, group members, and how the group will undertake its task. In the forming stage a group often is quiet and members speak hesitantly. The formation stage is characterized by constant examination of the goals, norms, and relationships within the group.

*Storming.* The second stage, storming, is characterized by conflict and disagreement. The intensity of conflict range from almost nonexistent to fairly intense. The conflict that may emerge is normal in groups. It results from group members' questioning their roles, others' roles, and the purpose of the group. As the potential conflict begins to get resolved, group members reestablish relationships and make a transition to the next stage.

*Norming.* During the norming stage group members become comfortable with role expectations, relationships, and the group's purpose. Communication networks and structural characteristics are solidified. Group cohesiveness, trust, and leadership are developed, along with new commitment to the group's goals. At the conclusion of this stage, group members are ready to undertake the task the group is to accomplish.

*Performing.* In the stage of performing, group members work on the tasks of the group. Discussion includes pertinent feedback, which allows for appropriate decision making.

*Adjourning.* The final stage, adjourning, comes as the task is completed, and relationships are redefined as closure takes place. This last stage is accompanied by an increase in self-esteem if the goals are met.

Although these stages are linear in their description, they are manifested in a dynamic manner. Groups can move back and forth across these levels of development as the group confronts new issues or the membership changes. If group membership changes often, the group has difficulty carrying out its business because of the continuing need to go through the developmental sequence.

**Group Functions**

All group members should possess several skills for a group to function satisfactorily. Many of these functions can be categorized into task functions and maintenance functions.

*Task functions* allow a group to move toward completion of the task. These are described briefly here (Hames & Joseph, 1986).

- *Initiating.* Initiation is a skill involved in beginning a group. It includes things such as imposing an agenda and defining the group goals.
- *Seeking information.* In seeking information, one requests facts, ideas, beliefs, and suggestions to expand upon the information provided or to ensure accurate representation of the group members.
- *Providing information.* In providing information, one offers facts, ideas, and new information related to the group's task.
- *Clarifying.* When seeking clarification, one requests elaboration or new information from group members.
- *Consensus testing.* Group members are checked to determine whether they are ready to reach a decision or if a unified position—consensus—is being established.

- *Summarizing*. Restating ideas or information generated in the group should produce a concise summary of what the group has accomplished.

*Maintenance functions* facilitate the group process and keep the focus on the task. These are as follows.

- *Gate keeping*. Gate keeping is a process that ensures the participation of all group members. If one or more individuals are dominating the group discussion, they are called upon to curtail their discussion so other group members can participate more fully.
- *Encouraging*. Comments and information of group members are accepted and, when appropriate, praised. Encouraging facilitates full participation by all group members.
- *Harmonizing*. In harmonizing, differences among group members are arbitrated or mediated. The intent is to reduce tensions among group members and to create an atmosphere in which all members feel supported.
- *Standard setting*. Standard setting means reinforcing the group's intent. It includes reminders of group goals and progress toward reaching these goals.

## ■ RESPONSIBILITIES OF GROUP MEMBERS

Group members may believe that task and maintenance functions are the primary role of the leader or facilitator. This is unfortunate because, although the leader or facilitator must be skilled in task and maintenance functions, groups are far more effective if all members assume responsibility. When all members share responsibility for these functions, they take ownership of the group process, and this ownership contributes to the group's being able to accomplish its purpose.

### ROLE OF FACILITATOR

Perhaps the most important member of a group is the facilitator. The facilitator must have strong leadership characteristics. The group's success depends on the facilitator's ability to organize group activities, create the communicative environment, and synthesize outcomes. The facilitator is responsible for maintaining a positive, cohesive atmosphere among a diverse group of people embodying varying levels and types of knowledge and personal biases. The leader also must have a clear sense of the purpose of the group and be able to communicate it clearly. He or she should be trustworthy. This person also must be a skilled listener who can motivate and empower group members to accomplish group goals (Bennis, 1984).

A *participatory* style of leadership usually is the most effective approach. This is a leadership style in which the leader encourages group members to participate and take meaningful roles as the group accomplishes its tasks. The skill of the facilitator impacts on both the quality and the timeliness of decisions made by groups (Abelson & Woodman, 1983). When conflicts arise, appropriate problem-solving techniques must be applied to guide the group through the difficulties toward the defined goals in a timely manner (Margolis & Shapiro, 1988). The facilitator must:

- be skillful in group facilitation, arbitration, and conflict resolution.
- have the ability and willingness to deal with complex issues simultaneously while generating an atmosphere of comfort and flexibility for all members of the group.
- be skilled at group development with individuals from varied disciplines.
- have the capability of developing true group rapport.
- project unity of concern for group members, addressing a problem from the unique perspective of disciplinary or individual orientation.
- facilitate group interactions and be strong enough to maintain group cohesion if conflict among the group arises.
- be able to engender a humility of spirit in group members so their own needs do not compete with those of the group.

As the stages of group functioning evolve, the facilitator's role must change to match the group's needs. At the onset of group functioning, the facilitator should serve as a guide and administrator. In time this role becomes less and less directive. In a group's forming stage the facilitator must serve as a director and administrator to orient the group to the tasks at hand. As the group moves into the storming stage, the facilitator must handle difficulties that arise, such as role ambiguity, questioning of authority, conflicting goals, and other potential problems. In this stage the facilitator uses problem-solving skills to negotiate arbitration and mediation among group members. In the norming stage a sense of group cohesiveness and trust is established and the facilitator can become less directive and more able to serve as a fellow collaborator in problem solving and task completion.

Although facilitators are responsible primarily for leading the group, their decision-making role is equal to that of any of the group members. After the task of the group has been accomplished in the performing stage, the adjourning stage is reached, and the facilitator should bring the meeting to a close by summarizing the results of the discussion. The leader should state specifically which group member will be responsible for carrying out each recommendation, and before the meeting adjourns dates should be set for initiating and completing of those tasks. This step is critical to allow for opportunities for correction or clarification.

## ROLE OF GROUP MEMBERS

The strength of the group approach relies on participation by all group members. Effective use of members' skills and resources should be one of the primary objectives of group functioning (Abelson & Woodman, 1983). Efficiency is more likely when group members realize their collective purpose and the specific short-term and long-term goals of the group (Zander, 1971).

Group effectiveness can be enhanced by collaborative goal setting that results in appropriate short- and long-term goals. Frequently, specific goals are not apparent immediately, but members usually can agree on abstract goals. Abstraction allows group members various interpretations of the goal. Because premature discussion of specific goals is more likely to divide the group, goal development should proceed from abstract to concrete and general to precise. Agreement on specific goals is most likely when cooperative interaction has taken place and abstract, general goals are agreed upon (Margolis & Shapiro, 1988). When setting goals, groups will confront two issues: content and process.

Content issues deal with specific tasks at hand, such as discussing a classroom concern, whereas process issues involve the means of attaining these specific tasks, such as the most appropriate means of addressing the classroom concern. When agreement is reached about content, problems that will interfere with process are identified and considered (Abelson & Woodman, 1983). Decisions must be practical, appropriate, and efficient logistically for all group members, including any child and family involved. If members are unwilling to reveal all pertinent information, decisions may not be appropriate. Group members should be encouraged to express their opinions in an accepting environment. If defensiveness, power struggles, or past interpersonal problems cause conflicts, these should be dealt with as they occur and before they become more intense.

Establishing the role relationships and norms that define individual and group functioning is of paramount importance. Most group members have specified skills and knowledge that give reason for their membership and help define their individual roles within the group. Effective group functioning requires clear role expectations. Undefined or unrealistic role expectations can prevent group members from contributing positively to the group process. In contrast, clearly delineated roles with realistic demands provide opportunities for successful interaction. When the group is made up of individuals from a variety of disciplines, a transdisciplinary approach is crucial to successful sharing and problem solving. This is an approach in which the skills and roles of team members are shared.

Group members should have a clear understanding of the process of group functioning and of the organizational and decision-making process of the group. They need to understand and anticipate the dynamics of group processes, such as the stages of group development, common characteristics of groups, types of problems group members face, and strategies to diminish the effects of those problems.

## ■ POTENTIAL SOURCES OF GROUP CONFLICT

Conflict is a strong force that must be reckoned with in most groups. Although conflict can affect a group negatively by preventing the group from undertaking its task, for example, developing an intervention program, it also can have a healthy effect on a group by allowing differences among group members to be addressed and resolved, thereby building consensus and commitment among group members. Butler and Maher (1981) defined two types of conflict:

intrapersonal and interpersonal. Although one thinks of the latter most often, it is not always the case that two parties are involved in conflict.

## INTRAPERSONAL CONFLICT

Intrapersonal conflict emerges when an individual has one or more concerns that are mutually contradictory (Margolis & Shapiro, 1988). These often are in the form of role ambiguity and role conflict. *Role ambiguity* occurs when a member is uncertain about his or her purpose for being in the group. *Role conflict* arises when a group member has been given incompatible expectations about his or her role in the group (Butler & Maher, 1981; Hebert & Miller, 1985). For instance, if a psychologist is viewed by one member of the group as a therapist and by another member of the group as a psychometrist, conflicting signals are being sent and the psychologist is likely to be confused and frustrated. This frustration may escalate and turn into an interpersonal conflict between these individuals.

Additional sources of internal conflicts often stem from irrational ideas, overgeneralization, and dichotomous reasoning. These conflicts can cause a group member to perceive group goals as incompatible.

Conditions of the organization can reinforce intrapersonal conflict. For example, when an institution requires more from a person than is possible, it produces *role overload*. A person experiencing role overload can become frustrated and feel unsupported by group members because they do not seem to be undertaking their share of the tasks.

In groups with a facilitator who is experiencing role overload members may feel frustrated because the leader will not share tasks. These feelings can be compounded if group members interpret the facilitator's behavior as resulting from his or her lack of trust in their abilities or views. In addition, group facilitators can experience intrapersonal conflict because of their competing roles within a group. On the one hand, the facilitator must be responsible for the product of the group, but on the other hand, the facilitator's decision-making role is equal to that of others in the group. As with many intrapersonal conflicts, if this overload is not resolved, it may intensify and turn into an interpersonal conflict.

Differentiation of function leads to dissonance and increases the likelihood of intrapersonal conflict. Individuals may be uncomfortable with new modes of operation or lack an appreciation of different ways of operating. As a result, the new way of performing creates an internal conflict with the way things used to be done. This also may happen when group members are unable to adjust to changes in the structure of the group, such as the addition of new members, the loss of a member, or the addition of new issues or topics for the group to address.

## INTERPERSONAL CONFLICT

The more familiar type of conflict is interpersonal conflict. Thomas (1976) defined this type of conflict as a situation in which a person perceives that another person is frustrating to deal with or is complicating a situation or concern. Role conflict and role ambiguity also can lead to this type of conflict. Unless roles are defined clearly, group members will not know their individual responsibilities or the responsibilities of others. Interdependence among group members also may contribute to interpersonal conflicts. The greater the interdependency, the greater is the impact of the relationships on the process outcome.

Personality characteristics of individual group members have a significant influence on interpersonal relationships and conflicts within the group. One of the most challenging tasks a leader must take on is to persuade disruptive members to become functioning members of the group. In most situations preventive action is the best strategy for addressing disruptions. By following good leadership etiquette, one can neutralize disruptive interaction styles. In some instances the leader might talk with disruptive members outside of the group to understand concerns that may be of a personal nature and not part of the group dynamics.

Five common types of disruptive interaction styles are: consensus blocking, power seeking, recognition seeking, time dominating, and clowning (Hames & Joseph, 1986). Each of these styles of interaction and suggestions on how to address them are discussed below.

*Consensus blocking.* In this style of interaction, an individual consciously or unconsciously attempts to bring in extreme or extraneous information to inhibit or block group consensus. This individual may become angry or aggressive, change the topic, or go back to reexamine previously established parameters. When a group disagrees with this individual, he or she will not accept compromise and will continue the argument.

When this kind of behavior occurs, several strategies are possible. If a person raises previously addressed issues, he or she can be told that the group has covered the issues and it is time to move on to another topic. If an individual brings extraneous information to the attention of the group, he or she should be told firmly that it is irrelevant to the issue being discussed and that it will be considered after the current issue has been addressed. Finally, if a person displays extreme emotions, these cannot be ignored. Sometimes the meeting may have to end and the emotional matter discussed privately. If any of these distractors is part of a recurring pattern, the group should bring this to the individual's attention.

*Power seeking.* Individuals other than the designated leader may attempt to seek control of the group. They might do this to gain authority over the situation, or it may be a personal trait in which the person feels a need to be in control. This problem also can surface if the leader is not fulfilling his or her role adequately. Someone within the group may then attempt to take over the leader's role, trying to help the group function. The result tends to be counterproductive because the group now is being dually led with no one in real control. The group then becomes dysfunctional.

Having clear role definitions within the group helps to avoid this problem. If it continues, a frank discussion among group members regarding role expectations can clear the air and help get the group back on track. Sometimes if the group leader makes a concerted effort to elicit opinion of the individual seeking power, this can defuse his or her need to take control.

*Recognition seeking.* Someone in the group may make inappropriate statements or display inappropriate behavior to bring attention to himself or herself. Sometimes this individual talks for a long time, and other members of the group are unaware of what contribution this discussion will make. These departures may be in the form of stories that place the speaker as a star. Setting limits on the amount of time each member "has the floor" can stymie attempts to gain recognition. Another strategy is to talk to these individuals outside of the group to help them understand how their behavior is being perceived.

If recognition seekers are interested in changing their behavior, the leader may be able to establish a subtle signal that will let them know they are perceived by their peers as seeking recognition. A signal sometimes works, because individuals who engage in power seeking often are unaware of how their behavior is being perceived.

*Time dominating.* Dominating time is related to seeking recognition. This individual monopolizes the communication by making long speeches that are, at best, tangentially related to the conversation. This individual cannot seem to say anything concisely. Time dominators are different from power seekers and recognition seekers in the sense that they seem to dominate because they can. They are not seeking authority, nor are they seeking to bring personal attention to themselves. The strategies for working with recognition seeking individuals also can be effective with time dominators.

*Clowning.* A clown is someone who actually is nervous in the situation and uses jokes or puns as a way to deal with it. Although it can relieve the intensity of the group, persistent joking can be distracting and can communicate to others that the work of the group is unimportant. Helping the individual feel more at ease can relieve the anxiety and need to clown around. Having a frank, discreet discussion with the person also can help.

Lack of commitment of members within a group also can do much harm to effective group functioning and may lead to interpersonal conflicts as well. Commitment to the task at hand is required of all group members. Everyone should be involved actively in the group's tasks. All group members must share responsibility in developing and delivering tasks (Abelson & Woodman, 1983).

Finally, time is an important factor in group decision making and, if it is not managed carefully, can result in conflict. Differing schedules must be adjusted, and flexibility often cannot be stretched far enough. Groups typically take longer than individuals to reach decisions on issues. Time constraints are an unfortunate reality, and on occasion time limits will affect the facilitator's management style, potentially decreasing the effectiveness of the group (Abelson & Woodman, 1983).

## ■ CONFLICT RESOLUTION

Solutions must be reached through discussion and then consensus. Imposing decisions on group members will create resistance, lack of commitment, and withdrawal from further group interactions. Resolving conflicts in an open, supportive manner, on the other hand, typically strengthens commitment and group cohesion. As two requirements for group members to invest in a solution to a problem: (a) they must believe that the solution will bring about the desired conditions, and (b) they must have a vested interest in the outcome (Margolis & Shapiro, 1988).

Arbitration and mediation are two useful techniques for resolving conflicts. These may be new to you because they are derived from the field of industrial relations, but they have their place in all group dynamics.

## ARBITRATION

When a conflict arises, the leader can structure the discussion to allow for arbitration. Kolb and Glidden (1986) defined arbitration as a formal decision-making procedure that identifies specific, immediate issues presented by the competing parties. As positions are defended and supporting arguments are presented, the facilitator may intervene with questions or clarifications, but the facilitator primarily listens. After the different viewpoints are presented and after all positions are articulated, the facilitator summarizes the opposing positions, the group then votes, and the majority position is the one that prevails.

---

*A new program is being introduced into a privately funded preschool program to support families that have been adjudicated for abuse or neglect. Several agencies are involved in the funding of this program: Head Start, Children's Services, and the local schools. The facilitator of this group is Bonnie (the preschool director), and the other group members are: Arlene (Head Start), Peggy (local schools), and Bob (Children's Services). A disagreement emerges between Peggy and Bob that is preventing the group from moving forward. Bob would like the children to be grouped together in their own class, and Peggy would like them to be integrated across the current classes in the program. Arlene and Bonnie are neutral on the issue. Bonnie decides that unless this issue is solved, the group will not be able to settle on other issues*

*associated with this collaboration. Bonnie decides to arbitrate*
*this issue and the following discussion occurs.*

Bonnie: It's clear that we have to settle this issue on integration before we can do anything else. I would like
Peggy and Bob to provide concise statements in support of their positions. Each also will have the opportunity to respond to each other's position. Please limit
your discussion to the issue of integration. Once their
positions are clear, we will vote on the issue. The
majority will prevail, and we can put this issue to rest.
Can we all agree on this approach?

Group: (Everyone nods in agreement.)

Bonnie: Bob, why don't you start?

Bob: Look, I'm all in favor of integrated programs, but we
must face the reality of funding and expertise. Our
agency has limited funds, and we must be sure the
funds we are providing for this effort are used for our
students and not for the general program. Moreover,
these kids and their families have unique needs, and I
don't believe your teachers have that expertise.

Bonnie: Bob, it seems your main concerns relate to keeping
funds isolated from general program funds and the
ability of the current teachers to meet the needs of
the children and their families. (Bob's body language
indicates that Bonnie got the essence of his position.)
Peggy, where do you stand on this issue?

Peggy: I'm concerned that if we segregate these kids, they
will be in an artificial environment that at best will be
sheltered and inhibiting. At worst, I worry that they
will model each other's inappropriate behavior, making it harder for them to make the transition to a regular classroom. I agree with Bob that funds are limited,
but I believe that with some work we can ensure that
funds are spent where they are intended. I also think
the teachers are knowledgeable and we can find
ways to support them as they work with these kids
and their families.

Bonnie: Peggy, you're concerned that segregation is harmful
to the kids. Also, you believe we can keep funds
straight and find ways to support teachers. (Peggy's

> *body language indicates that Bonnie got the essence of her position.) Does everyone understand the two positions? Okay, let's vote.*

---

In this example Bonnie sets up a situation that allows Bob and Peggy to state their positions before the group. By voting on the issue, the group can make a decision and move on to other issues. In most cases arbitration should be limited to issues that are fairly simple or for which no compromise is possible.

## MEDIATION

The previous example represents a complex situation and some compromise may have been possible. A better strategy may have been to use mediation. Mediation adds the dimension of compromise to the decision-making process. Concerns other than those at hand can be introduced into the discussion as long as they are relevant to the decisions to be made. Because all of the issues are not equally important to everyone, the facilitator structures the discussion in such a way that the adversaries are accommodated somewhat on their issue of most concern and are convinced to concede on issues of lesser importance. Proposals then can be made that will form the basis for agreement (Kolb & Glidden, 1986). When initial positions are being presented, the facilitator's role in structuring the dialogue is similar to that of the arbitrator. After the positions have been presented, however, the facilitator becomes active with individuals, isolating key issues and finding ways to compromise. Consider the previous example with a mediation twist.

---

*Instead of voting, the facilitator (Bonnie) begins to mediate between Peggy's and Bob's positions.*

*Bonnie:* *Bob, do you agree that segregating these kids has potentially harmful aspects?*

*Bob:* *Of course, that would be like being against Mom, Apple Pie, and the flag. I don't think we'll be able to keep the funds straight and who has the resources to support these teachers! Peggy is always coming up with suggestions that ignore reality.*

> *Bonnie:* We need to limit our discussion to the potential harm-
> ful impact of segregation. We'll examine the other
> points one by one. Can I surmise from your com-
> ments that, like Peggy, you see problems with segre-
> gating these kids?
> *Bob:* Yes.
> *Bonnie:* If we can find a way to keep the funds straight and to
> support the teachers adequately, would you consider
> supporting an integrated approach?
> *Bob:* If those concerns can be addressed, I'm willing to
> talk.

In this example Bonnie is able to identify the key issue to be addressed and reach a compromise. She does this by getting everyone to agree on the most important issue, namely, what is best for the children and their families. Once she has this agreement, the context for a compromise is established. Although much more has to be discussed and negotiated, the group is well on its way to a compromise. In this example, Bob initially resorts to a personal attack, which is a common way to derail a mediation. Bonnie and the group ignore the attack, which allows the group to get to the point. If the group had been unable to ignore the attack, Bonnie should have intervened and said something like, "If we're going to solve this issue, we must refrain from personal issues and stick to the problem." When engaging in mediation or arbitration, the facilitator must listen carefully and use summarization to clarify conflicting positions.

## ■ WORKING EFFECTIVELY IN GROUPS

Groups are a basic organizational structure in which humans participate. In schools a great deal of work occurs within groups. If you are going to be a competent collaborative professional, you must have the ability to function as a productive group member. Whether you are the leader, facilitator, or a participant, you have a responsibility to participate in the group in such a way to ensure that group is able to achieve its goal. Effective groups do not occur by chance. They result from hard work and commitment on the part of group members.

## ■ REMEMBER...

1. The four types of groups are: conversational, instructional, decision-making, and discovery. A specific form of decision-making groups is the group formed to engage in problem solving.
2. Good communication among group members is the foundation of a successful group. Without open and honest lines of communication, the group is not likely to maximize its effectiveness. Open channels of communication are the means by which groups establish norms, role expectations, and group goals.
3. The three critical components of group dynamics are: structure, process, and function. Structure refers to the framework of the group. Process is its developmental growth pattern. Function relates to the tasks a group undertakes to achieve its purpose.
4. Groups proceed through a relatively predictable sequence as they attempt to accomplish their purpose: forming, storming, norming, performing, and adjourning.
5. Skills that group members should possess for a group to function effectively typically are categorized into task and maintenance functions.
6. Conflict is an important force that can inhibit or facilitate group development.
7. Efforts to resolve group conflict should move from the abstract to the concrete and from the general to the specific. Conflict resolution should be seen as a problem-solving endeavor that results as group members become mutually satisfied with the outcome.

## ■ ACTIVITIES

- Get three or four primary puzzles that have 6–10 pieces and randomly give them to group members. Have them work together to solve the puzzles, but without speaking to one another or taking any pieces from another person. Participants must freely give pieces to another group member. Once the puzzles have been completed, group members discuss how they worked together to solve the puzzles. Point out aspects that inhibited or facilitated the group process. Also discuss the roles individuals assumed in the activity.

- During the next week record the types of groups in which you participate. Describe the developmental process of one of these groups and the role the group leader took to facilitate the group development.
- Describe any disruptive group members you observed, and reflect on how they were dealt with by group members.
- Reflect on the groups in which you have participated, and describe the role conflict has played within the group. Focus on the positive aspects of this conflict.

# PART THREE

# COLLABORATION IN PRACTICE

# 7

# COLLABORATION
# AS
# SPECIFIC
# PROBLEM SOLVING

**W**hen we think about what collaboration looks like in practice in the schools, we most often think about small groups of teachers getting together to solve specific problems. Historically, this kind of collaboration has centered on the needs of a specific student who is having difficulty achieving in general education classrooms because of behavior or academic problems. For most of us, then, probably the first image we call up is that of two teachers—most likely a classroom teacher and special education teacher or a school psychologist—putting their heads together to develop classroom-based interventions that will increase the student's chances for success.

In contrast to team teaching, which will be covered in the next chapter, collaboration as specific problem solving is based on the notion that, on a temporary basis, bringing together pairs or small groups of teachers to pool their varied expertise is a valuable way of dealing with a wide variety of problems teachers face. Ideally, collaboration creates a sense of mutual responsibility within the entire school staff for the full range of students who attend and helps build classroom teachers' capacities for and confidence in working with all the students they encounter.

Groups of teachers that form for the purpose of collaborative problem solving may meet only once, or they may get together at regular intervals to consider the progress of the situation in which they are interested. They may be made up of only two teachers or a larger group of teachers. Some groups may adopt formal structures or models to facilitate their work. Others might prefer to work informally. Once the immediate problem is solved, or at least is on its way to being solved, that specific configuration of teachers might dissolve and different groups of teachers might join together to address other issues. The specific form and duration of the pair or group of teachers that undertakes problem solving depend chiefly upon the problem being addressed.

What approaches to collaborative problem solving have you observed or participated in during your field experiences or in your teaching? What was the purpose of the collaboration? How comfortable do you think the participants were in the process? How well did it seem to be working? What problems did you observe?

## ■ DIFFERENTIATING CLASSROOM-SPECIFIC AND SCHOOLWIDE COLLABORATIVE PROBLEM SOLVING

In general, short-term collaborative interactions fall into two broad categories of problem solving: *classroom-specific* and *schoolwide*. As we already have said, collaboration as we usually know it is initiated because of a specific difficulty within a specific teacher's classroom. The student clearly is the focus of the interaction and usually is considered to be the source of the problem at hand. This is what we mean by classroom-specific collaborative problem solving. In contrast, every school confronts many issues that transcend individual classrooms and individual students. When teachers get together to work on these more far-reaching classes of problems—which might include creating a new disciplinary climate, for example—their interaction is a form of collaborative problem solving as well, but on a schoolwide basis.

The collaborative dynamics that participants bring to bear to these one-on-one or small group interactions are similar, even if the sources of the problems differ. Although distinguishing between classroom-specific and schoolwide issues that deserve collaborative problem solving seems easy enough, more often than not the two are strongly related, and classroom-specific problems often emerge out of larger, schoolwide practices that themselves might be diminishing students' chances for success.

## CLASSROOM-SPECIFIC COLLABORATIVE PROBLEM SOLVING

Teachers who initiate classroom-specific collaboration may already be considering referring the students about whom they are concerned for some type of special service, or the student may be labeled already as having a specific disability. When teachers recognize that alone they are not capable of solving the difficulties a student is having, they may call on a colleague to help. This assistance might involve interactions between classroom teachers and speech and language specialists, counselors or school psychologists, specialists in visual and hearing impairment, specialists who provide support for the integration of students with severe and profound disabilities, or those who are charged with the education of students labeled as having mild disabilities. It also may include interactions with teachers whose specialization is bilingual education, reading, or mathematics education. What these various situations have in common is that the focus of teachers' problem solving is the specific need of an individual student or a small group of students within their classrooms.

Because it often brings together a specialist and a classroom teacher, classroom-specific collaborative problem solving most closely resembles what commonly is known as consultation. These interactions also might come under the rubric of *prereferral intervention*, denoting that the teacher and specialist are trying, through their interactions, to improve the learning situation within the classroom for a specific student and, thus, prevent unnecessary referrals to special education. We, however, choose to use the umbrella term *collaborative problem solving* to denote this kind of periodic, student-specific interaction. As we argued in Chapter 2, collaboration better describes the ideal nature of interactions among school staff members and is more consistent with the general movement toward building collegial learning communities among all adults who work in schools. Further, collaborative problem solving promotes the notion that all members of a community, no matter what their specific title or expertise, enter into the dynamic as equals with varying and distinct contributions to make to the situation at hand.

A variation on classroom-specific collaborative problem solving occurs when ongoing support is needed to facilitate the integration of students with enduring problems, particularly those with disabilities, within general education classrooms. In a collaborative relationship between, for example, a specialist for students with severe disabilities and a classroom teacher, their collaboration is not the result of reacting to a specific problem that requires immediate action. Rather, it stems from the agreement to work collegially over time to maintain a high-quality, maximally inclusive program for the student in question, even though the specialist and classroom teacher may not be teaming per se. In this kind of collaborative relationship, the two teachers involved may meet regularly over the course of the year to monitor the student's progress, make necessary adjustments in program or curriculum, or plan for future activities. This role does not preclude team teaching.

In the following example of classroom-specific problem solving, a classroom teacher relies on a trusted colleague to help construct a solution. Which dimension of collaboration is operating here?

---

*Carol is a third-grade teacher at Sunshine Elementary School. She is considered to be one of the stronger teachers in her district. This year, however, she is challenged by Sarah, a child the second-grade teachers have warned her about. Sarah is not a child who acts out but, instead, is isolated and gets little work done. Carol's colleagues suggest that she should expect little from Sarah, although she is identified as a student with potential.*

*At the start of the year, Carol begins to see the same pattern in Sarah's behavior. She isn't getting her work done, and she seems to have few friends. Determined not to buy into her colleagues' views, she enlists the support of the reading teacher, Nathan, whom she always has felt she could trust to lend a sympathetic ear to her problems. In explaining the situation to him, she focuses on her desire to help Sarah break out of her isolation and reach her potential.*

*Nathan poses several questions for Sarah to think about, and Sarah poses several more to herself as well. They talk about Sarah's interaction patterns, her reluctance to talk in a large group, her unkempt look that seems to isolate her even more—but also the sparkle in her eyes when Carol has the time to work with her one-on-one. Carol begins to see that if Sarah is going to succeed, Carol herself will have to structure some sort of peer interaction carefully and slowly, and select a peer who won't push Sarah too fast. As she discusses these issues with Nathan, they both identify Lily as a student who is ideal. Lily is a bit more mature than the other students, is always willing to help, and is a good worker. She is a leader, but in a quiet way.*

*With Nathan's encouragement, Carol decides to talk with Lily about being her special helper for Sarah. Carol is to rearrange the cooperative groups so Sarah and Lily are together, and Carol will give them some private time each day to talk about their work. Sarah will know that she can ask Lily for help, and Lily's job is to encourage Sarah. Carol will talk to the girls together periodically, and she also will plan a time each week to meet privately with Sarah to keep track of her assignments. The other aspect of this plan is that Carol will buy Sarah a comb and brush to keep at school, and a few hair ribbons. Sarah can come in a few minutes early each morning and get help fixing her hair.*

*As the first weeks progress, Nathan often stops by to talk to Carol about Sarah's progress. Sarah is beginning to come around after a few weeks, and Carol feels confident that she is on the right track.*

## SCHOOLWIDE COLLABORATIVE PROBLEM SOLVING

What kinds of problems deserve schoolwide attention? Perhaps a school's reading teachers find that the methodology used in a given subject area is not achieving results. They might engage in collaborative problem solving with their peers to identify the specific dimensions of the problem and develop new directions for the school's reading practice in the content areas. Other groups may develop informally around similar interests, working to iron out the bugs in implementing new methods of teaching other subjects, or initiating interdisciplinary approaches to curriculum. Sometimes whole school staffs may meet to discuss a general problem—for example, schoolwide discipline—and splinter off into temporary working groups to come up with multiple suggestions for addressing the challenge. Classroom teachers also might meet to discuss problems with the existing curriculum at a certain grade level and its impact on the achievement of specific students. Other groups may form when the staff realizes, for example, that a disproportionate number of minority students are being referred for special education.

In short, schoolwide collaborative problem solving is initiated when a school staff recognizes that it holds responsibility for improving the entire educational program the school offers. Schoolwide collaboration builds a school's capacity to move forward, even if the status quo seems to be working well enough. It also creates an atmosphere in which teachers are encouraged to take the risks associated with trying out new practices and seeing if they actually represent an improvement. With schoolwide collaborative problem solving in place, problems stemming from ineffective practices potentially can be minimized.

In the following example of schoolwide problem solving, the entire staff participates in the process. How is this an example of collaboration?

---

*At Cosby High the teachers are participating in their first meetings of the year. At the end of the previous year, they had begun to discuss their frustration with the short 45 minutes they have for each class. The principal, Ms. Clanton, remembers their frustration and brings up this issue as one potential goal for the year. In their discussions today, they are reviewing the problems they talked about last spring. Although everyone agrees about the problem, finding an acceptable solution seems to be much more difficult. Some teachers want to overhaul the curriculum completely. Others basically like their work they way it is, although they do admit that having more time with each class would be helpful.*

*To move the process ahead, Ms. Clanton asks that a set of study groups be set up, enlisting teachers from various subject areas. Four small groups are formed, each of which is assigned the task of finding out how other schools have moved away from the traditional schedule. The groups all contain some teachers who are "gung ho" for radical change and others who are less inclined. Their tasks involve talking with teachers from other schools, reading articles about secondary school reform and curriculum reform specifically, and polling their colleagues about specific aspects of schedule and cur-*

riculum reform. These study groups are to meet monthly during the fall semester in faculty meetings reserved for discussion and debate.

Through these meetings the teachers as a whole become well informed about their options. It becomes clear that, though many are interested in curriculum reform as represented by interdisciplinary instruction linking—for example, social studies/literature and math/science—some are far more ready for this shift than others. Given all of the options they studied, at the start of the spring semester the faculty decides to plan for implementing a double period schedule the following fall. In this format only four classes will meet each day. Given the current seven-period schedule, each class will meet for double the time but only every other day. The new eighth period will be used for talent development groups, enabling students to choose activities in which they have a particular skill or interest.

In this plan the extended time per class will allow for faculty members who wish to team to do so but will force those who were not interested in this interdisciplinary work to create new forms of instruction that lend themselves to the extended time period. Through their conversations each faculty member has agreed to identify one aspect of his or her teaching to work on changing in the coming fall. The spring semester is to be devoted to developing individual or interdisciplinary plans. Also, it is agreed that in the coming year monthly faculty meetings will be devoted to sharing the progress of interdisciplinary teaching teams.

The original study groups disband in the early spring. These give way to pairs of teachers working together to develop individual plans for the coming year.

---

## ■ THE RELATIONSHIP BETWEEN CLASSROOM-SPECIFIC AND SCHOOLWIDE COLLABORATIVE PROBLEM SOLVING

These two general categories of collaborative problem solving—classroom-specific and schoolwide—typically are not addressed in relationship to one another in the context of teacher collaboration.

From our perspective, however, they are linked inextricably, are not mutually exclusive, and ideally should co-exist within a building. If one of the major goals of collaborative problem solving is to improve the broader educational climate for a wider and wider range of students, this means recognizing the delicate interplay between teachers' improving their own teaching practice and schools' recognizing what has to be accomplished at a macroscopic level in terms of schoolwide norms for how curriculum and instruction can change to meet students' needs. One would not want to create structures for collaborative problem solving for specific classroom problems without the complementary notion of schoolwide collaboration designed to keep problems from occurring in the first place.

Schoolwide collaboration emerged as a professional expectation in the context of the educational reforms of the 1980s and 1990s, when school staffs were encouraged to engage in collegial deliberation about the school's curriculum and instructional practices. Because to date it has been practiced least in schools, this kind of professional collaboration traditionally has not been stressed in preservice teacher education. In contrast, collaborative problem solving in reaction to a specific student's academic, behavior, medical, or family problems, or language diversity—problems that are seen as requiring the involvement of a specialist working together with a classroom teacher—is a far more common practice and in most cases has preceded large-scale school reform. In schools that practice full inclusion of students with disabilities, collaborative problem solving to support their continued inclusion also is becoming far more widespread than in the past.

To foster classroom-specific and schoolwide collaboration alike, teachers have to be skilled in the four dimensions of collaboration that make up the framework of this book, and know when each might be called for. For example, when collaborating about schoolwide problems, teachers often enter together into a new arena of educational methodology or philosophy. Therefore, *support* for this new endeavor and a means to *facilitate* its acquisition on an ongoing basis probably are in the forefront. Specific *information* likely is needed, and a specialist or consultant from outside of the school might be brought in to provide that information and work as a facilitator to impart this knowledge. Some forms of direct *prescription* regarding how to proceed methodologically are likely to accompany such a change.

When collaborative problem solving is initiated in response to a specific classroom problem, other dimensions move to the forefront. First, a pair or small group of teachers and specialists must work together to *facilitate* problem solving on the part of the teacher who seeks assistance and to support the teacher during that time. Joint ownership for the problem and its solution remain with the teachers. If you are a specialist, this means controlling the tendency to be prescriptive and, instead, working with teachers to build on the strengths they already bring to the situation.

In our experience, only rarely have we *prescribed* a sequence of steps. In the case of collaboration to support ongoing integration of students with enduring disabilities, *support* and *information* usually are most relevant, with *prescription* and *facilitation* following closely when a serious challenge presents itself. Thus, not all situations call for the same dimensions of collaboration. Teachers must rely on all four dimensions, however, to solve the broad range of problems they encounter in their attempts to work with students.

## ■ GENERAL FEATURES OF COLLABORATIVE PROBLEM SOLVING

No matter for which purpose it is initiated, all forms of collaborative problem solving retain some common features:

- the shared nature of the interaction.
- the presence of two or more individuals with various kinds of knowledge and expertise recognized as being germane to the problem at hand.
- joint recognition and acceptance of the need to engage in collaboration as a dependable and effective way of addressing a specific problem or goal.

This last feature means participants acknowledge that the results of their joint problem solving probably will be superior to each trying to solve the problem individually. Irrespective of the various titles participants in collaborative problem solving may have, once they come together for a specific purpose, they should function as a team and honor the various strengths that each brings.

Further, no matter what the reason for initiating collaborative problem solving, all participants in these interactions can benefit from bringing to the group the basic communication skills addressed in

Chapters 3 through 6. Although specific collaborative problem-solving relationships will look different depending upon the teachers involved and the issue in which they are interested, they all should be identifiable by the presence of these common features. In addition to these overall features, collaborative problem-solving interactions also rely on the four dimensions that make up the framework of this book and on a step-by-step problem-solving process.

## ■ GENERAL STEPS FOR PROBLEM SOLVING

Most problem-solving models, whether they are team or one-to-one models, contain a series of basic steps to help structure the interactions. These steps have become so widespread that they almost always are cited in the collaboration literature as the underlying process for problem solving and usually include: (a) some form of problem identification or description, (b) development of interventions, (c) implementation, and (d) evaluation.

The problem-solving model we suggest is a variation on this process based our own work in collaborative problem solving (Pugach & Johnson, 1990b). This problem-solving process utilizes the following seven steps:

1. Articulation of the problem.
2. Consideration of contributing factors.
3. Development of a problem pattern statement.
4. Generation of possible solutions.
5. Selection of the solution.
6. Development of an evaluation plan.
7. Implementation and monitoring of the identified solution.

### ARTICULATION OF THE PROBLEM TO BE SOLVED

A problem is a dilemma, concern, or challenge that a teacher wishes to resolve. This challenge need not be child-centered. It could be curriculum-centered, teacher-centered, or be a concern of the broader school community. To focus on deficit concerns alone would be a mistake. Although curriculum has not been given much attention in collaborative problem solving, the focus of collaborative problem solving need not always be the child's problem or those things children can't do or are having difficulty doing. Many challenges relate to refining and enhancing the curriculum and should be part of the consideration in developing interventions to enhance student success (Warger & Pugach, 1993).

This step in the process requires developing a brief statement that articulates in general terms the problem area to be examined. More specific statements should not be forced, nor should they be encouraged because, in narrowing the focus quickly, they tend to inhibit full examination and exploration.

## CONSIDERATION OF CONTRIBUTING FACTORS

One of the most critical components of any problem-solving process is time for reflection. You must allow time and a process in which an individual can explore all the factors that might be contributing to the problem and reflect on how they relate to the issue being addressed. For example, in the process of peer collaboration, we facilitated reflection through a structured dialogue in which teachers developed and answered their own questions related to the issue. A peer partner monitored questions to ensure that the partner was asking what, when, where, and who questions and, if needed, the partner provided prompts to facilitate the process.

In this step, teachers who initiate the problem-solving process must stay focused on issues over which they have control. Although there may be some merit in exploring contributing factors over which the teacher has little control; in the long run these factors often prove to be distractors. If the teacher is unable to control or change these factors, he or she is not going to be able to develop an intervention that addresses them. If, on the other hand, the main contributors to the problem are outside of the teacher's control, this should clearly indicate that outside expertise and resources should be brought to bear on the problem.

## DEVELOPMENT OF A PROBLEM PATTERN STATEMENT

After exploring contributing factors, the teacher who is seeking a solution indicates that it is time to move on and develop a pattern statement for the problem. The pattern contains three components:

1. A brief description of the problem and its underlying factors.

2. The individual or group response to the problem.
3. A list of controllable areas that relate to the problem identified.

Those who are collaborating with this teacher should take notes and record the questions raised and the pattern established.

## GENERATION OF POSSIBLE SOLUTIONS

Once the problem pattern has been identified, possible solutions can be proposed, using the notes generated during the reflective period of this process and reexamining the answers to the questions that have been posed. These can be summarized for the teacher or given to the teacher to read so he or she can begin to consider possible solutions. One strategy is to have the teacher generate at least three solutions that he or she can use in beginning to work on the problem. This is a good strategy because it encourages teachers to take ownership and develop strategies that are within their repertoire of teaching skills.

Sometimes, however, you may wish to access the expertise of a group to assist in problem solving. This can be done in a brainstorming session. When brainstorming, the following rules apply:

1. Criticism is not acceptable.
2. Brainstorming encourages participants to offer ideas freely and willingly, generating many ideas without judgment.
3. The facilitator should combine related ideas to generate more fully developed ideas.
4. "Killer phrases" should be avoided at all cost. Phrases such as "That's ridiculous," "But that will cost a lot of money," and the like can derail a strategy or an approach before it is fully developed. More importantly, it can diminish a teacher's motivation for trying something new.

If a brainstorming technique is used to generate possible interventions, the teacher should be allowed to pick two or three from the list. The group should withhold judgment as to the merit of any chosen intervention. We must remember that *the teacher with the problem owns the problem and owns the solutions.* He or she must have the right to select what, in his or her professional judgment, seems to be the most appropriate solution.

## SELECTION OF AN ALTERNATIVE SOLUTION

At this point, the classroom teacher has explored all facets of the problem and now is at a point at which he or she must select a reasonable intervention. The teacher should be most actively engaged in the selection of an appropriate intervention, and the partner or group should play a background role. One strategy is to have the teacher select three of the interventions proposed and predict what is likely to happen when these are used in the classroom. Through these predictions, teachers reexamine their biases, fears, and concerns and try to forecast what's likely to transpire in their classroom. Typically one strategy emerges as more workable than others. Going through this process should help the teacher select a strategy to implement in the classroom.

## DEVELOPMENT OF AN EVALUATION PLAN

To verify the success of an intervention, classroom teachers must develop some plans to establish that the situation has changed as a result of its implementation. More important, they must establish that they have implemented the intervention as they have stated. This approach need not entail rigorous charting or recording of behavioral changes, but it must be something that can convince both the teacher and his or her collaborative partner that the evaluation had been monitored (process evaluation) and that the intervention was successful (outcome evaluation).

## IMPLEMENTATION AND MONITORING OF THE ACCEPTED SOLUTION

A timeline should be established, identifying when and how long the intervention will be implemented before making a decision about its effectiveness. If everything seems to work out, the follow-up meeting can be brief, and the participants can share their success. If, on the other hand, things are not working as projected, teachers and their partners need to decide whether to bring in a consultant's expertise or reexamine steps in the problem-solving process to see if a key issue was missed that could produce a more successful strategy.

In general, this approach to problem solving places the most emphasis on the description of the problem by allowing ample time for the teacher to reflect on the various factors that might contribute to the problem—primarily as a means of seeking out appropriate strategies for intervention. The step-by-step process introduced here provides a framework for how professionals might spend the precious time they have to engage in problem solving.

Once participants are familiar with these steps and have internalized them, solving problems should begin to feel less like a formal process and more like a conversation, but a focused conversation. Further, although the process may seem at first to take a lot of time, the time required becomes shorter with practice. Problem solving, of course, *does* take time, and one of the goals of collaborative schools is to reorganize resources to maximize that time.

## ■ STRUCTURES TO SUPPORT CLASSROOM-SPECIFIC COLLABORATIVE PROBLEM SOLVING

Because classroom-specific collaborative problem solving has been practiced already in the context of special education and school psychology for at least two decades, many models with varying degrees of structure have been developed to facilitate problem solving as it relates to teachers' capability and willingness to accommodate students with disabilities and other students who seem difficult to teach within a specific classroom. These structured models, which proliferated in the 1980s, come under various names, including teacher assistance teams (Chalfant, Pysh, & Moultrie, 1979), intervention assistance teams (Zins, Curtis, Graden, & Ponti, 1988), peer collaboration (Johnson & Pugach, 1991), and mainstream assistance teams (Fuchs, Fuchs, Bahr, Fernstrom, & Stecker, 1990).

What these models have in common is the goal of bringing together teachers with other teachers or specialists to improve the school experience for specific students who are having difficulty. Despite this broad, common goal, however, the models themselves vary greatly, specifically with respect to how the expertise of specialists and classroom teachers is conceptualized and the roles various participants play in the process of problem solving. Because they are so different in this regard, selecting a collaborative problem-solving model is a very crucial decision for a school.

When schools seek greater integration between special and general education, they often begin by selecting and implementing one of these collaborative models. Because different models of classroom-specific collaborative problem solving place different weight on the roles of participants, the selection of a specific model reflects how collaboration is defined in that building and influences the kind of relationships that develop in the context of that model.

For example, if the model selected to guide the interaction between specialists and classroom teachers is heavily weighted toward *prescription* by specialists, the classroom teacher's expertise may never be recognized properly. On the other hand, if the model is weighted more heavily toward *facilitation* of teachers' expertise, other relationships and strengths may develop. In our experience, the "default" form of interaction, when a specialist and a classroom teacher get together, seems to be the direct dispensing of answers by specialists, no matter how collaborative the interaction is intended to be. Therefore, selecting a model that already fosters the prescriptive approach limits the growth potential of teachers in the building.

We would argue that the relationship between creating schoolwide norms of collaboration and selecting a specific collaborative model to enact those goals has to be recognized from the outset so that selection of a specific model for collaboration is informed by the school's prior commitments and goals. In this way, each model can be measured against the schoolwide goal before any specific one of them is selected, to see if it is consistent with the direction the school wishes to take. With the school as the critical context for developing and sustaining the commitment to collaboration, pairs or small groups of teachers become subunits working toward the same goal with whatever model the school chooses.

Given a prior commitment to schoolwide collaboration, the various models become tools to reach the overriding goal of schoolwide collaboration, and *not* what defines the overall relationship between special and general education. The schoolwide context within which these specific, special-education-oriented collaborative models operate is crucial to their success, and the school should be considered the primary unit of mutual commitment to collaboration as a means of meeting the needs of all the students in a building.

## MODELS FOR COLLABORATIVE PROBLEM SOLVING

Because so many structured models for collaborative problem solving have been developed to facilitate educational programming for students regarded as difficult to teach, presenting them all here is not possible. Instead, we have selected four examples that illustrate fundamental differences among the models. In your work you are likely to come across various interpretations of these and other models for collaborative problem solving, initiated in reaction to specific student problems in the classroom. They may operate under the names described here, or under a general rubric such as *prereferral intervention*, or the district or school may have developed a local name for the interaction.

Under whatever name these interactions take place, what you should be looking for are the underlying assumptions of the model in practice and how consistent they are with the school's prior commitment to collaboration. How are these models alike? How do they differ? With which would you feel most comfortable?

### Teacher Assistance Teams

The intent of the teacher assistance team (TAT) is to place decision-making authority in the hands of classroom teachers in a team format (Chalfant, Pysh, & Moultrie, 1979; Chalfant & Pysh, 1989). The TAT approach was one of the earliest attempts to stem the tide of referrals to special education, and it did so by emphasizing the important contributions of classroom teachers to problem solving at the classroom level.

TATs were developed in the 1970s in response to increasing numbers of referrals for special education, a situation which highlighted the need for collaborative problem solving (Chalfant et al., 1979). In this model two or three skilled classroom teachers are elected to become members of a permanent problem-solving team. Administrators and specialists are invited to participate only as the team deems appropriate. Any teacher who encounters a problem for which help is needed can self-refer to the TAT to receive assistance from the team. Teams typically meet for 30-minute problem-solving sessions (Chalfant & Pysh, 1989).

Research on the outcomes of implementing the TAT approach suggests that it is successful in reducing the number of inappropriate referrals to special education (Chalfant & Pysh, 1989). Using this approach, teachers seem comfortable generating intervention goals, and teachers who participated in the 15 TATs studied in Arizona, Illinois, and Nebraska reported that, for 103 of the 200 students they served, the interventions that were implemented were successful.

The benefit of a TAT approach to collaborative problem solving is that it encompasses multiple teachers and a group of teacher experts within the building to whom others can look for collegial advice. Valuing the role of classroom teachers and placing the decision-making authority in their hands regarding who else in the school might contribute to problem solving are important if classroom teachers themselves are to be full participants in collaboration. This teacher-centered orientation is purposive (Chalfant & Pysh, 1989) and functions as a built in, ongoing source of support for a variety of classroom and school-based problems.

**Peer Collaboration**

In the same period of research activity, the peer collaboration model was developed (Johnson & Pugach, 1991; Pugach & Johnson, 1990b, in press). The assumption underlying this model is that in many cases classroom teachers themselves have ample expertise to come up with effective solutions, but what they lack is the time for reflection and the structure within which to do so. Peer collaboration provides a format for engaging in a structured dialogue between classroom teachers specifically for the purpose of problem solving for students with mild learning or behavior problems. It also is based on the assumption that teachers need to engage in some form of internal dialogue to raise their own awareness of the problem in all its complexity and of the range of options available to them within their classroom and school. Thus, peer collaboration promotes reflection on the teacher's part in a supportive context and utilizes the strengths of other classroom teachers.

Initially designed for use by two classroom teachers, peer collaboration has been applied successfully to other job-alike pairs—for example, two special education teachers. Each participant takes on one role, as either initiator or facilitator. The initiator is the teacher who has a problem to be addressed; the facilitator guides the peer as her or she reflects on the problem and comes up with solutions. To begin the interaction, the initiator prepares a brief written description of the problem as he or she sees it. Then the pair (or triad, as appropriate) begins the cycle of peer collaboration. The four general steps of the process are:

1. *Clarifying questions.* The facilitator begins asking questions to assist the initiator in clarifying the problematic situation. To ensure that the initiator is engaging in reflective thought about these questions, the facilitator re-forms the question to make it more meaningful, and the initiator responds to it. This step is intended to turn over ownership of the process of clarification to the initiating teacher, as he or she has the most information about the situation. The facilitator guides the peer to consider basic areas around which to ask good questions. Once the problem is clarified to the satisfaction of both partners, they proceed to step 2.

2. *Summarization.* The initiating teacher reframes the problem based on the clarifying activities just concluded. Often participants in collaborative problem solving assume that the problem as stated by the teacher is an accurate description of what is going on. In peer collaboration the assumption is that, given the time and structure to clarify multiple aspects of the situation, the problem may look different than it did initially. The format for summarizing the problem anew includes: (a) establishing the pattern of behavior, (b) acknowledging the teacher's feelings about the problem, and (c) identifying classroom and school variables that are under the teacher's control. The last aspect of summarization directs attention to things the teacher can do about the situation instead of dwelling on things over which he or she has no control.

3. *Interventions and predictions.* At least three potential interventions are generated, and predictions are made regarding the outcomes of each. After assessing each possibility, the initiator chooses the one he or she feels most comfortable implementing. The facilitator continues to ask clarifying questions about the interventions, models the development of interventions if necessary, and ensures that predictions are made about each.

4. *Evaluation.* A two-part evaluation strategy is developed: (a) an implementation strategy and a means to keep track of it;

and (b) a plan for accounting for the student's progress. The partners plan a meeting two weeks following to consider progress or redesign the intervention, possibly taking into consideration the other alternatives generated in step 3.

Research on peer collaboration (Johnson & Pugach, 1991; Pugach & Johnson, in press) suggests that, for 86% of the teachers who participated, the problems on which they worked were alleviated. In addition, the referral rates by teachers who used peer collaboration were significantly less than rates of their comparison group counterparts. Teachers who participated in peer collaboration sessions expanded their conception of what social behaviors they considered appropriate in class and became more confident in handling classroom problems.

This research suggests that many relatively mild learning and behavior problems can be solved when classroom teachers themselves have the opportunity to be creative and flexible in their thinking about the kinds of interventions that can be developed. Peer collaboration research also seems to indicate that specialists do not have to be present to solve all problems, and that their specialized expertise can be reserved for more complex situations.

Although in this model the process is structured by the steps of the dialogue, its content is not structured directly. Instead, it affords a great deal of self-determination and ownership on the part of the teacher partners. This classifies peer collaboration as an indirect approach to collaborative problem solving, one that encourages a high level of active cognitive participation and involvement. It is designed to build teachers' commitment to implementing the strategies they develop. Developing this sense of commitment through active participation means that teachers are less likely to resist implementing the strategies. After all, they are the ones who developed them.

A potential drawback of peer collaboration comes when teachers follow the steps as a rote exercise and do not take the time to engage substantially in rethinking and redefining the problem. This usually occurs when facilitating partners fail to encourage their peers to ask clarifying questions properly or have difficulty generating appropriate follow-up questions. With adequate training, however, these problems can be minimized.

## Mainstream Assistance Teams

The mainstream assistance team, or MAT (Fuchs, Fuchs, & Bahr, 1990), is an example of a highly prescriptive approach to problem solving that always includes specialists as consultants and classroom teachers as consultees. Students, too, are often included as members of the team. The underlying assumption of the MAT approach is that efficiency in changing classroom teachers' behavior is of utmost importance. As a result, in the MAT process teachers are provided with a list of prescribed interventions from which to choose. In so doing, the researchers "sacrificed some consultation-teacher autonomy and collaboration to help ensure accurate implementation of judiciously chosen interventions" (Fuchs et al., 1990, p. 496). During the interactions consultants follow written scripts. Classroom teachers are required to use student self-monitoring, sometimes in conjunction with a teacher-student contract, as the format for the intervention, with much emphasis on the degree to which teachers follow the prescribed steps.

This prescriptive approach, based on a model of behavioral consultation, relies on four common problem-solving steps: (a) problem identification, (b) problem analysis, (c) plan implementation, and (d) problem evaluation. Problems are described in behavioral terms, the existence of the problem is documented, and once a plan is jointly developed, the consultant monitors the implementation. This degree of structure was implemented in response to the needs of the participating teachers for efficiency. They were impatient to have the problem "solved" and did not seem to want to participate in an interactive process of problem solving (Fuchs et al., 1990).

Research on the MAT model (Fuchs et al., 1990; Fuchs, Fuchs, & Bahr, 1990) suggests that about 70% of the daily behavioral goals were met using this model. On a 5-point rating scale participating classroom teachers rated the process between 3.00 and 3.82 for its effectiveness in achieving positive academic or behavior changes.

What are the benefits of this approach to problem solving? As its developers intended, it provides an efficient way to identify an intervention, and its directive format means that classroom teachers get advice easily and rely on the specialist to guide the changes specified. Therefore, teachers are freed of much of the responsibility of reflecting on their own teaching practice and can wait for a specialist to provide the "right" answer.

From our perspective, situations do arise that require specific, prescriptive action. That is why prescription is one of the fundamental collaborative practices included in our framework. In our experience, however, these situations are the exception and not the norm. Although interventions should be as expedient as possible, as the teachers who used MATs wished, in this approach teachers are less likely to figure out how to bring their own skills and experiences to the problem-solving process. Therefore, a model such as the MAT should be utilized only sparingly, and only in schools where a solid collaborative foundation and real collegiality already exist among staff members.

## Intervention Assistance Teams

Intervention assistance teams (Zins, Curtis, Graden, & Ponti, 1988), or IATs, represent a collaborative model from the school psychology literature. In this model the teacher who wishes assistance meets with another classroom teacher, a specialist, and an administrator. The problem-solving steps IATs follow include: (a) clarifying the problem and defining it behaviorally, (b) analyzing the problem's components, (c) exploring various intervention options, (d) choosing an intervention, (e) specifying how the intervention will be implemented, (f) implementation, (g) evaluation, and (h) as necessary, identifying next steps. Zins and colleagues state that, in most cases, permanent teams are formed at each school building. Some teams are small and add members as needed. Others are as large as six or seven members.

Developers of the IAT model stress the importance of good group dynamics, especially because of the relatively large size of many teams. Stability of group membership is encouraged. Further, they suggested that teams develop and disseminate standard policies regarding (a) how to access the team; (b) preparation for meeting with the team, particularly the kind of documentation teachers should bring and in what specific form it should be written; and (c) procedures for IAT meetings.

To guide interactions of the specialists, collaborative consultation is applied in the context of the IAT. The terms "consultant" and "consultee" describe the various participants in an IAT. The developers see them as equal partners with varying forms of expertise and information to contribute to the problem-solving process. Preferably, the consultee is the one who initiates the request for assistance.

In contrasting the collaborative consultative arrangement with the more hierarchical, expert model, IAT proponents see the collaborative model as more constructive, resulting in more potential interventions and greater involvement of and ownership by the consultee in relationship to implementing and evaluating the intervention. Like other prereferral models, interaction with the team is expected to occur before formal referrals are made for special services, with the intent that many problems will be rectified through the IAT process, reducing unnecessary referrals.

## SIMILARITIES AND DIFFERENCES AMONG COLLABORATIVE PROBLEM-SOLVING MODELS

These four examples are based on different conceptions of how directive collaborative problem solving should be. They also have different implications for how the concept of teacher resistance to change plays out.

These models can be seen along a continuum of directiveness, with TATs at one end as an example of a highly nondirective approach and MATs at the other as an example of a highly directive approach. On the continuum, peer collaboration falls close to TATs, with IATs falling between peer collaboration and MATs. As we have seen, TATs and peer collaboration are both based on the fundamental assumption that teachers themselves have a great deal of expertise, expertise that has to be recognized and utilized for solving many classroom problems. Specifically, peer collaboration stresses the role of teacher reflection in understanding the problem and creating solutions. The lesson of TATs and peer collaboration is that we cannot always make the assumption that classroom teachers need specialists to solve problems; instead we need to recognize the degree to which classroom teachers are professionals capable of coming up with solutions for themselves or for their colleagues. As a result, specialists' time may be used for more intensive problems.

Both the IAT and the MAT models require the participation of the special education teacher or school psychologist. The assumption underlying these approaches is that problems cannot readily be solved without the specialist's presence. Unlike MATs, however, the IAT process is not nearly as prescriptive; its proponents stress the need for voluntary teacher participation.

Limitations of the TAT model revolve around the structure of the meetings themselves. Typically, the format for problem solving is to brainstorm various solutions. Although TATs do seem to result in usable interventions and the open structure of the meetings may allow for more latitude in developing interventions, more structure than is described in the TAT literature may be desirable to ensure that the meetings are efficient in facilitating teachers' thinking about how to approach the problem they are addressing. Peer collaboration provides a structure for the process, but a balance has to be struck between the structure of the dialogue and teachers' freedom to engage in a conversation-like interaction.

Resistance is another issue around which there is a clear distinction between more and less directive models of collaborative problem solving. Managing resistance is a common theme in the literature on collaboration and consultation (see, for example, Aldinger, Warger, & Eavy, 1991; Friend & Cook, 1992; Zins et al., 1988). Its prominence reveals an overriding concern that many teachers are likely to resist the suggestions of specialists and consultants, suggestions that place on the recipient the expectation for changing his or her classroom practice. Much of this literature on resistance makes reference to the "acceptability" of suggested interventions (e.g., Witt & Elliott, 1985).

In models such as the MAT, commitment to implementing the solution typically is seen as the point of resistance. Resistance is considered to be an issue after the solution is developed—a byproduct of the process. In these more directive models, building teacher skills through efficient and prescriptive means precedes the issue of building commitment. By contrast, in less directive models such as the TAT and peer collaboration, building commitment is related integrally to the process itself. Teachers are seen as having the skills and knowledge to generate effective interventions, an assumption that provides a basis for one's commitment to the intervention itself.

In a sense, in less directive models resistance is dealt with at the front end of the process by emphasizing the teachers' expertise and willingness to try to work out solutions, not by their lack of skill. Teachers may need to learn new skills, but they do so in a context in which their contribution and professional commitment is recognized from the outset. We believe that resistance is counteracted by having teachers choose to intervene for educational improvement at the classroom level and at their own levels of professional development, but within an overall school climate that favors such change.

If the goal of collaborative problem solving is to build teacher flexibility and enhance the teacher's repertoire of instructional or behavioral interventions, the teacher himself or herself must be committed to implementing whatever changes are developed as a result of the collaboration. This is the case whether the interaction includes a specialist, another teacher, or a small group. Lasting change occurs because teachers feel comfortable taking the risks associated with trying the new behaviors themselves. In addition to these models, other structures have been developed to support problem-solving schoolwide.

This view of teacher resistance is not meant to imply that change comes without conflict. On the contrary, conflict during the process of change can be an indicator that free and open dialogue is taking place within a school staff. Our point here is simply that the schoolwide context itself can intensify or limit resistance to change.

## ■ STRUCTURES TO SUPPORT SCHOOLWIDE COLLABORATIVE PROBLEM SOLVING

As school staffs begin to move away from the isolated, individualized notion of teachers' having responsibility for a single classroom alone, structural changes to facilitate proactive, schoolwide collaboration are being implemented more frequently. These schoolwide structures may be either formal or informal depending on the nature of the problem to be addressed, and they are more or less successful depending upon how closely the staff and administrators function according to the philosophy of shared governance and participatory management.

The purpose of shared governance in schools is to encourage teachers to work collegially to make decisions regarding how the school operates both philosophically and substantively. Shared governance often is defined by the presence of site-based management, a managerial approach that means decisions no longer are made by the principal and handed down to teachers. Instead, teachers work in a participatory fashion with each other and with their administrators as part of a unified community to make decisions about their school— consistent with the vision they set out. One of the foremost goals of shared governance is to enhance the professionalism of the teaching staff and increase teachers' direct responsibility for what goes on in terms of instruction within a school building.

Making a verbal and cosmetic commitment to site-based management and actually reaching the goal of shared governance characterized by collegial, collective decision making are distinctly different (Conley & Bacharach, 1990). In schools where teachers participate actively in decision making, they work together to make decisions about issues such as the philosophical character of the curriculum, the specific methodologies teachers practice, the extent to which instruction is either child-centered or teacher-directed, ways to increase parental involvement, and so on. Another example of schoolwide collaboration is a decision to restructure delivery of services to students with disabilities to promote full integration; the planning and instructional changes necessitated by that shift entail a lot of schoolwide discussion, consensus-building, and specific work by subgroups of teachers.

Ironically, some schools always have been managed in a way that fosters participatory decision making and problem solving, chiefly because of the principal's leadership style. Others, under the rubric of site-based management, have structures in place wherein staff members and administrators meet regularly to engage in what is supposed to be collegial decision making, but in reality the principal continues to make top-down decisions, invalidating the concept of participatory decision making. Teachers may sit on site-based management councils weekly or biweekly but feel uncomfortable on a day-to-day basis raising questions about instructional or disciplinary practices in the school. Therefore, more important than the title "site-based management" is the quality of professional interactions and workplace structures that exist in a school to make it work as a collegial entity.

## PICTURING THE COLLABORATIVE SCHOOL

When teachers and administrators work together as members of a community to improve the educational program for which they are responsible, what do schools look like? In her exemplary study of the social organization of schools, Rosenholtz (1989) identified several characteristics of vital, energetic, professionally renewing schools—schools in which schoolwide collaboration is the professional norm:

1. Staff members at these schools had identified clear goals for their students. What went on in individual classrooms clearly was related to a set of mutually defined schoolwide expectations. This means that time had been taken to discuss schoolwide goals and reach consensus on what they would be.
2. As a means of reaching these goals, teachers provided assistance to their peers without hesitation. Teachers were not expected to find their own, isolated answers to problems or struggle in isolation to acquire new methods. Structurally, this means that time has to be made for teachers to exchange knowledge and perhaps observe in each others' classrooms and coach each other in acquiring methodology consistent with schoolwide goals.
3. An atmosphere was fostered in which teachers' ongoing learning was expected and accepted. Structurally, this means professional growth opportunities must be developed that allow teachers to practice new instructional skills and receive feedback on their progress, rather than just listening to "how to" inservice programs.
4. The principals incorporated the expectation for teacher learning in the evaluation process, chiefly as a means to communicate the importance of this value in the school and to recognize where support for weaker teachers could be marshaled.

Along with these underlying structures comes an increase in teacher commitment and certainty, apparently because the potential for positive change seems attainable and within the collective powers of the school's teachers and staff to influence. As a result of these basic characteristics of schools, teachers begin to feel more confident taking the risks that will enable them to solve problems more creatively and try new approaches. This is the essence of schoolwide collaboration. In any specific situation that might arise, the ethos of a collaborative school dictates that ingenuity and experimentation by the collective staff is to be expected in the context of reaching the school's goals.

In schools that practice shared governance, teachers meet regularly to discuss professional issues, and they do so with encouragement for their leadership and impunity for challenging the status quo. Staff meetings or other designated meeting times are set aside specifically to reflect on progress toward the school's goals and to identify new issues requiring the staff's attention. Through the mechanism of open communication, issues to be resolved have a forum in which to be addressed.

In some schools a committee structure might be formed within which smaller groups of teachers collaborate and report to the entire staff. In other schools grade- or multi-age-level team meetings take place regularly to identify specific issues. The common thread is that meetings take place at regular intervals for the purpose of improving school practice, are purposeful, and have an eye toward reaching schoolwide goals. Finally, teachers form and re-form such groups as needed.

Implementation of consistent, shared governance is what can lead teachers to reconceptualize their work as a collaborative enterprise. Although the specific structures that facilitate collaborative outcomes may differ from school to school depending upon the relationship that develops between the principal and the teachers, the general qualities we have described—well-defined common goals, frequent communication, an atmosphere that honors experimentation, and ongoing learning and support for learning among the staff—are found in all schools that practice schoolwide collaboration.

The kind of collaborative problem solving we have just described entails no step-by-step procedure. Rather, if a school practices collaborative problem solving, it pervades the school, and the entire atmosphere is imbued with a sense of professional support and interdependence. In a sense, you know it when you feel it, and you are painfully aware of its absence when you don't. A collaborative ethos is self-renewing. New teachers are socialized to the prevailing norms. If those norms are collaborative as they relate to addressing building-wide problems or challenges, new teachers will shed the age-old belief that teachers must "do it alone" and will begin to participate in the various forms of schoolwide collaboration that are available.

## THE ROLE OF PEER COACHING IN COLLABORATIVE SCHOOLS

One effective means for creating a schoolwide climate of change and supporting teachers in those efforts is peer coaching (Joyce & Showers, 1988). Joyce and Showers made clear that acquiring any new teaching method takes time—much more time than traditional patterns of inservice education foster. Further, they recognize the important role feedback plays in assisting teachers as they embark on such changes. Once a school adopts a specific direction intended to accommodate student diversity more effectively, teachers can form dyads or triads to support each other as they experiment with new methods or make more substantive, broad-based changes such as selecting an entirely new curriculum.

The purpose of peer coaching is to provide that support, not in an evaluative manner, but in a way that stresses the importance of collegial sharing in the process of acquiring new methods. The process begins with acquiring knowledge, in initial training sessions, regarding new methods and practices. Then the emphasis shifts to applying the method within the classroom. At this point, "coaching conferences take on the character of collaborative problem solving sessions, which often conclude with joint planning of lessons the team will experiment with" (Joyce & Showers, 1988, p. 86). The term "coaching" is used purposefully to denote the gradual development of skill, through practice, with the guidance and feedback so often associated with the coaching role.

Teachers involved in peer coaching relationships learn new methods together, watch each other practice those methods with their students, and critique each other's progress by watching videotaped lessons jointly. The group becomes the support mechanism by which informal discussion related to growth, problems encountered, and variations on method can be shared and discussed. Most important, helping each other learn new ways to work is accepted and valued as a schoolwide norm. This benefits not only classroom teachers but specialists, too, because if teachers and specialists alike learn new techniques together, they necessarily function as equals within the school. This diminishes the tendency toward creating hierarchies within the school staff.

Research on peer coaching suggests that teachers who participate in coaching use new methods more often, more appropriately, and with longer retention than their noncoached peers (Joyce & Showers, 1988). Coached teachers also show greater cognitive understanding of the purpose of the new methods (Joyce & Showers, 1988).

Peer coaching as conceptualized by Joyce and Showers is not meant to be evaluative at all but, rather, is complementary to the effort to create a supportive environment for school improvement. The principles associated with peer coaching—namely, support and feedback by peers—deserve a place in school restructuring as a fundamental means of creating an environment in which teachers are willing to try new approaches to meet the needs of the diverse students they teach.

## ■ INTERACTIONS BETWEEN SCHOOLWIDE AND CLASSROOM-SPECIFIC COLLABORATION

Schoolwide and situation-specific collaboration are not mutually exclusive. Both have to be present in a school that is committed to meeting the needs of all of its students. Schoolwide awareness and planning are the most expeditious means of meeting the needs of students who are difficult to teach. Even with the best curriculum and teaching in place, some students will always need accommodations and teachers will have to be flexible in their expectations and demands. At times those demands revolve around the needs of students with disabilities. At other times they relate to other children labeled at risk for school failure. In both of these cases a specialist probably will be needed to help create a successful situation for the student, or pairs or small groups of teachers will have to work together.

Sometimes, however, problems that seem to require one-to-one interaction to meet the needs of a specific student actually stem from larger issues that require schoolwide attention. "To what extent is the problem really the student's, and to what extent is it a problem with the way things are conceptualized and operationalized at the school?" Collaboration is labor-intensive, and it doesn't make sense for lots of individual, teacher-to-teacher collaborative interactions to go on if the solution lies in broad-based changes at the school level.

This distinction is important because it relates directly to the issue of resistance we discussed earlier. Our position is that, within a supportive context for schoolwide collaboration, resistance to innovation either (a) diminishes, or (b) is part of a series of smaller skirmishes with resistance that can be addressed from a schoolwide perspective and not singularly on the specialist's part. We recognize that teachers often are reluctant to take the risks associated with trying new teaching approaches. When these changes are expected *and* supported schoolwide, however, a climate can be created in which the norm shifts from the status quo to one of experimentation. As a result, experimentation stands a better chance of becoming the norm, not the exception. But when an individual teacher alone is expected to do things differently, within the relatively lonely context of a one-to-one relationship with a specialist, he or she might well resist the change.

Therefore, we see resistance more as a problem of the school context in which it occurs and believe that the greatest potential for reducing resistance is to create a school context that consistently supports the risk taking needed to improve one's teaching. Thus, if the specific problem a child is encountering is really a problem for many students or is a problem with the school's general approach to a specific issue, then it is that issue that should be addressed. All the energy that goes into individual collaborative interactions might better be redistributed around greater change schoolwide.

We can think of three areas of possible confusion regarding whether the focus of collaboration is schoolwide or classroom-specific: (a) the curriculum, (b) inclusive education as a schoolwide goal, and (c) creating conducive environments for teacher change. These three areas point to the importance of nesting the act of collaboration within the larger context of the school—both for the sake of efficient problem solving and for reducing the potential for resistance. By doing so, short-term change that takes place classroom by classroom is integrated with long-term change schoolwide to which each classroom teacher contributes. The act of change within schools always will occur on two levels at once, schoolwide and individual. Still, building a climate of proactive, schoolwide collaboration eliminates the need for so much reactive, situation-specific collaboration.

## THE STUDENT OR THE CURRICULUM?

One of the most common reasons for initiating a cycle of collaborative problem solving at the classroom level is that a student is "behind" or can't get his or her work done on time. Once it is decided that the student actually is capable of completing the work but chooses not to, an immediate determination must be made: Is the work worth doing? In his book *Growing Minds: On Becoming a Teacher*, Herbert Kohl wrote that one of the most important disciplinary tools a teacher has is the students' desire to be included in daily activities *because they are worthwhile* in the students' eyes (Kohl, 1984). In the most immediate sense the problem on which the teacher wishes to collaborate really does exist in the classroom. In the greater sense, however, if the curriculum is dull, decontextualized, and requires students to engage in meaningless tasks in which they have no personal investment, one wonders why even more students are not getting their work done.

Although not all students who have trouble achieving in school are victims of a dull curriculum, current curriculum reform efforts in all of the major subject areas suggest that the traditional, lockstep curriculum is a big part of the problem for most students. If you are consulting with a teacher who is trying to make a dry curriculum more palatable to a student who is not readily interested in it, you face a question of principle when you engage in the joint development of interventions that may never address the curriculum schoolwide.

In the short run, plans that you may develop in collaboration may put a stop to the immediate problem, but the question you probably want to ask yourself is: If the curriculum for the grade or the school is the problem, why are we developing sophisticated means of designing and implementing individual interventions and not attacking the fundamental issue itself? By failing to address the larger curriculum question, the interventions developed for several students in several classrooms may be duplicating the effort to "make do" with a bad curriculum.

When curricula are based entirely upon the mastery of basic skills, students often do not see the reason for their labors. Instead, when the study of basic skills—which is often the concern of teachers with students who are having difficulty achieving—is embedded in meaningful academic work (Means, Chelemer, & Knapp, 1991), the motivation for getting actively involved is likely to improve. If, for example, students read interesting books and write interesting stories and reports, the messages they get about the purpose of schooling are far different from the messages they get when they experience reading as decoding and mathematics as the acquisition of basic facts.

Until we sort out whether individual students' difficulties stem more from the curriculum than from internal problems they may have, developing an individual intervention skirts the larger issue. That is not to say that an intervention of this sort might not be an appropriate stop-gap measure. Nevertheless, working proactively on curriculum change and renewal schoolwide, rather than engaging in multiple cases of reactive problem solving, probably is one of the best ways to allow school to be a successful experience for diverse learners.

## INCLUSIVE EDUCATION AS A SCHOOLWIDE GOAL

Often, in one-to-one collaborative problem solving, one of the goals is to increase the range of student diversity with which a teacher feels comfortable. Teachers might also have the goal of working together to serve a child with an identified disability more effectively. Or the goal may be learning to work with students whose dominant language is not English. Finally, teachers may be learning to work more effectively with students whose socioeconomic status differs from students with whom a teacher has worked in the past.

The commitment to inclusive education, however, gains far more power if it is undertaken as a schoolwide rather than an individual goal. A teacher may be having difficulty developing the flexibility to work with students whose needs differ from those other students. Making those changes within a school context where everyone is addressing the same problems and where a group forum exists for discussing them removes the pressure of being singled out, of being the only one who may be trying to change. Questions of students' acceptance outside of the classroom, in special classes, across the school, provide the opportunity to see broader progress toward schoolwide goals. This is not to say that individual change will be neglected but, rather, that this change is more likely to happen when it is part of a buildingwide effort and a stated commitment by the principal and the teachers. Without prior commitment, the potential for changing norms schoolwide diminishes.

## CREATING CONDUCIVE ENVIRONMENTS FOR TEACHER CHANGE

Sometimes teachers request one-to-one, classroom-based, situation-specific, collaborative problem solving, but they seem uninterested in making real change. For example, a teacher seems to want help with instructional methods or classroom management, but, upon collaboration, has difficulty or chooses not to follow through. Sometimes teachers ask for more and more help, collaboration, and assistance, but no progress seems to be forthcoming. In these cases the pressure to change focuses entirely on individual teachers and those with whom they collaborate.

If these kinds of interactions occur in a school where experimentation and change is not the professional norm, the responsibility lies solely with the two collaborators to make progress. If, however, the school itself is a workplace where experimentation, teacher improvement, and professional renewal is the professional norm, teachers who are uncomfortable with change have two choices. *First*, they may decide they have absolutely no interest in changing and they look for another school in which to work. They are uncomfortable with the school's changing professional norms. In our experience, this happens infrequently, but it does occur. *Second*, and more common, is that teachers may begin to take small steps toward change, venturing out from their comfortable routines rather slowly, trying out new approaches first in the safety of their own classrooms and then discussing them with a colleague. In the second scenario, support can be found within the school even if the change is focused on a single classroom.

Perhaps the most critical thing to understand is that changing the practice of teaching comes slowly, that the concept of intervention means different things for each teacher depending on his or her point of professional development, and that just because a pair of teachers or a teacher and a specialist have decided on some course of action does not mean the action will take place. When the problem is taken out of the context of the individual classroom and placed into a schoolwide context that supports changes in teaching, somehow taking the chance to try something new doesn't seem as intimidating. Given the overall difficulty in fostering changes in teaching, creating a supportive environment schoolwide seems a necessary precursor to expecting change to occur for a single, specific situation.

## ■ ACHIEVING A BALANCE BETWEEN SCHOOLWIDE AND CLASSROOM-SPECIFIC PROBLEM SOLVING

As collaboration is recognized increasingly as a valued means of school improvement, we hope a balance between classroom and schoolwide collaborative problem solving can be achieved. We believe that, as teachers gain more and more experience with collaborative professional relationships across the range of challenges each school presents, problems associated specifically with creating hierarchical, rather than collaborative, relationships should diminish considerably. As a school becomes more and more collegial and working jointly with others to solve problems becomes part of the professional norm, all teachers should have multiple opportunities to feel comfortable engaging in the four roles collaboration requires and not see themselves only in the role of one who receives others' prescriptions. By the same token, with experience all teachers should feel comfortable receiving advice in a collegial fashion.

Although solving problems is certainly a common outcome when educators collaborate, we pointed out in Chapter 2 that not all forms of collaboration are meant to result in problem-solving interactions. Collaboration designed to solve specific problems is based on the assumption that expertise from various individuals is needed *temporarily* to deal with the situation properly or fully. Collaboration as problem solving connotes a specific, relatively short-term goal. In contrast, team teaching, which we address in the next chapter, is a form of collaboration in which specific teachers share the direct work of teaching on an ongoing and permanent basis. Other forms of collaboration—for example, the school-university collaboration described in Chapter 9—are meant to support teachers' growth in understanding their own practice or acquiring a new methodology rather than to solve a specific problem.

## ■ REMEMBER...

1. Collaborative problem-solving techniques can apply to schoolwide or to classroom-specific challenges.
2. Establishing collaborative problem solving as a schoolwide norm provides the capacity for a school staff to identify and solve its own problems and use creative approaches to improving schools.
3. By solving problems jointly, the results can be superior to those arrived at in isolation.
4. Because models of classroom-specific collaborative problem solving differ greatly in philosophy, and thus define collaboration differently, selection of a model should come after a school has established its goals.
5. Problems that seem to require classroom-specific solutions

may be a function of practices that should be changed schoolwide.

6. One important outcome of collaborative problem solving is to create a support structure for teachers to improve their own classroom instruction.

# ■ ACTIVITIES

- Divide up into groups of five or six people. Take the first initial from each member's name and combine the initials to create an acronym for an organization with a name and a specific purpose. After this has been done, reflect on how well your group collaborated. What skills did you use?
- Divide into small groups. For each group select a school (real or fictitious). Generate a list of resources available to you in the school, and decide how to reorganize, redistribute, or redesign these to help a wider range of students.
- Divide into groups of four or so and select one group member to be the problem identifier. This person is to describe a specific problem (real or fictitious) that he or she is encountering with a student. Through discussion and asking questions, try to determine whether this is more a schoolwide or a classroom-specific problem. If time permits, repeat the activity with other group members.

# 8

# TEAM TEACHING
# AS
# COLLABORATION

One of the most powerful forms of collaboration is team teaching. When teachers decide to become part of an instructional team, they make a commitment to open the classroom door, to make their teaching a more public act, to seek and give support to their colleagues on an ongoing basis, and to recognize the mutual strengths each has to contribute to their students' success. In contrast to a problem-centered view of collaboration—one in which teachers come together to work on a specific challenging learning situation for a certain student or group of students—those who teach in teams collaborate as a regular part of their daily work to design and carry out educational programs that foster students' growth and, as much as possible, prevent problems from developing. When problems do occur, as they inevitably do, the team itself is an ongoing, ready-made resource for problem solving within the context of its larger, year-long educational goals. That is why we sometimes think of team teaching as proactive collaboration.

Team teaching has had a spotty history in the American educational system. Pockets of team teaching have existed for some time. Interest in team teaching appeared in the early 1960s and was documented in the educational literature at that time (Cohen, 1981) but slowed soon after. A resurgence of interest in team teaching has emerged in the 1990s in conjunction with widespread attempts to restructure and reform education. In this context team teaching in schools is found most often in two forms: (a) as the foundation of the middle school concept, and (b) teaming between remedial/special education teachers and general classroom teachers. Teams also are found in elementary and high schools, but they are not as common in these settings.

In middle schools teachers from various subject areas share responsibility for planning and teaching a specific number of students, often from 100 to 150, a model that permits teachers and students to build learning communities in which students feel a sense of belonging. In this model students have the opportunity to build a relationship with their teachers over time rather than to shift from class to class every 45 or 50 minutes. Also, creating student and teacher teams builds on the natural developmental preference that preadolescents and adolescents have for participating in a strong peer culture.

Team teaching has become a preferred model for collaboration between special or remedial education (e.g., Chapter 1 programs) teachers and classroom teachers. This kind of teaming, sometimes called collaborative teaching or cooperative teaching (Bauwens, Hourcade, & Friend, 1989), has emerged in reaction to the problems with both special and compensatory remedial education models in which students traditionally have been identified permanently as low achievers, have been pulled out of their regular classrooms for individual instruction in basic skills, and have had fragmented social and educational experiences as they travel back and forth between remedial and general education classrooms. Special education and Chapter 1 classes often function as a lower academic track, and teaming is seen as one way of overcoming this problem.

Another premise of the co-teaching model is that not only students labeled as needing special or compensatory education have difficulty achieving in school but also many other students who are not so labeled but have trouble academically. This kind of team teaching allows specialized teachers to work with more heterogeneous groups of students and, as a result, helps to eradicate the stigma associated with permanent placement in a pull-out program. The decision to initiate team teaching often, but not always, originates with special education teachers who recognize the problems their students have as they participate in conventional mainstreaming.

Although team teaching as a form of collaboration may originate from different purposes and at different levels in the educational system, many of the dynamics in any team teaching situation are similar. This chapter presents principles that should characterize good team teaching situations. These principles do not represent an absolute formula for success. Instead, they form a set of criteria against which the practice of team teaching can be judged.

# ■ WHY TEAM?

Before you decide to enter into a teaching team, you should consider the conditions under which teaming makes sense as an instructional arrangement.

---

*One of the LD teachers at Elm Street School, Sally Long, has been reading about the value of team teaching and has talked with a few LD teachers in neighboring districts who raved about the relief in scheduling and the great support that team teaching provides. Sally is brimming with enthusiasm to try this new approach. Because most of her students are third graders, she approaches a third-grade teacher, Angelina Garcia, who enthusiastically agrees to try teaming the following year. Together they design a workable schedule for sharing the teaching load, identifying which subjects each will teach and how they will interact during the lessons. They plan to have the LD students assigned directly to Angelina's class from the start of the year and to teach jointly four hours each day. Although they will have 30 students altogether, rather than the standard 26, with 8 formally identified as LD, they believe that the four hours Sally will be in the room daily will make up for the larger class size.*

*As they begin to discuss the specific subject areas, Sally and Angelina find themselves spending a lot of time talking about math. Sally is comfortable teaching math, so she wants to take a major role in this curriculum area early on. They discuss how difficult the concepts of multiple-digit multiplication and long division are and how much trouble students have understanding the meanings of the divisor, dividend, and quotient. They also discuss the problem of how slowly they work out each problem in all of their workbook and practice pages. They agree that both teachers are needed in the room to help the large numbers of students they know will have problems in these areas. With two of them in the room, the chance of success for all of the students who are having difficulty with these and other mathematics skills should improve. They believe that together they can assist many more students in achieving the goals of their school's traditional curriculum.*

Given these plans, how will teaming improve the overall educational situation for students who may have difficulty learning? For students labeled LD in particular? Specifically in mathematics? Do you think this plan is valid? Might these two teachers plan for mathematics instruction in any other ways? Can you think of analogous situations for other subject areas?

## TEAM TEACHING AS CURRICULUM REFORM

Much of the failure students encounter can be traced to problems with the lock-step curriculum and the rigid, graded organizational structure in which teachers traditionally have worked (Cuban, 1989). Often, when students are having difficulty, the apparent intractability of the traditional curriculum is at the root of the situation. An advantage of team teaching is that it permits students to receive additional assistance in the traditional curriculum. Therefore, even though teachers like Sally and Angelina may have misgivings about the quality of the curriculum they are directed to use, they see team teaching as a way to make it more palatable.

When team teaching is initiated, it usually involves a response to a curriculum in which many students are not achieving, may not be motivated, and may not see the value of what they are being asked to do in school. These students may be labeled as having learning disabilities or behavior disorders, or they may carry the more general label of "at risk." As a structure for teaching, teaming certainly can be beneficial to students in these situations by making two teachers available to assist them in acquiring skills and small chunks of subject-by-subject knowledge as represented in the traditional curriculum. The potential of team teaching, however, seems much greater than simply making a bad curriculum more accessible by providing two teachers to help students through it (Pugach & Wesson, in press).

The real ai m of team teaching should be to create teaching and learning situations that represent the most motivating and effective approaches to curriculum available to teachers. This means shifting away from a decontextualized curriculum based on acquiring separate skills and facts to a curriculum building on the natural interests children and youth bring to school. With this natural motivation as a backdrop, basic skills can more naturally be embedded within a framework of meaningful educational experiences. Team teaching should be the means to provide teachers with the opportunity to create model classrooms in which students who previously have had difficulty learning are successful.

In making the commitment to participate in teams, then, the primary goal ought to be *a joint effort to improve the teaching/learning process by implementing the most effective contemporary approaches to curriculum and instruction available*. A commitment to team teaching should mean a commitment to improving the whole act of teaching, particularly when existing approaches to curriculum and instruction have led to large numbers of children and youth having difficulty in school. When this commitment exists, teaming has the potential to prevent many learning problems from arising in the first place—not just for students whose difficulties have been formally identified as having disabilities.

Why is this commitment a concern particularly with respect to making the decision to participate in team teaching—and not just a function of each individual teacher's decision to enter the profession? It is because teaming provides the natural support teachers need to implement new curricula and instructional approaches that have the potential to counteract the rigid educational structure that has led to so much school failure. The resources of two individuals are available on a continual basis to select and implement improvements.

Team teaching becomes the means by which teachers can challenge themselves and jointly take the risks needed to improve the quality of teaching and learning for their students. It enables teachers to be flexible and to shift their teaching from routine, skill-driven, subject-by-subject instruction to nonroutine and more complex instruction—instruction that challenges their typical, day-to-day routine (Cohen, 1981). The flexibility and support that team teaching affords are squandered resources if these attributes are not used to fuel basic changes in curriculum and instruction (Pugach & Wesson, in press). With this commitment comes the responsibility to communicate the benefits of such change to colleagues throughout the school.

The commitment to improving educational practice as a basic assumption of team teaching should not be seen as a call for changing everything at once. Rather, teachers who team ought to set specific goals for various curriculum areas, working to gain skill in one and then applying those skills to other areas of the curriculum. Or they may begin by experimenting with one thematic unit and gradually incorporating others. Teaming is an effective form of professional collaboration only if the question, "What is the purpose of collaboration?" is answered with, "The purpose of collaboration is to promote the most effective teaching possible for the greatest number of students."

## TEAMING AND IMPROVING THE CONDITIONS OF WORK

In addition to improving student achievement, team teaching also has a goal of improving working conditions for teachers, conditions that perhaps are most challenging for those who teach to ever more heterogeneous groups of students. In this case, the benefits of teaming include greater power to do the job well, a sense of shared responsibility, and a partner with whom to share frustrations as well as successes. Others have identified a heightened sense of survival and power, more freedom, an increased sense of belonging, and simply making teaching more enjoyable (Thousand & Villa, 1990). For a profession that traditionally has been grounded in isolated teaching in separate classrooms, these benefits are important. The collegiality that has to be constructed for teachers who work in isolation in their own classrooms is not at issue for those who team teach; a community of adult learners begins to exist by virtue of the decision to team.

Further, the dimensions of collaboration described in Chapter 2 are integrated because, in team teaching, members continually move back and forth from direct to indirect support within the context of working as equals, even if their respective backgrounds and training differ. In this way, teaming naturally resolves some of the problems associated with seeing support teachers as "specialists" and classroom teachers as less worthy "generalists."

Finally, teachers who team also seem to benefit from the synergy generated by their own joint efforts. In one case we know of, the teachers' enthusiasm, expressed openly in their teachers' lounge, created envy among their colleagues who were teaching in isolation!

The potential for curriculum reform and for improving the conditions of work are two benefits of team teaching. Take a moment to consider all of the other benefits this approach offers. What other benefits can accrue for students? For teachers? For school improvement as a whole?

## ■ PRINCIPLES OF TEAM TEACHING

We obviously believe that team teaching has many benefits and that the benefits clearly outweigh the extra time and effort that might be required to participate in this kind of teaching structure. After making the commitment to team teach comes the question of actually how to go about doing it. The following principles for team teaching serve as our basis for its implementation.

1. *Team members challenge themselves to improve their teaching.* Although teachers can challenge themselves when they are not involved in team teaching, rising to the challenge is easier with the built-in support mechanism teaming affords. After making the decision to team, teachers must set this common, broad goal of instructional and curriculum improvement in whatever subject areas the team members select. Improving teaching for all students is the foundation for the decision to team teach.

2. *Team members share responsibility for all students.* That the students with whom team teachers work "belong" to all teachers involved should be axiomatic. Particularly when classroom teachers and specialist teachers (e.g., in learning disabilities or Chapter 1 classes) enter into teaming arrangements, however, they might have a residual tendency to see the students as "my" group and "your" group. Although for administrative reasons students still may have to be identified by a certain label or as "belonging" to a particular teacher, these distinctions never should be made during the day-to-day operation of the classroom. One of the most important outcomes

of team teaching is to create a sense of community within the classroom, a community to which all students belong (Pugach & Wesson, in press). Especially when team teaching is initiated deliberately to reduce various forms of academic tracking or to integrate a student with enduring disabilities, the students must be seen as a unified group, and the teachers (as well as the students) as having responsibility for everyone in it.

A commonly reported outcome of teaming seems to be the inability to distinguish, either initially or after some time, students who formerly were segregated, particularly in LD resource rooms, from other students. If groups are identified as belonging primarily to the special or general education teacher, the stigma and low achievement of special and compensatory education students is seriously diminished.

---

*Near the end of the school year at Mesa Middle School, part of the sixth-grade team is in the library to use computers to complete a series of assignments in English. This team was formed the previous summer specifically to integrate students labeled as having learning disabilities. The teaching team consisted of two general teachers and one LD teacher, who teach approximately 60 students. The teachers, Rachael, Joan, and Chris, worked hard to use instructional methods that enabled all of the students to be successful. They used cooperative learning, attended to individual student's needs, and shifted their literacy program from the traditional basal approach to a more integrated program based on trade books and a lot of writing. The teachers never identified the students who were labeled LD, and the students never raised the issue during the year.*

*On the day in question that May, Dan was having trouble spelling some of the words for his composition. He was getting a little frustrated and asked his teacher how to spell the word "glass." His classmate, Maria, overheard his question and said in a sassy voice, "You don't know how to spell that word? That's an easy word!" Without missing a beat, Dan replied, "Well, I have a learning disability and spelling is hard for me, so if I need some help, I ask for it." With an astonished look,*

*Maria said, "You have a learning disability? You can't be in our class! You need to go to a special school!" To which Dan replied, "No, I don't. We're in a special program this year. The LD kids are with everyone else, and we're making it. If I have to go to a special school, so does Carlos. Right, Carlos?" Carlos piped in, "Yeah, I have a learning disability, too. And if I have to go, so do Samantha and Kayla."*

*Maria had a shocked look on her face, because Kayla was one of the top math students in the class and Maria was among the lowest. She said, "I can't believe this. Not Kayla! All of you fit right in." Despite her initial surprise, she went back to work with a shrug of her shoulders. The LD students had made it to May without a problem, and it seemed they would get through the next few weeks the same way.*

---

The issue of shared responsibility should not be interpreted to mean that all members of a teaching team have to do everything. Clearly, one of the benefits of teaming is that the work of teaching can be divided. This division of labor has to take place within the framework of unified commitment and a sense of responsibility to and accountability for student progress. Otherwise, what is going on really isn't teaming but, rather, is parallel teaching, in which teachers work side-by-side but aren't committed to a common goal. When parallel teaching substitutes for real teaming, both participants can forget to set common goals and work toward them jointly. In real team teaching, decision making becomes a shared responsibility.

3. *Team members share responsibility for instruction.* Sharing responsibility for the same group of students means sharing responsibility for their instruction as well. Instruction can be divided in several ways. Teachers who team may choose to teach specific subject areas in which they excel, or they may share all subjects, taking turns in the leadership role. The most important aspect of decision making around the issue of shared responsibility for instruction is that each teacher involved in teaming should take major responsibility for some portion of instruction. This is especially critical in teams wherein one member was formerly the remedial or special education teacher and may be perceived as working only with students who have problems. In these situations, shifting the status of a specialist teacher to one who teaches all students depends largely on his or her willing-

ness to take on major teaching roles in the various subject areas. If this does not occur, the former specialist runs the risk of always being seen as a helping teacher rather than a "real" teacher.

Coordination of instructional responsibilities is a critical feature of teaming. Cohen (1981) and her colleagues discussed two kinds of interdependence in teaching teams, each requiring different amounts of coordination and communication. The first, *throughout interdependence*, takes place when teams of teachers split the instructional tasks, with each taking responsibility for specific groups of students. In this kind of interdependence, teachers do not necessarily have to interact around substantive issues of instructional method or philosophy.

The second, *instructional interdependence*, is defined as two or more teachers' working with the same group of students in the same subject. This form of interdependence is more demanding and requires that teachers spend time together directly involved in developing and coordinating instruction. Cohen's (1981) research documented that this more challenging form of interdependence, which places teachers in a reciprocal relationship with regard to instructional stimulation and feedback, is far less common than interdependence of scheduling, discipline, or other more routine aspects of teaching. Therefore, if teachers who choose to enter into teaming arrangements are not conscious of the need to aspire to instructional, or reciprocal, interdependence, they may find themselves simply dividing up the work and never really benefiting from the challenges they are able to take on as members of a team.

Specifically, then, sharing responsibility for instruction also means identifying challenging instructional goals for the team. Teachers who team should specify the areas in which they wish to grow each year and work together toward attaining those goals. This puts all team members in the position of learning new skills together. For example, in the scenario presented earlier, Sally and Angelina might want to move toward a problem-solving, more conceptual approach to the teaching of mathematics rather than an approach based primarily in computation. This represents a major instructional change and probably will absorb a lot of their energy. Working on this goal together, however, should provide the support they need to see it through.

Sharing responsibility for instruction also means figuring out the most effective ways to balance the needs of individual students who may be having trouble achieving success with the needs of the group as a whole. Unlike teachers who work in isolation, teachers who team have a great deal of flexibility in how they group students. An important benefit of this kind of teaching structure that you may not have identified yet is the capacity to form and re-form small groups on an as-needed basis for instructional support, for both remediation and enrichment (Pugach & Wesson, in press). Flexible grouping means that, for any given subject, students are pulled together as needed for intensive assistance. What distinguishes this approach from traditional grouping is the concept of flexibility, which Mason and Good (1993) called "situational adjustment," to denote that grouping decisions are temporary depending on the topic, and require constant teacher monitoring to determine future group membership.

With shared responsibility for instruction, benefits also accrue to the teachers. One LD teacher who teamed with several middle school colleagues unequivocally supported teaming because it ended her own isolation as an LD teacher, placed her much more in touch with the regular staff and the regular academic curriculum, made her feel like a more valued member of the school, and seemed to counteract the perception that she was a lunchroom aide!

4. *Team members communicate regularly about the progress of their work.* Although a tremendous amount of communication among team members takes place informally in the day-to-day operation of the class, a regular meeting time must be set aside for discussion and planning. In a job as demanding as teaching, to use scheduled planning time to "blow off steam" and wind down from the hectic daily pace is tempting. Nevertheless, time must be identified for reviewing progress and for future planning. Of course, the amount of energy team members put into their planning fluctuates, but the general rule ought to be to meet regularly, to meet often (at least weekly), and to use the time productively. In one study of collaboration, teachers used a form called the "Meeting Tamer" to give structure to their discussions and to ensure the productive use of time (Ellis, 1990). To maximize your ability to communicate, the guidelines in Chapters 3 through 6 should help.

Setting weekly times for communication is easier if teams are structured as permanent working groups. This becomes more difficult, however, if a compensatory or special education teacher teams with several classroom teachers. Nevertheless, this aspect of teaming is crucial if the partnership is to be successful.

Another critical issue related to communication among team members is what teachers in these teams communicate *about*. If, as suggested earlier, teams set complex instructional routines as their goals, regular meetings will more likely serve a real purpose in terms of reflecting on the progress of these efforts. Without prior commitments, though, time likely will be devoted to routine tasks that may be performed more effectively by a routine division of labor. Every decision, particularly a trivial one, does not have to be made through laborious debate. Instead, energy should be conserved for stimulating discussion on and making decisions about instruction and curriculum issues. Most important, a relationship seems to exist between the introduction of more complex forms of instruction and the amount of collaboration in a school (Cohen, 1981). Therefore, collaborative teaming and instructional innovation are naturally complementary activities.

One attribute of communication that is essential to a healthy team is being open about problems. Problems may involve how a team member is interacting with students, with his or her team members, parents, or administrators. Or a problem may stem from an instructional difficulty a teacher is having. In each case, ground rules, set from the beginning, should encourage airing problems openly and as soon as they appear so they don't escalate and produce a dysfunctional team.

Another vital aspect of communication is the ability to handle different viewpoints among team members respectfully. Team members should expect, from time to time, to engage in heated discussions with their peers about the best way to approach various classroom situations. Discussions of this sort often lead to solutions that are more creative than if they had been developed by a single teacher alone. One of the strengths of teaming is its ability to promote discussion and debate, pushing each team member to the outer limits of his or her creativity. This aspect, according to Cohen (1981), is what can save the occupation of teaching from becoming "fossilized."

5. *Teachers who team support their partners.* Even though mutual and reciprocal support should be axiomatic in team teaching, it should be highlighted as one of the fundamental principles of teaming. Team teachers acknowledge that daily support will be an ongoing feature of their work. When things are going well, support takes a background position. When things are not going smoothly, support assumes a more prominent role and may take more time. In the latter case, taking the time to support each other is well worth the investment.

Support takes many different forms in a teaching team. It might be as simple as an informal, "That was a great lesson" or, "I'm really glad we tried that new approach. It seems to be working well." Or it may be support in the face of a botched lesson. Still another kind of support is needed when a student has difficulty or is especially hard to control, or when a testy parent or administrator is around. Those who elect to teach in teams should anticipate support from their colleagues and at the same time expect to provide it.

A different kind of support comes when teachers are working actively to acquire a new skill and need to coach each other in their progress. This kind of support usually comes under the general rubric of peer coaching, a technique we described in Chapter 7 developed by Joyce and Showers (1988) to encourage practice in and feedback on the specific steps of new teaching approaches. In team teaching, the general strategies associated with peer coaching are applicable when one team member wishes to acquire skills his or her teammate already possesses, or when both wish to acquire a new skill or method together. An important thing to recognize about teaming is that each member brings a different kind of expertise, and one of the inherent values is the ability to learn from each other.

6. *The team teaching agenda requires actively working to include all learners.* When teaching alone, one of the standard complaints teachers make is how much trouble they have trying to meet the needs of all of their students. As an organization, schools have created ways of alleviating these pressures by introducing various forms of tracking: special education, Chapter 1, and ability grouping. With the introduction of team teaching, teachers can work actively to implement curriculum and instructional methods that do a better overall job of meeting the needs of all their students. Teachers who team need to make this goal central to their work. In one team we know, the teachers decided to target five students a week as a way of systematically attending to every student's individual needs— in addition to their other efforts to change and improve their overall instructional approaches. During weekly meetings time might be designated specifically to talk about the progress of individual students in relationship to the group and group needs.

These six principles, then, form the backbone of team teaching:

1. Challenging yourselves to improve your teaching.

2. Sharing responsibility for all students.
3. Sharing responsibility for instruction.
4. Communicating regularly.
5. Supporting team members.
6. Actively working to include all students.

In the absence of any one of these principles, teachers who team teach will have difficulty meeting the challenge associated with teaching diverse groups of learners.

## ■ CHALLENGES FOR TEACHERS WHO TEAM

Team teaching is not without its challenges. Particularly for teachers who have taught in isolation for many years, team teaching presents a major change in their work. *First*, someone is watching you teach on a regular basis. This is the greatest change team teaching involves. Difficulties surrounding this challenge manifest themselves in different ways. Some teachers simply might not know what to do with themselves when their team member is delivering a specific lesson, and they need to structure their tasks in this regard. Grading papers or leaving the room while a team member is teaching violates the intent of teaming in the first place. Still other teachers may feel uncomfortable asking a peer to do a specific job. Teachers who are used to being in the specialist role, without their own large classroom group, may be reluctant to take the lead role and may consistently put off "taking the plunge" to instruct and manage a whole class of students.

Despite the discomfort of shifting job responsibilities, the power of watching and being watched while teaching is more than just a challenge. One LD teacher told us that she thought having someone watch her teach was a luxury, because she received regular feedback on her work. Communicating from the start and regularly thereafter about how it feels to be watched, until all team members feel comfortable, is essential.

*Second*, you no longer have your "own" room. You share it with another teacher. Some teams dispense with teachers' desks altogether; others move two desks into a single room. Whatever arrangement you choose, decisions regarding space, traffic patterns, rules, and how to create a stimulating physical learning environment are no longer decisions you will make alone. Because at least some of these decisions reflect personal preference—as contrasted with those made on the basis of mutual agreement on professional matters—they may cause unease.

Each member of a team must be clear on what he or she is and is not willing to compromise when sharing a classroom. One of the most common concerns involves different personal levels of tolerance for noise. Others may involve individual styles of record keeping. A more complex issue relates to different styles of planning. Still another involves disciplinary styles. Team members must discuss all these things from the outset to avoid unnecessary problems.

What aspects of your own personal style might you need to address if you are to team teach? On which would you be willing to compromise?

A *third* challenge involves philosophical differences. In making the decision to become part of a team, teachers, we assume, either know each other well enough to recognize that they have compatible educational philosophies or at the least have discussed these issues before formalizing their commitment. Many teaming decisions are made simply because teachers already have beliefs in common about teaching (Cohen, 1981). If this is not the case, the professionals involved should talk about their preferences for instruction, management routines, and the extent to which a child-centered or a subject-centered approach dominates their teaching style.

The issue of philosophical differences diminishes in importance, however, once teachers agree to move *together* toward alternative, contemporary approaches to teaching and learning. In some teams we have seen, teachers with diametrically opposed and irreconcilable philosophical differences have been placed together involuntarily and never have been able to find a comfortable way of working together. These involuntary situations should be avoided, as they lead to dysfunctional teaming. At the same time, teachers who at first may not seem likely partners should be given the opportunity to explore the potential teaming offers. They may choose to participate in good faith on a trial or partial basis and discover that their philosophies may be more compatible with those of some of their peers than they believed at first.

A *fourth* challenge involves different levels of expertise. As we discussed earlier, one of the functions of teaming is to provide support in acquiring new skills. Teachers who team should expect to learn from and to teach their teammates the various skills and knowledge they possess. This does not mean that, as a result of teaming, all participating teachers should look like carbon copies of each other. Instead, teaming should be conceptualized as providing the opportunity to share expertise. The challenge comes when one team member feels threatened by the expertise of one of his or her peers. Open communication about these issues should dispel many of these potential problems.

What is the array of expertise among teachers who team? If the collaborative teaching situation involves a group of classroom teachers, individual expertise might exist for specific academic curriculum areas, for contemporary organizational structures such as cooperative learning, or for newer approaches such as integrated thematic instruction, process writing, or whole language. If the collaborative teaming situation blends remedial or special education teachers and classroom teachers, classroom teachers are likely to have more expertise in subject matter and group management. Specialists, on the other hand, may be knowledgeable in a few of the subject areas—typically limited to reading and mathematics—but may have expertise in individual approaches to management or tutoring. Specialists for students with enduring disabilities are likely to have expertise in communication modes and technological assistive devices, as well as a range of functional curriculum materials usually associated with students with moderate to more severe disabilities.

Whatever expertise instructional professionals bring to the team constitutes resources upon which the whole team can draw. Unless all teachers see themselves as those who can learn *from* as well as those who can *provide for* their peers, however, these expert resources run the risk of being lost amidst the insecurities team members may have about being in the position of learning from their teammates.

## ■ TYPICAL PLANNING CONSIDERATIONS

In addition to these principles and challenges, teachers who have experience as team members identify a number of specific issues that cross levels and have to be addressed to facilitate their work. The first is to include families from the outset of planning a shift to team teaching, particularly when integrating special education students. The collective experience of the teachers with whom we have worked is that families are nearly uniformly supportive of teaming once they see its benefits for their children. This applies to children with disabilities and those without disabilities alike. Some districts begin by offering families of children with disabilities a choice of resource room or full integration into a team-taught classroom. Others simply integrate all children at a specific grade level.

Another common planning consideration revolves around how many students who are formally identified as needing remediation or as having disabilities are "too many" for a single team. This is a tricky question, because many students never before have had the opportunity to participate in a "normal" classroom as a full participant in the life of that classroom community. Thus, the extent to which they will challenge the teachers in a given team is relatively unknown. In a study of one elementary team teaching situation (Pugach & Wesson, in press), the majority of LD students who were integrated did very well and did not seem to be a burden to the teachers, even though many of those students formerly had been in resource room settings for their entire school careers.

The point here is that, in planning for team teaching, one cannot make assumptions or set hard and fast expectations about the behavior of students labeled as having disabilities until we give them the chance to be educated in as stimulating, motivating, and supportive an educational environment as possible (Pugach, 1993). What this does mean, however, is that during the first year of transition to an integrated setting, students might need a period of supported transition (Pugach & Wesson, in press) to allow them to gain the confidence needed to function within the larger group.

Further, many of the teachers with whom we have talked believe it is important to start off slowly, with volunteer teachers who are willing to take the time and effort to make heterogeneous grouping work well. Teachers who seem to resist teaming are often teachers for whom isolation as a condition of work has become the only professional mode they can imagine or who seem to lack flexibility in instructional planning. The door should remain open to teachers who previously have doubted the potential of team teaching. Once the benefits become apparent schoolwide, more and more teachers likely will show an interest in becoming a member of a team.

Next, we should retain a place for students who have periodic behavior problems to "cool off." And crisis intervention probably will be needed at times, until students labeled as having emotional/behavioral disorders can see themselves functioning effectively in regular classrooms with peer role models. In short, we cannot predict the degree to which special services ultimately will be necessary for students with behavior disorders.

Finally, once a grade level shifts to teaming, particularly in situations where specialists join with classroom teachers, we must think and plan ahead for the kind of classrooms into which the students will be moving in subsequent years. If, for example, the fifth grade initiates a team, is a team of sixth-grade teachers preparing for the coming year so special education students do not have to return to a segregated, resource setting the following fall? Unfortunately, these situations have occurred, and students have been forced to seesaw between segregated and integrated classes because long-range planning did not take place. Ensuring that classes in subsequent grades are prepared to continue team teaching requires long-range planning and the solid commitment of the school's administration at each step of that process. This kind of planning is crucial particularly when students are making the transition from elementary to middle school or from middle school to high school.

## ■ SETTING UP TEAMS

How do these principles and challenges play out in practice as teachers begin setting up team teaching situations? And what might teaming look like at various levels?

If the purpose of teaming is to foster the inclusion of students with learning and behavior problems, decisions about team teaching may depend upon how many specialists are available to work with the classroom teachers in the school. In our experience, specialists include special education teachers, speech and language teachers, Chapter 1 teachers, district-funded reading and other remedial teachers, and various state-funded teachers. Rather than looking at teaming as simply a function of integrating special and general education teachers, thereby limiting the potential for teaming to the number of special education teachers available, we suggest first looking at the staff schoolwide to determine who might be in a position to begin teaming. In this way, one team teaching situation might be formed at each grade level (for elementary) or one per subject area (secondary), making it possible to begin to accommodate students who formerly have been pulled out for special education or other remedial services.

This type of schoolwide approach is effective only when specialists are not tied to a specific category of disability or a specific category of low achievement. For example, if an LD teacher works with all students in that grade who are labeled as having learning disabilities, behavior disorders, or cognitive disabilities, another specialist is available to work at another grade level or in a specific subject area. By coordinating the work of most special and remedial/compensatory education teachers, teaming can usually be arranged in at least one classroom per grade level. This depends, of course, on the willingness of specialists to work across the various categories of low-achieving students.

The most successful teams we have observed are those in which the teachers take turns working with large and small groups but all planning takes place jointly. On whatever schedule the teachers set up, one takes major responsibility for the lesson as a whole while the other works to identify groups of students who need assistance— be it remediation or enrichment—associated with that or related lessons.

During actual teaching time the most effective teaching partners are comfortable when both contribute to the lesson even though one takes the lead. The decision on how to divide the responsibilities usually is contingent upon the subject matter and the extent to which the specialist teacher feels comfortable with the subject matter. What seems to work best is having specialists begin large-group lessons with the subject areas in which they feel most comfortable and observing and studying subjects in which they feel less so. As stated earlier, the goal is to ensure that both adults are seen unequivocally as teachers, not one as a teacher and the other as only a helper.

## ELEMENTARY TEAM TEACHING

At the elementary school level, team teaching may take various forms. Given the current age-graded organizational structure of most elementary schools, the most common format we have observed is one specialist teacher working at one grade level with a general education teacher. We also know of teams in which one special education teacher formed a partnership with two general education teachers who shared some of the basic academic subjects. This means that, if teaming is to become the format for serving heterogeneous classes of students, eventually at least one specialist will be needed per grade level all the way through school.

When fewer specialists are available, we may conceptualize elementary teaming in two other ways. *First*, and preferably, is to form multi-age classrooms in which one specialist teacher works with various "labeled" students at multiple grade levels. The trend toward multi-age grouping is beginning to reappear with greater frequency nationwide, often in the primary years, and known as "ungraded primary." The reason for this approach is that we know that developmentally children are not all at the same point simply because they all end the second grade, for example, on June 15. Ungraded primary settings provide a block of several years for children to develop the knowledge they will need in the intermediate grades. Further, these settings maximize the natural help and modeling that older children offer to younger ones. A natural extension of this educational trend is to form a teaching team that includes a specialist and that enables a group of students at multiple age levels to be assigned to that class.

The *second* way to structure team teaching at the elementary level is to split the specialist's time between two classroom teachers at two different grade levels. This is the less favorable route, as it leaves one teacher without his or her partner for a portion of the school day. Depending on the "personality" of the class, however, a specialist might team only in certain subject areas or for some integrated thematic units.

## MIDDLE AND HIGH SCHOOL TEAMING

The structure of true middle schools easily lends itself to teaming between specialists and classroom teachers. Based on the concept of interdisciplinary academic teams, often middle school teachers integrate one specialist into their "house" of students. The division of labor depends on the various areas of expertise the classroom and specialist teachers share. Because peer culture is such a prominent concern for adolescents, team teaching provides the sense of belonging that often is absent in impersonal, decentralized settings and may be felt most vividly by preadolescents and adolescents in the middle school years.

If teaming is being planned for a more conventional junior high school or high school, team teaching still can take place with each specialist working directly with one or more teachers in a specific subject area. Similar to the set-up in elementary schools, specialists across the various compensatory and remedial programs could be teamed with various teachers or subjects to spread the practice of teaming across the school. Once teaming is initiated at the middle or junior high school level, and on into high school, it presents a special challenge with respect to subject matter for specialist teachers who never have taught advanced skills in, for example, science, literature, or mathematics. Typically at least a semester is required for a specialist to begin to feel comfortable with a new subject area. Nevertheless, teaming at the high school level is becoming one of the hallmarks of reform, exemplified in some of the more well known successes like Central Park East in New York City (for a discussion of secondary school reform, see Sizer, 1989).

In some cases specialist teachers run special study halls for their students, especially when students are beginning to make the transition from a resource to an integrated team teaching situation. This provides the security students may need until they feel confident in their abilities to perform comfortably in the regular school program.

## ■ POWER OF TEAM TEACHING AS COLLABORATION

We began this chapter by calling team teaching one of the most powerful manifestations of professional collaboration. We believe this is the case because team teaching changes the basic conception of teaching from an isolated task to one in which collaboration among professionals is built right into teachers' daily work. Once some form of team teaching is established in a building, endless possibilities open up for developing new configurations of teachers for different teaching goals.

Although some school staffs may make the transition to teaming easily, others are likely to hold onto the old norms of isolation, resisting the changes teaming requires. At each stage of the transition, the mutual support of teachers and administrators at varying levels is needed to emphasize the potential of teaming. Sometimes administrative support builds slowly and only after the demonstrated success of team teaching, much like the process with skeptical teachers. At other times administrative support is universal, and the challenge is to bring along teachers who lack the confidence to make their teaching more "public." In some cases teachers may hold onto the isolated mode of teaching as a means of keeping private their skill levels, which may fall below what is considered adequate for the school. Whatever the reasons for resisting the transition to teaming, in our view continuing to work toward team teaching should be a schoolwide goal. Even more important, team teaching is a structure that has the potential to transform the basic configuration of the profession.

Each team, of course, will have its own personal character, forged by the personalities of the individual teachers who make up the team. Personal creativity and variation are some of the hallmarks of teaching. Teachers need not and should not lose these individual qualities as teaming takes on a larger role in the schools. Instead, the personal and professional strengths of all participating teachers are shared in team teaching. This increases the potential for improving the educational experiences of the children and youth for whom we make these changes in our professional lives.

## ■ REMEMBER...

1. Team teaching provides a permanent collaborative arrangement to support teachers in their work.
2. Team teaching provides the natural support to challenge and encourage teachers to practice and use new instructional strategies.
3. Teachers who team share full responsibility for all of the students in their classrooms.
4. Team teaching requires full appreciation for the varying kinds of expertise each team member has to offer.
5. Team teachers need to build a strong working relationship

by becoming familiar with each others' teaching styles and by participating in joint planning regularly.

## ACTIVITIES

- In a small group, each member is to identify the personal and professional skills he or she would bring to team teaching. After the list has been compiled, decide what other skills, if any, might be needed. How could you get access to those other skills?

- One of the most important issues teachers who team have to cope with is reconciling different styles. In a small group, plan a week-long summer vacation together. When you're done, go back and discuss your planning styles, preferences, and so on. Draw analogies to team teaching.

- Make a list of all the things that obstruct progress for some of the most challenging students with whom you have worked. Now, in small groups, prioritize which problems you would tackle first if you were in a team teaching situation.

- Prepare a brief presentation with one other person. Begin by identifying your strengths and weaknesses. Develop the presentation jointly to maximize those strengths and to complement the weaknesses. When the two of you have completed the presentation, explain to your audience how you decided to make use of your strengths and compensate for your weakness.

- Interview a teacher who has entered into a team teaching situation recently. Ask him or her to contrast the job of teaching before and after teaming. What are the pros and cons of teaming for this teacher?

# SCHOOL-UNIVERSITY COLLABORATION

U p to this point we have discussed various ways in which teachers might collaborate with each other on a variety of problems and issues they face teaching diverse students in our schools. Another trend that is becoming apparent in the broad context of school reform is school-university collaboration. You might ask why a book on teacher collaboration would include school-university collaboration. We believe that, in the current climate of restructuring schools, a valid question to ask as we seek to become skilled in collaboration is: What contribution might school-university partnerships make toward fostering professional collaboration among teachers? In this chapter we explore the current and fast-changing nature of school-university relationships and provide specific examples of collaborative activities that have the potential to strengthen teachers' capacities to work with the heterogeneous groups of students they serve.

## ■ SCHOOL-UNIVERSITY COLLABORATION AS A REFORM STRATEGY

Recognizing the serious nature of the problems facing schools as the population becomes increasingly diverse, schools and universities have begun to enter into partnerships as a means of refocusing "teacher development so that it becomes an overall strategy for professional and institutional reform" (Fullan & Stiegelbauer, 1991, p. 321). Historically, the relationship between schools and universities has been characterized by periodic interaction whereby, in general, university faculty looked for research sites or placements for student teachers but had little interest in long-term commitment to

**199**

school improvement. They might visit every few weeks to supervise a student teacher or to collect research data. Likewise, schools called upon university faculty to provide "one-shot" inservice workshops and often expected teachers to change as a result. Clearly, this kind of episodic relationship had one fundamental fault: the absence of a common goal that would unify the efforts of schools and universities alike.

As reform efforts have progressed since the early 1980s, one of the most significant changes is the call for redefining the relationship between schools and universities. The purpose of this redefinition is to create supportive partnerships wherein the interests of university faculty—teacher education and educational research—and the practice of teachers in classrooms interact to inform each other mutually, with the common goal of improving education for all students. As partners, both contribute unique perspectives to these joint efforts. University faculties provide constructive criticism and an insistence on reflection on practice, while school staffs tend to be more action-oriented in their goals but may be less used to taking a reflective, critical stance (Goodlad & Sirotnik, 1988). By bringing together these approaches in a collaborative partnership, the potential for real reform, not just cosmetic changes or small improvements, increases significantly. The aim of partnerships like these is to retain the contributions of each of the partners but to do so in the context of a common goal that both wish to achieve (Goodlad, 1988).

 There are many specific strengths universities bring to the schools, and the schools bring to university-based teacher education. Take a minute to think about what these strengths are. Make two mental lists, one defining university strengths and one for the schools.

One basic tenet of school-university collaboration is to link the development of prospective and practicing teachers alike. This approach highlights the continuum of development over the course of a career in teaching. Without continuous development the kinds of changes needed to improve our schools are not likely to come about.

For example, staff development, typically thought of as workshops or dreaded "inservice" sessions, shifts the conceptualization to ongoing professional growth, growth that should characterize the lifespan of all teachers from their initial decision to enter the profession. The most important outcome of ongoing professional development is that, as a result, schools develop the internal capacity to go on growing and teachers to go on learning.

A second tenet is that inquiry into the problems and processes of education is not the domain of university faculty alone. It also should be conducted as a joint effort with teachers and administrators, who are just as interested in improving educational practice and who have major contributions to make in terms of conceptualizing, implementing, and interpreting classroom-based research. Some have called this *collaborative inquiry* (Sirotnik, 1988).

Given the intention of such partnerships to overcome the traditional separation of teacher education, research, and school improvement, prospective and practicing teachers, at the least, will have much greater interaction. Further, the experiences gained in schools should be used, ideally, as a basis for reflecting on, and thus learning from, practice itself.

When these two basic aspects of school-university relationships— *a continuum of ongoing professional growth and development* and *continuous inquiry*—are in place, the potential exists to create the kinds of workplaces where, as we described in Chapter 1, teachers are encouraged to experiment for the purpose of improving the education their students receive. In a building where it is accepted that everyone can improve and that seeking systematic improvement through inquiry into the practice of teaching is appropriate, staff members support each others' change efforts in the context of whatever schoolwide goals are set. Workplaces then can become places for lively intellectual interchanges among all those concerned with education and, thus, can begin to promote the general value of professional collaboration as a means for sustaining the interchange on a daily basis. How schools look when they foster collaboration to enhance how teachers meet the increasingly complex needs of their students is the topic of this chapter.

As we embark on this discussion, we would do well to remember Fullan and Stiegelbauer's (1991) comments on school-university collaboration:

> University partnerships, if they are to work, are a new way of life, not just another project. In the process, the culture of the school and the culture of the university change and begin to overlap in organic ways. (p. 323)

Precisely what these new organic relationships look like will differ from school context to school context. The process of creating partnerships, however, should be based on a set of principles that transcends individual context. At the end of this chapter, we offer guidelines for initiating these partnerships as a means of supporting professional collaboration in schools.

## ■ SCHOOL-UNIVERSITY COLLABORATION AND THE CONTINUUM OF TEACHER DEVELOPMENT

There may be many names for these new partnerships, but probably the best known rubric to describe this new concept of school-university collaboration is the *professional development school* (Holmes Group, 1990) or *professional practice school* (Levine, 1992). Some partnerships function as part of a network—for example, the Coalition for Essential Schools (Sizer, 1989)—and may or may not carry the title of professional development school (PDS) or professional practice school. The name given to the relationship is a secondary consideration. What is important is the quality and character of the activities the partnership supports. We wish to paint a picture here of how the work of schools and universities looks different when they engage in collaboration toward a common goal. For purposes of this discussion, we use the general term professional development school to denote sites where schools and universities have entered into a collaborative partnership.

Structurally, perhaps what best distinguishes a PDS from a traditional school is that teachers, administrators, teacher education students, and university faculty are present and work together at the school site regularly. This in itself is a radical departure and represents the "organic" nature of the changes Fullan and Stiegelbauer anticipate. The logical question that flows from this new structure is: What do teacher education students and faculty do when they collaborate in the schools? What they do is related directly to whatever common goals for improvement the school staff and university faculty have set jointly. For the partnership to work, whatever is done is done collaboratively. Because it provides the conceptual framework for the activities that take place, goal setting is a crucial step in defining the parameters of the partnership between university and school representatives.

Consider an example from one PDS in an urban setting that defined improving literacy instruction as the initial goal of the partnership (Jett-Simpson, Pugach, & Whipp, 1992). The philosophy adopted jointly was that of a strategic approach to learning based on the overall goal of developing independent, lifelong readers. The following scenario describes what you, on any given day, might observe taking place with respect to the goal of improved literacy instruction.

As you read the scenario, look for the various ways in which collaboration is taking place. Write down all the things that went on in the building that day that seem different from "business as usual" in a school. Then note specifically all the different instances of collaboration that occurred at this PDS on this Tuesday. Between whom did they occur, and for what purposes?

## ■ A Day in the Life of a Professional Development School

On Tuesdays at Central City Elementary School, a school of about 650 students ranging from kindergarten through fifth grade in a large metropolitan district, literacy learning is apparent everywhere. Students are busily reading books, writing their own stories, having them typed on computers so they can be "published," or preparing for their multicultural literature competition, "Battle of the Books." Each Tuesday two faculty members ("liaisons") from the partnership university, who spend about a day and a half each in the building in lieu of one course taught at the university, are here as well. In the morning they stop in the office to talk briefly with the principal or vice-principal to determine where their efforts should go next.

This particular day the discussion has to do with planning a half-day professional development session on team teaching, as this is the first year Chapter 1 reading teachers have been working directly with the teachers in their classrooms each morning. The principal, reading teachers, and faculty members see a need to develop and discuss guidelines for team teaching, and they role-play what it looks like now that the teachers have had the chance to "get their feet wet." They also have a brief conversation about the need to secure a substitute teacher a month from now, because one of the teachers will be making a presentation at a professional conference with one of the two faculty members who work in the building.

At the same time you can find about 15 teacher education students working directly with students in reading and writing as part of their methods courses and, later in the morning, meeting with their professor, who is one of the two assigned to the building, to process what they have been working on during the past week. Teachers in whose rooms these students work have volunteered to host them because the teachers themselves are interested in implementing the techniques the students are learning in their reading methods class.

Later in the semester these teachers are to participate in evaluating their students' professional portfolios for reading methods, together with faculty members from the elementary teacher education program. As the end of the semester approaches, several of the reading students request to return to the building for student teaching in the coming year.

This semester the school also is hosting three student teachers. In most cases student teachers and their host teachers work as members of a team rather than in the traditional arrangement. Some of the host teachers are relatively new themselves, and the opportunity to team with a student teacher helps them move more systematically toward their instructional goals in literacy. Although a student teaching supervisor is formally assigned to the school, the faculty liaisons visit the student teachers regularly and talk with them and their host teacher often, as they do on this day.

In the teachers' lounge you can find a sign-up sheet where teachers have requested informal meetings with faculty liaisons. Some want to meet during their preparation time. Others have requested that a specific reading or writing technique be demonstrated in the classroom. Still others have prepared to teach a lesson jointly as a way to gain confidence with a new method. Also located in the lounge is a professional development library containing recent professional journals in all subject areas and many recent books, which serve as resources about contemporary approaches to literacy teaching.

Throughout the day teachers and faculty liaisons can be found talking about the progress Central City's students are making, about problems they are having implementing a new approach, about courses they might take the following summer related to literacy learning. These informal discussions also take place at lunchtime. In the afternoon one of the professors and the school's lead reading teacher together teach an informal class for the building's paraprofessionals—teaching them specific roles related to individual reading with students consistent with the school's literacy learning goals. After this class the two meet to discuss a session they will hold at the university on Friday with the school's Chapter 1 reading teachers to allow them time to gauge the progress of the team teaching model they instituted for the first time that year and also to discuss the support various teachers need as they continue to try to alter their literacy curriculum.

In addition, about 20 other students are participating directly in classrooms as part of their first field experience in schools. They are greeted by the professor who instructs the course for which this field assignment is required. Their informal chats on Tuesdays allow the students and the professor alike to get a sense of their progress. The professor also checks with the host teachers to see if things are going smoothly. As part of their work, these students interact with family members, community members, the principal, and the vice-principal. One is assisting with a special project to prepare a group of fourth and fifth graders to act as guides when guests come to visit the school. This project is run jointly by a teacher and a faculty liaison. Once or twice during the semester, members of this group meet to discuss the structure of their students' experience and ways to improve it in coming semesters.

Two of these students are spending time in both special and general education classrooms, and one of the professor's responsibilities is to clarify the linkages between these programs. The special education teachers, who in this school teach in the fields of learning disabilities and behavior disorders, are implementing literacy programs consistent with the rest of the school. The school's special education teachers have asked to meet with the professor this afternoon to begin exploring the possibility of more extensive inclusion of their students in general education classes using a team teaching model. The principal supports this idea and believes it will strengthen the teaming concept that is taking place with the Chapter 1 teachers.

Because these teachers are all in their first or second year of teaching, the principal asks if the professor will work with them to construct an implementation plan. The teachers already had identified colleagues who were interested in trying team teaching on an experimental basis for the coming semester. The special education teachers are planning to attend a districtwide support meeting for teachers who already are involved in or are planning to begin team teaching in the near future.

One of the faculty liaison's roles has been to provide descriptions of experiences from schools in other districts that have implemented team teaching successfully, articles on process and on curriculum issues (particularly related to changing concepts of literacy curriculum in special education), and support. The teachers themselves deem the work in alternative approaches to literacy learning important because they believe it will provide motivating experiences for their students in literacy instruction, not just basic skills. This is consistent with the school's goal for literacy learning, too. The faculty member and a doctoral student assigned to the building work regularly with these teachers in the planning phases of this change in service delivery, and nurture their desire to learn more about the literacy methods being used.

After school the two faculty members work with a group of volunteer teachers who are interested in portfolios as a means of assessing their students' progress in literacy learning. Members of this group meet about once a month. Before the meeting they read professional articles related to this topic. On their way out of the building, the faculty members make plans to return to see a special performance several classes are putting on later in the week related to a thematic unit on the rainforest. The faculty members then return to their university offices and meet to discuss their work for the coming week related to their school responsibilities.

## ■ THE RANGE OF COLLABORATION IN SCHOOL-UNIVERSITY PARTNERSHIPS

This PDS scenario represents one instance of a contemporary approach to school-university collaboration. But exactly how does this partnership support collaboration and at the same time work to support a continuum of teacher development from preservice teachers to beginning teachers to experienced teachers within the building? Several examples from the scenario illustrate the interactions between teachers, faculty members, administrators, and prospective teachers that contribute to a climate of ongoing professional growth and development. Each instance of collaboration is important, but what is perhaps most important is the changing nature of the school as a place to work. Experimentation, reflection, and open discussion about instruction characterize the various kinds of collaboration in this school. Multiple opportunities for professional growth are starting to become a regular part of what happens in this school.

### COLLABORATION BETWEEN PROSPECTIVE AND EXPERIENCED TEACHERS

This PDS affords multiple opportunities for collaborative relationships between those who are planning to teach and those who are in the profession already. As a PDS, the school is committed to a large presence of university students at various levels of preparation. It is not always the traditional relationship between highly skilled, experienced master teachers and novices (although this kind of interaction certainly occurs). Instead, beginners and experienced teachers alike are simultaneously learners and teachers to each other.

As they collaborate, several things are happening. For one thing, experienced teachers are one of the first contact points for students' initial field experiences; they open their doors to enable teacher education students to get a sense of what teaching is about. Also, teachers who work with reading methods students benefit from observing the new techniques their students are practicing and the feedback they receive from their reading professor who, as one of the faculty liaisons, is a trusted colleague. This whole configuration of students and teachers fosters the implementation of the literacy goals for the school. In addition, teachers contribute directly to the preparation of teachers by their participation in portfolio evaluations. Further, the teaming that characterizes student teaching in this building means that teachers and student teachers are more like colleagues from the outset. Equally important, the team provides much-needed support for implementing some of the complex teaching strategies in literacy the teachers wish to accomplish.

In summary, collaboration between prospective and practicing teachers is woven into the fabric of the building in a number of ways, and the reciprocal nature of the relationships benefits the school's students, teachers, and university students as well. Perhaps most unique, teacher education students who work at this school observe teachers in the process of their own growth and development and may begin to see this as a part of what it means to be a teacher. Likewise, teaching in this building is a public act; teaching is observed regularly by teacher education students, other teachers who team (specifically Chapter 1 reading teachers), faculty liaisons, and visitors to the building. Multiple opportunities to be observed while teaching result in multiple opportunities to talk about the practice of teaching with those who are observing, whether it be for the purpose of providing advice, explaining to a student teacher why a certain practice is used, or debriefing on a lesson that had been co-taught as an experiment with a new teaching technique.

## COLLABORATION BETWEEN BEGINNING TEACHERS AND UNIVERSITY FACULTY

Collaboration between faculty and beginning teachers is exemplified in the work of the special education teachers. As they consider embarking on an integrated service delivery model based on team teaching, collaboration with university faculty liaisons is an immediate source of support for such changes. First-year teachers often are reluctant to make such sweeping changes, or they may not know how to proceed expeditiously. As part of a collaborative relationship, they are able not only to get information quickly, but also to gain a perspective on linking their plans with existing work being done on teaming in Chapter 1 services.

## COLLABORATION FOR BUILDING INTERNAL LEADERSHIP

Another type of collaboration in this PDS is collaboration to build stronger internal leadership. For example, the school's reading teachers are working together not only to initiate new forms of service delivery (for example, team teaching) but also to provide leadership regarding better ways to meet the literacy goals set jointly by the school and the university as part of its PDS work. To this end, several activities are taking place: co-teaching the class for paraprofessionals, planning the professional development meeting on team teaching, and holding regular meetings to discuss progress on schoolwide literacy projects. The goal of these activities is to support the reading teachers and to build their strength as a collaborative team of literacy leaders in the school.

## COLLABORATION FOR DIRECT INCREASES IN TEACHERS' KNOWLEDGE

Access to all formal avenues for knowledge building is open to university students and teachers alike. Use of the professional development library and participation in meetings and after-school "classes" characterize activities of prospective and practicing teachers. Teachers select topics related to the school's literacy goals and work on increasing their knowledge base. These activities encourage teachers to reflect on how the teaching of literacy is progressing and gain other perspectives from their colleagues and university faculty. As the teachers gain confidence with their literacy work, several participate in professional presentations and conferences—another means of clarifying the processes taking place in their classrooms.

# ■ SCHOOL-UNIVERSITY COLLABORATION AND ONGOING INQUIRY: ACTION RESEARCH

Teachers in professional development schools participate in many different forms of inquiry: inquiry related to their role in teacher education, into changing curriculum patterns, into changing norms of interaction with dynamics such as team teaching, and so on. How such inquiry is structured in terms of collaboration and to what degree it is systematic also have a role in redefining the relationship between schools and universities.

When teachers think of inquiry, or research, they often think of university faculty members working alone in their offices, poring over statistical analyses, or figuring out how to establish a relationship with a school so data can be collected for their study. In reality, in the last several decades educational research often became separated from the very classrooms it was designed to help. Consequently, teachers traditionally have not thought of themselves as being involved in research or, to be sure, as capable of being researchers themselves. More often they have seen research as something esoteric and out of their realm.

But another research tradition, *action research*, has as its explicit purpose collegial, collaborative inquiry into classroom practice by teachers. Action research can be thought of as an integral part of professional growth and development and has been called "the missing link in the creation of schools as centers of inquiry" (Holly, 1991, p. 133). As teachers participate collegially in systematic inquiry into their own teaching practice, they are better able to see and implement the kinds of changes that may best improve education in their own school. The term "action" implies that research in the social sciences should be linked to social action (Lewin, 1946) and directly involve those who practice in social institutions in the study and improvement of their own work. Therefore, the purpose of research is to inform action, and the process belongs to the practitioners, or teachers, themselves.

Action research, then, is based on the idea that teachers themselves can and should be undertaking research, but not in isolation. Instead, action research, which recently has been called "interactive research and development" (Lieberman & Miller, 1984), is meant explicitly to bring together groups of teachers as investigators who collaborate with university faculty members to study problems *defined by teachers* as being important to *teachers'* work.

Therefore, action research has the potential to "demystify" research (Holly, 1991) and can promote collaboration on two levels. *First*, teachers are encouraged to work with teacher partners on practice-oriented investigations. In this aspect of action research, teachers collaborate to discuss the kinds of issues about which they need to know more, various ways of studying them, and the impact of their school context on the study of a given problem. Further, by engaging in action research jointly with colleagues, ongoing support for the work is embedded in the process of participation itself.

*Second*, teacher-researchers collaborate with academic researchers to acquire the skills needed to formulate problems skillfully, investigate them in meaningful ways, and share the work and recognition of writing up findings and presenting them professionally (Oja

& Pine, 1989). This aspect of action research is clearly distinguished from conventional university research in that problems to be studied are those that are meaningful to teachers and are not defined in isolation by researchers, as has been the case traditionally.

Because action research is designed to foster teacher inquiry and professional interest in school improvement, it can be thought of as integral to the goal of ongoing professional growth and development. When teachers inquire regularly into what they themselves are doing, at both the classroom and the school level, they create intellectual interest in and responsibility for what goes on in their workplace—one of the hallmarks of a healthy collaborative school. And when they do this collaboratively, as action research is intended to be carried out, the process of inquiry becomes a collective act to be supported and shared. The school as a workplace then becomes a community of inquiry, wherein all participants are encouraged to raise the level of discourse about their work to include improving it through systematic study. Equally important, university faculty begins to see research as linked intimately to school practice and takes a major role in assisting teachers to develop the skills needed to carry out classroom and school-based studies.

If you were to have the opportunity to study some aspect of your teaching in an action research format, what would it be? What do you want to know more about? What do you want to change? How might faculty members from a local university help you?

## THE PROCESS OF ACTION RESEARCH

But how exactly can action research be implemented? Typically, action research is thought of in a series of stages that follow the basic guidelines set forth by Lewin (1946). They include:

- identifying and defining the initial idea or problem, including "reconnaissance."
- developing and implementing a plan, or solution, to the problem.

- evaluating the effect of the solution by making sense of, or analyzing, the data collected.
- revising and reimplementing.

We can see that action research is cyclical in nature, beginning with identification by teachers of what they wish to examine systematically and ending with a reconsideration of the effect of the plan developed as a result of studying the problem. The attraction of this process, naturally, is that it is generic. Whatever issue needs attention can be formulated into a problem for study. Let us consider each step in greater detail and the role of collaboration in those steps.

1. *Identifying the initial problem.* To begin the process of action research, a small group of teachers and one or two university colleagues join together to begin discussing issues in the school or classroom that demand attention. This might start with each of the teachers discussing general issues about which they are concerned. For example, a teacher might say, "I wish I knew why more of my students aren't 'getting' the concept of division." Another might ask, "How can I give my students more time to read independently each day so they will feel comfortable with it?" A third might say, "It's so difficult for Caroline to get started on the tasks I give her each day. I wish I knew how to help her with this." These are examples of the kinds of "general ideas" (Elliott, 1991) that form the basis for teachers' action research.

Obviously, not all ideas lend themselves readily to the conditions in schools under which action research takes place. Problems selected for study ought to be worthwhile and feasible (Holly, 1991), and they also should represent a situation that "(1) impinges on one's field of action and (2) is something one would like to change or improve on" (Elliott, 1991, p. 72).

Selecting a problem to study is critical, because in conducting action research teachers spend a good deal of time thinking about and working on the problem. What seems to be a problem at first, however, may represent, upon further reflection and clarification, only an aspect of a larger or different problem (Pugach & Johnson, 1990a). Working collegially from the outset in discussing these general ideas is a way of getting different perspectives on the problem from colleagues. Especially if the problem is schoolwide, varying perspectives certainly will aid teachers in the way they think about problems. Therefore, a complementary step to identifying initial problems may be what Lewin (1946) called "reconnaissance," or fact-finding, to help clarify what the problem really might be. Reconnaissance is an informal type of data gathering to assist teachers in the next stage, "imagining a solution."

2. *Imagining a solution.* According to McNiff (1988), the next logical step is "imagining a solution" (p. 60). Once you realize what the problem you wish to study will be, you have to decide what you wish to do differently to improve the situation. Imagining a solution means developing a general plan for action (Elliott, 1991). Developing a plan for a solution through action also means considering (a) who else, if anyone, should be included in the planning and implementation phase, and (b) what resources might be needed to carry out the action plan (Elliott, 1991). Implementing the solution, which follows directly from imagining or constructing it, is part of this phase. It is the stage when practice itself changes or is modified. Further, when developing a plan, one has to consider what kind of evidence will be collected to determine whether the plan, or solution, is having the desired effect.

Colleagues are essential to this step because they provide a sounding board for teachers to contemplate issues such as feasibility and appropriateness of the plan. Most important, they provide support for making the changes, or doing things differently as a means to improvement—precisely the goal action research wishes to achieve. Further, throughout the stage of implementation, colleagues meet regularly to talk about progress, share problems, and support each other through subsequent phases of the action research projects—the supportive dimension of collaboration.

In general, the kinds of evidence, or data, that are collected in action research usually are qualitative (Holly, 1991), including: logs and diaries (dated and kept regularly), which in essence are field notes about the progress of the action research; analysis of documents (lesson/unit plans, student work, curriculum materials); video or tape recordings of lessons (including transcriptions of relevant portions); running notes taken by outside observers; interviews (with students, other teachers, parents, teacher education students, and so on); and questionnaires or checklists (Elliott, 1991).

Selection of a method for gathering evidence depends on the nature of the study and the context in which it is carried out. For example, if the problem a teacher wishes to investigate concerns on-task behavior for the whole class and the teacher is working actively to increase motivation by linking lessons to the students' life experiences, videotaping and then analyzing the lessons would provide an accurate record of the teacher's capacity to motivate the students and keep them engaged. The teacher would not want to record every lesson but, rather, develop a pattern of observation on a regular basis or select representative lessons.

At this point, collaboration with university faculty becomes important as a source of information regarding how to structure these various forms of collecting evidence. Equally important, teacher colleagues provide a realistic check on when and how to collect the needed evidence efficiently.

---

*Barbara Miller, a fourth-grade teacher, wishes to build her students' capacity for independent reading. She decides to structure the selection of books carefully and set up a daily period, with a timer, during which she charts for her students the amount of time they are able to sit quietly and read. She sets a 12-week period for collecting evidence. Her evidence will consist of number of pages her students read independently, number of books read, and an actual tally of the time they spent reading. In addition, she decides to enforce the practice of reading silently by using herself as a model, which she has not tried before.*

*At their biweekly action research meetings, her colleagues suggest that she also might want to have one of the school's reading teachers interview a small group of her students to see how they feel about their capacities as independent readers. Barbara asks the reading teacher, Anita, to help her by doing this. During the implementation period Barbara continues to attend biweekly meetings to discuss progress and make sure everyone is on track with the plan to collect evidence.*

---

These periodic meetings are essential if action research is to encourage the goal of reflection, which is an outgrowth of the action research process. Sometimes, action researchers organize themselves into more formal "study groups" (Kyle & Hovda, 1987), or informal graduate courses with the participating faculty members, with university credit attached to participation.

3. *Evaluating the effect of the solution by analyzing evidence.* In this phase of action research, teachers and faculty colleagues work together to consider what patterns have emerged from the evidence that has been collected. Data analysis, conducted collegially, enables novice action researchers to have support for the kinds of hypotheses and conclusions they may have reached tentatively upon initial consideration of the evidence. In our example, Barbara may see that on some days her students are more able to sustain silent reading than on others and that the overall trend is an increase in the time they read silently. In looking over the data, however, her colleagues note that the students seem to be reading only books that are easy for them, and have trouble reading books that are even slightly challenging. They brainstorm ideas for renegotiating the selection of books to ensure a broader range of difficulty.

In another crucial aspect of evaluating the effects of the new actions, a time is allotted to share the results of the action research, or report on it. Reporting on action research means not only sharing the results but also sharing the process. Writing out reports formally for dissemination provides an opportunity for teachers and faculty members to co-author the writing, further solidifying these collaborative ties. Such complete reporting is critical for several reasons. *First*, it is a means of illustrating how teachers can conduct their own systematic inquiry. *Second*, it provides a model of what can be accomplished with collegial support for changes in practice. *Third*, it may stimulate others to realize that they are concerned about problems similar to those studied thus far. *Fourth*, reporting on the results of their work gives the teachers involved the chance to revisit their work and clarify their thinking about why they undertook this investigation and the benefit of the results achieved. Frequently, action research is reported as a case study of teacher change in a specific classroom.

4. *Revising and reimplementing.* Revising and reimplementing are done when, during the process of conducting action research, the initial solution, or plan, is not resulting in the desired changes. Through periodic monitoring, the results of which are shared in regular meetings with colleagues, teachers conducting action research have the opportunity to assess progress informally and determine whether the general solution, or plan, has to be revised.

With the input of colleagues, the plan might be revised and different or additional ways of gathering evidence might be initiated. This step of revising and reimplementing characterizes the cyclical nature of action research: the results feed back into making additional changes to improve even further the practices teachers are using. During a cycle of action research, revisions and reimplementation actually may take place more than once before the results are reported.

## COLLABORATIVE OUTCOMES OF ACTION RESEARCH

Action research has been studied in the United States, Great Britain, and Australia. One body of research has been conducted by Sharon Oja and her colleagues at the University of New Hampshire (Oja & Pine, 1989). In their work they specifically studied the collegial outcomes of a group of teachers who participated in an action research project over several years. They identified the following outcomes for teachers regarding collegiality:

- creating new patterns of communication.
- learning the dynamics of collegiality and sharing among members of the action research team.
- learning about the influence of collegiality on schoolwide problem solving.
- becoming more willing to communicate about problems and to experiment with alternative solutions.
- getting daily support from colleagues.
- participating in the development of a common body of knowledge.
- developing greater capacity for dealing with the pressures of school.
- in general, developing greater interest in creating schoolwide collegiality.

Action research has great potential to foster the kind of professional collegiality that can build internal strength within a building for continuous school renewal. From this kind of school-university partnership, a culture of experimentation and collaboration can emerge, one in which teachers take more responsibility for improving the quality of education in their own schools and faculty assist them in developing the skills of action research as a means of professionalizing teaching.

## ACTION RESEARCH AND COLLABORATION BETWEEN SPECIAL
## AND GENERAL EDUCATION

One of the more rapidly growing forms of professional interaction is that between special and general education teachers. The dynamics of action research can be applied to a common form of special-general education interaction—namely, one-on-one collaboration between a special education teacher and a classroom teacher. Typically, the purpose of such one-on-one interactions is to work with classroom teachers, assisting and supporting them so their teaching becomes more accommodating of students who have difficulties in school, either with academics or behavior. Although the reason for initiating such a collaborative relationship is usually a specific problem the classroom teacher is having with one or two students, more often than not some general practice in the classroom is at the root of the problem.

Elsewhere we have argued that, when the problem to be solved affects more students than the specific one a teacher might target, action research likely holds more potential for real, consistent change (Pugach & Johnson, 1990a). Action research places ownership for change squarely with the teacher, minimizing teacher resistance. Further, if special and general education teachers participate together as members of an action research study group, they are instantly on equal footing as colleagues supporting one anothers' action research. As a result, both are in the position of inquiring into the quality of their own practice and working to improve it.

As we discussed in Chapter 7, resistance to change is a lot less probable when a group of teachers work on change together and create a school climate where change is the norm. Action research is one way to shift from the traditional norms of the status quo to norms of experimentation, bypassing the need for some of the formal, one-on-one interaction that goes on between special and general education. Particularly when problems affect many students—for instance, motivational problems based more on the general nature of the instructional activities than the student's inherent unwillingness to participate—action research can provide a safe, supportive context in which to address these far-reaching changes in teaching practice.

## ■ GUIDELINES FOR SCHOOL-UNIVERSITY COLLABORATION

One of the major goals of school-university collaboration is to create schools as places where teachers inquire continuously into their practice. Action research is a wise complement to building solid school-university relationships in the context of professional development schools. How do these partnerships get started, and what guidelines can we follow as a way to build collaborative schools?

*First*, partners from the schools and universities who wish to enter into a collaborative relationship need to recognize that they must go through a period of *trust building* (Pugach & Pasch, 1994). This is essential to get past the stereotypes each person carries about the other. During this time, they should be asking questions like, "What will we as a school get out of this? What will I as a faculty member get out of this? What's in it for us as partners?" (Goodlad, 1988). Taking enough time for this stage will allow all of the ensuing activities to take place in a relatively positive atmosphere. At the school level the trust-building stage may mean that faculty members spend more time in the building getting to know the teachers, students, problems, and personalities. At the same time, teachers have the opportunities to discuss their concerns and see if they can work together with the designated university faculty.

The *second* guideline is *to establish both a university person and a school person to broker the interactions between the two institutions and their resources.* Most PDS structures identify a faculty liaison and a teacher liaison to facilitate the work. Thus, if a specific project within the partnership requires specific human, fiscal, or academic resources, the liaisons can work together to secure them. This may mean identifying teachers who wish to work with teacher education students at any given time, or it may mean soliciting the participation of another faculty member to provide input on a specific problem.

*Third*, regular *opportunities for dialogue* have to be built into the interactions between teachers in the school, their administrators, and university liaisons. These sessions become the basis for emerging common goals that will form the backbone of partnership activities in the future. Equally important, they become the means by which new goals are set and initiated as the partnership develops.

*Fourth*, at some point following the initial relationship-building as represented by the first three guidelines, *common goals have to be set* to focus the participants' energy. In the PDS scenario presented earlier, the goal of radical change in teaching literacy was set, but only after a period of "roaming around" establishing strong school-university relationships. Goodlad (1988) specifically warned against setting common goals too soon, as this might prevent the necessary dialogue from occurring in the first place. What is needed, he continued, is a healthy tension between engaging in dialogue and goal setting, so that thinking and reflecting carefully before acting become the norm for decision making in the school.

Obviously, for school-university partnerships to be successful, another layer of relationships has to exist beyond the school building. The commitment of district and university administrators is vital in providing leadership and stability for individual schools that participate in partnerships. This level of commitment is essential for securing fiscal resources to enable teachers and faculty partners to have the time to engage in dialogue and meet regularly. We appreciate the essential nature of partnerships at this level, but our interest here is in the effect of these partnerships at the school level and their ability to foster professional collaboration among teachers, teacher education students, and university faculty members. Once agreements are in place among administrators, the various players at the school sites have to develop the relationships that enable them to gain from such a partnership.

One other point should be mentioned as a key element in promoting healthy school-university partnerships. Participating in a partnership means making a commitment to changing the way teaching takes place in your building. This is a long-term commitment. Those who take part in school-university collaborations have to be aware that *change is usually a slow process.* If change is not taking place rapidly, participants may believe the partnership is not working. This is precisely when a more reflective, long-term view may be helpful. As long as progress toward change is taking place, teachers and faculty can feel good about the work they are doing together. Therefore, those who enter into school-university partnerships must understand the process of change in which they are participating (Goodlad, 1988) and be willing to accept the pace at which change occurs.

## ■ REVISITING COLLABORATION IN SCHOOL-UNIVERSITY PARTNERSHIPS

School-university partnerships represent an unprecedented opportunity to support real and lasting change in schools by supporting the creation of highly professional workplaces characterized by ongoing professional collaboration. A climate in which teachers, prospective teachers, and university faculty explore and act on the problems of educational practice together maximizes the potential to find far better ways of organizing schools and classrooms to meet the needs of a diverse student population. In the context of a school-university partnership, teachers can find support for asking difficult questions about the school's practices, structure ways to solve them, and together see what really makes a positive difference.

With these partnerships the school itself becomes the unit of change. In this way, we can move beyond changing only one program—special education, for example—and look at needed changes from a schoolwide perspective. School-university partnerships enable working on specific programs within a building, but in the larger context of improving educational practice schoolwide. Perhaps most important, given the dialogue that is essential to professional growth, this partnership forces consideration of where one's own interests intersect with those of one's colleagues across the building. If these partnerships are successful, collaboration can be an unmistakable and much welcomed outcome.

## ■ REMEMBER...

1. Like any other form of collaboration, school-university partnerships pool different kinds of expertise.
2. School-university collaboration can foster the development of a climate wherein teachers feel free to experiment and are supported in their efforts.
3. As one example of school-university collaboration, professional development schools (PDSs) bring together the preparation of new teachers with the ongoing development of experienced teachers.
4. Collaboration is based on the development of mutual respect

for the contributions of schools and of higher education to the improvement of schooling.

5. Action research is a form of collaboration that encourages inquiry into the improvement of teaching.

## ■ ACTIVITIES

- As a group, record all the school-university partnerships in your area. Which ones exemplify the goals of collaboration advanced in this book?
- Assume that 20 student teachers are going to be assigned to your school, which has 18 classrooms (three each at grades K–5). How would you organize their semester-long activities to promote the most professional collaboration schoolwide?
- Revisit the four dimensions of collaboration. Which dimensions would be best facilitated by a school-university partnership?

# 10

# SCHOOL-FAMILY COLLABORATION

The family is the basic unit that defines and sustains our society. It is a group of individuals that exists to meet the collective and individual needs of members of the family. Developing a healthy partnership with families is one of the most important goals our schools can undertake. Without an active and positive partnership with families, we never can achieve a truly collaborative school. Our students are all members of families first and students second. Families are going to have the most lasting and powerful influence on the development of the students with whom we work. Consequently, we must have an understanding of families to lay the groundwork for effective collaborative relationships.

In the past our notion of family was narrow and revolved around a traditional unit consisting of husband, wife, and children. The basic family unit has changed drastically over the last several decades. Since 1950 the divorce rate has more than doubled and the number of children that must cope with a divorce has tripled (Office of Policy and Planning, 1992). In 1990 there were 2.4 million marriages and 1.2 million divorces (Ahlburg & DeVita, 1992). Currently one in every two marriages is destined for a divorce. Since 1970 there has been a 30% decrease in families made up of a married couple and children. During the same time period there has been a 97% increase in single parent families (Ahlburg & DeVita, 1992). From 1950 to 1990 the number of children in single parent families tripled from 7% to 22% with 57% of these families living below the poverty level (Office of Policy and Planning, 1992). Finally, in 1950 only 28% of married women worked outside of the home, while in 1990 74% of married women worked outside of the home (Office of Policy and Planning, 1992). Clearly, our notion of the family has to expand to encompass the various types of family units with which you will come in contact.

In this chapter we provide a framework from which to interpret and understand the demands placed on the family. Without an understanding of families and their unique needs and pressures, your attempts at collaboration may be misunderstood. After we have provided this foundational context, we explore barriers, real and perceived, that have inhibited collaboration between teachers and families. Finally, we provide practical suggestions on how to collaborate more effectively with the families of your students.

As you read this chapter, take a minute to think about all the different types of families with which you have had more than casual contact—the way they interact, solve problems, experience joy, and so forth. They could be families of close relatives, your own family, the families of friends. As you think about these families, identify three or four families that have different structures and styles. As you read about families, ask yourself how the issues discussed relate to or play themselves out with each of these families. Focus on both similarities and differences as you think about these families.

## ■ THE FAMILY DEFINED

The main purpose of the family is to meet its members' needs to nurture their fullest development. Even though families differ across cultures, the commonalities among family units worldwide are far greater than the differences. As LeVine, Miller, and West (1988) asserted, what parents want for their children is universal.

The family can be defined as a network of people who live together for an extended time because of a mutual commitment to the unit. This commitment can be by blood, marriage, legal means, or otherwise. The type of the commitment or how this commitment is made is unimportant. Rather, the fact that a commitment has been made and that it is a mutual partnership among family members is the overriding factor. As Galvin and Brommel (1982) pointed out, families exist in a number of forms, all of which are able to meet the needs of family members. These forms are:

1. *Childless:* two adults without children.
2. *Traditional:* two adults plus children from the union of these adults.
3. *Single-parent:* one parent and one or more children.
4. *Blended:* two adults and children from different unions.
5. *Extended:* relatives and friends who have a connection with the family unit.

Families can change from one form of family unit to another. For example, a childless family can become a traditional family and then, through a divorce or a death, can become a single-parent family and then can be joined with another single-parent family to become a blended family.

## ■ FAMILY SYSTEMS

As a system, the family is made up of members and a series of subsystems that are internally and externally related. If anything impacts a member of the family, it will have an effect on the rest of the family system. Similarly, changes in the broader structural system within which the family exists affect the family system. For example, a bad economy can create additional stress that can strain the family system and influence how a child functions in the classroom.

Likewise, what happens at school can affect the broader family unit. For instance, a child who receives a detention or some kind of school discipline also may be disciplined at home. If one of the adult members of the family considers this discipline too harsh, additional stress is placed on the marital subsystem. More specifically, when we ask family members to spend extra time with one of their children to support classwork, the extra time spent with this child detracts from other activities within the family. Although requests for support typically have positive outcomes, if the family is stressed already by spending long hours supporting the family financially, the added time we request for family members to work with the child actually may do more harm than good.

The family system is composed of a series of subsystems: (a) marital, (b) parental, (c) sibling, and (d) extrafamilial (Turnbull, Summers, & Brotherson, 1984). The interaction between subsystems depends greatly on the structure of the larger family unit. Single-parent families, for example, have no marital subsystem, and families with only one child have no sibling subsystem. Family systems are further defined as follows.

1. *Marital:* two primary adults within the family unit regardless of their marital status. These adults have needs and roles as adult partners. They plan for the family, support one another, play together, and share intimacy.
2. *Parental:* the adult primary caregivers and the children. As they interact with the children within the family, these caregivers assume a wide variety of roles: counselors, financial advisors, chauffeurs, disciplinarians, tutors, and so on. These roles can be explicit or implied and are fluid and changing constantly.
3. *Sibling:* children within the family unit. Siblings sometimes take on parental roles within the family and interact more like a parent than a child.
4. *Extrafamilial:* the family members in interaction with community members and members of the extended family. These interactions can be a source of support, or they can be a source of additional stress when members of the community place pressure upon the family to conform to their expectations.

Some families have extended families that provide a great deal of support; others may have become estranged from their extended families because of their geographic location or other reasons. As a result, these families do not have a natural support system they can rely upon. These families must create their own extended system from friends and neighbors. Some families are unable to create an extended support system at all.

In the next section we are going to discuss basic family needs. As you read this section think about the families of the students in your class or practicum. Do some of these families have trouble meeting their basic needs? How does not being able to meet family needs affect children at school? Can the school do anything to help the family meet its needs? Is this the school's responsibility? Are there any pitfalls in schools' providing resources to enable families to be better able to meet their needs?

## FAMILY FUNCTIONS

The tasks that families undertake to meet the needs of their members are called family functions. Turnbull and Turnbull (1990) described seven family functions: (a) economic, (b) daily care, (c) socialization, (d) recreational, (e) self-definition, (f) affection, and (g) educational and vocational. Families implement these functions to meet their current and individual needs and to transfer responsibility for meeting those needs from the older generation of the family to the younger generation. All too often we focus on the educational and vocational needs of the families and ignore their other needs. Families are complex and have diverse needs that must be met for the family to be effective.

### Economic Needs

All families must make decisions about how to obtain and spend money to meet their needs. When a family is having trouble meeting its economic needs, tremendous stress is placed on the family unit. This stress can accentuate negative behaviors of family members and strain their interactions. Maintaining a supportive environment is difficult when basic needs are not being met. If a family has a child with a disability who requires special care, the demands placed on the family can be even greater as a result of the costs of medical care or because of the extra efforts family members must expend to generate the additional finances needed.

When families are having difficulty meeting their needs because of economic problems, schools can do many things to help. A school can collect information and resources on financial planning and make them available in a family resource library. Schools can make community contacts to provide parents with specialized information such as estate planning, employment services, and financial planning. The school's parent organization might identify special speakers to address financial planning, saving for college, and other economic concerns. Parents who have successfully addressed issues such as planning for college can be asked to speak with other families that have similar problems. Secondary schools can make families aware of scholarships and college planning concerns (Turnbull & Turnbull, 1990).

**Daily Care Needs**

Perhaps the most important function a family performs is meeting the daily care needs of its members. The day-to-day tasks of cooking, cleaning, doing laundry, transporting, obtaining appropriate medical care, and the like, typically dominate family life. As with economic needs, if the family's medical and domestic care needs are not being met, the family has difficulty focusing on any other issues. When parents are trying to meet the daily care needs of their children, they sometimes overlook their own needs and become exhausted in the process.

When encountering such a family, schools might provide information, in areas such as health care, as part of the resource library. This should include psychological information as well as that pertaining to physical health. The school can introduce health promotion into the curriculum. If the school has a school nurse, he or she might work with parents to develop programs for parents. A simple but effective action is to examine food served at the school to ensure that it is consistent with best thinking about nutrition. Parents who have been successful in juggling the many demands placed upon them might share their strategies for success with other families (Turnbull & Turnbull, 1990).

**Socialization Needs**

The ability to socialize is a critical component of a family's quality of life. Families are the basis from which children learn to interact with others (Skrtic, Summers, Brotherson, & Turnbull, 1984). Families that have children with disabilities or behavior problems can be severely limited in their social options because of the undue stress upon the family when the child is in public.

Schools can do several things to expand socialization options for families. Respite care can be developed for families that have a child with severe disabilities, releasing parents from the constant demands on them and opening up socialization and recreation opportunities. The school can sponsor workshops on behavior management, offering strategies to help parents deal positively with their child's public behavior. The school can encourage family support groups that enable families to socialize with others in similar circumstances. Finally, the school can reconceptualize itself as a community center and offer workshops and other community activities for families in the neighborhood. Thus, the school becomes a place for families in the community to interact (Turnbull & Turnbull, 1990).

### Recreational Needs

We all need activities to unwind and divert our attention from the daily routine. The family is a primary source of recreational opportunities for its members. Recreational needs are met in various ways, from planned, structured vacations to simple walks or conversations during dinner. The suggestions for helping families meet socialization needs also apply to their recreational needs. Not only do those activities allow for socialization but they often constitute a recreational outlet for the family as well.

### Self-Definition Needs

Our sense of confidence and self-worth are key elements of our identity as individuals. The family perhaps is the most important system to help individuals develop their sense of their self-identity. School personnel must realize that the self-identity of parents is tied heavily to the abilities of their children. If a child has difficulty in school, for example, family members can internalize a sense of responsibility for the problem and develop feelings of inadequacy themselves. Helping parents identify and pursue their own interests is one way to help them nurture their own self-identity and move beyond associating so intensely with their children. Finding ways for parents to participate and be successful within the school community also is recommended. Family support groups, again, can help families address their concerns in relation to other families with similar concerns (Turnbull & Turnbull, 1990).

### Affection Needs

Families provide an essential environment for individuals to experience affection and physical intimacy. The family sends physical as well as emotional messages that communicate unconditional regard for and love to members. These messages are communicated through both verbal and nonverbal means. Nonverbal actions such as touching, hugging, kissing, and just being with one another are powerful.

Although we tend to think that meeting the affection needs of families is beyond the scope of schools, we can do some things to help families address these needs. For instance, making information on sexuality available can be a source of help. In particular, accurate information on AIDS and other sexually transmitted diseases is important for students. Counselors and support groups can help students as they confront issues of affection (Turnbull & Turnbull, 1990).

### Educational and Vocational Needs

The educational and vocational needs of the family probably make up the area that professionals emphasize most often. Many demands compete for families' time and efforts. We must be sensitive to the kinds of demands placed on parents and recognize that the child is only one of those demands. Families must be allowed to choose their level of involvement within the school. If the family's educational/vocational needs are not being met, the family cannot be involved extensively in the school. The suggestions related to economic needs could be expanded to include educational and vocational needs.

## ELEMENTS OF FAMILY INTERACTION

The main elements of interactions within the family are cohesion and adaptability. The extent of cohesiveness or adaptability of the family has a significant impact on the quality of interactions within the family. Cohesion is the emotional bond between members of the family. Adaptability is the capability of a family to modify or change in response to outside pressures (Olson, 1980).

### Cohesion

Cohesion exists along a continuum with high disengagement on one end and high enmeshment on the other end. A healthy family maintains a delicate balance between disengagement and enmeshment. This balance often shifts as new issues confront the family. When a family faces a crisis, it becomes more enmeshed. When children are trying to strike out on their own, the family becomes more disengaged.

*Enmeshment.* Families that are highly enmeshed are character-ized by overinvolvement and overprotection of family members. Family members are allowed little privacy, and most activities of family mem-bers are contained within the family. A family that becomes too en-meshed has a difficult time functioning effectively. In particular, members have difficulty developing their own sense of individuality. A certain degree of enmeshment is healthy and positive. It provides a safety net that allows individuals within the family to feel sup-ported and bolstered by the other family members. This environment can lay the foundation for risk taking and growth. If the family's level of enmeshment becomes stifling, however, it stifles risk taking and inhibits members from growing as individuals.

*Disengagement.* Families that are highly disengaged are char-acterized by underinvolvement. Members have few interests in com-mon, excessive privacy, and long periods of separation. In these families the members do not discuss individual decisions, and activities of family members rarely are family-focused. Disengaged families have rigid subsystem boundaries, and members of the subsystem do not interface with another subsystem (Turnbull & Turnbull, 1990). For example, one of the boys may have a new girlfriend of which the siblings are aware but the parents are not.

As with enmeshment, a certain amount of disengagement is healthy for family members. If individuals within a family are to de-velop autonomy and independence, they must have interests outside of the family. This is especially true as children reach their teen years and try to make a transition into adulthood. That each member within the family needs time away from other family members is important for adults within the family to realize. If a family becomes too dis-engaged, though, its cohesiveness as a family unit can be compro-mised because family members do not feel bolstered or supported by each other.

## Adaptability

Adaptability relates to the family's ability to adjust family roles and routines to new situations. Like cohesiveness, adaptability ex-ists along a continuum—here, from rigid to chaotic. Rigid families seem unable or unwilling to adapt to new situations. Chaotic fami-lies have little structure or apparent planning. In a functional family, as the needs of the family evolve, the family becomes more rigid or more chaotic to better to address the situation. A family must develop a careful balance between structure and chaos.

*Rigid Families.* This family has a high degree of control and structure with strict rules. Roles within the family are well defined and extremely inflexible with an overt power hierarchy. The emphasis on power and control can stifle the individuality of family members and inhibit appropriate risk taking. This type of family also has difficulty dealing with crises that are outside of the family's rules and expectations.

Even so, some structure and predictability, if applied appropriately, are essential for children to develop self-discipline. Children must learn that their actions can have either negative or positive consequences. For this to occur, consequences must be applied in a consistent and predictable manner. Actions that warrant negative consequences must result in negative consequences, and actions that warrant positive consequences must result in positive consequences. Through this structure and predictability children develop an internalized set of limits that contributes to their self-discipline. If these rules become rigid and unbending, however, children learn a narrow view of justice, often equating it with external controls. Rigid family systems stifle risk taking and inhibit an individual's development of self-discipline and worth. Children within a rigid system are apt to become dependent upon external rather than internal controls for their behavior.

*Chaotic Families.* Chaotic families have little control and structure. They impose few rules, and those rules seldom are reinforced. Promises and commitments are not kept, and family members learn at an early age that they cannot count on one another. This type of family lacks a hierarchical role structure among family members and subsystems. The result is confusion regarding role expectations. This ambiguity surrounding roles can be a source of tension among family members.

An appropriate amount of chaos within the family, on the other hand, is healthy. The most positive aspect of chaos is flexibility. The notion that roles can change within the family and that rules can be negotiated helps children learn a greater sense of fairness that takes the circumstances of a situation into consideration. Without clear leadership and with nondistinct roles, however, children can develop a sense of "learned helplessness" (Seligman, 1975). They believe they have little control over things that happen to them. No matter what they do, it doesn't seem to make a difference because outcomes seem to be independent of their actions.

## EFFECTIVE FAMILY INTERACTIONS

Although functional families vary greatly in their general structure and organization, certain characteristics of families seem to enhance their ability to be functional. These characteristics, described by Luterman (1987), are:

1. Communication among family members is clear and open. The issues are discussed clearly, and personal comments are directed to the individual to whom they are applicable. Messages are accompanied by appropriate content and feeling.
2. Although roles and responsibilities of family members are delineated clearly, the family has enough flexibility to address unique situations. For a family to run effectively, it must have clear boundaries that each member understands. Expectations and roles must be articulated clearly and fulfilled. At the same time, the family must be flexible enough to shift roles to meet unique challenges of the family.
3. Family members accept limits and resolve conflicts. Conflict is a healthy part of any family. Effective families resolve conflict at an individual level through fair and open means. Conflict is not denied, nor are the needs of one individual considered paramount to the needs of the family unit or other individuals within the family. Rather, a resolution is sought in which all family members can feel committed. Often these families have a successful face-saving mechanism that allows all family members to feel as if they are at least partially successful in resolving the conflict.
4. Intimacy is present, and a function of equal power transactions. A primary feature of the family is to provide intimacy to the members. Human beings need an environment with closeness and caring among other humans. Intimacy must be based on equal power and is not something to be demanded. All family members must have the ability to share their intimacy based on their individual needs as well as the needs of the family unit.
5. A healthy balance exists between change and stability. Families

must have a stable foundation and at the same time be willing to adapt to new challenges. A healthy family makes changes to accommodate challenges facing the family while it still provides stability for its members.

In the next section you will read about barriers that have inhibited collaborative efforts with families. As you read this section, think about these barriers. Identify those you have run into and those you have heard about from other teachers. In retrospect, could you have avoided or overcome the barrier? Have you ever changed one of your actions because a colleague or supervisor suggested that one of the barriers would prevent you from being successful?

## ■ BARRIERS TO FAMILY PARTICIPATION IN SCHOOLS

If we are to collaborate well with the families of our students, serious barriers must be overcome. Some of these barriers are perceived, and others are grounded in fact. Lynch and Stein (1982) studied these from a parent and professional perspective. Parents identified barriers related to logistics, communication, and misunderstanding by schools that give rise to feelings of inferiority and uncertainty about their child's unique problems. Professionals identified barriers related to issues such as parent apathy, lack of time, and the expertise of professionals.

### BARRIERS IDENTIFIED BY PARENTS

#### Logistical Problems

Families have substantial problems trying to arrange for transportation, babysitting, or time away from work to attend conferences or meetings within the schools. These are serious problems that, if recognized by the school, can be overcome. Rather than having family members meet within the school, schools might consider going to the family's home or meeting in a community center near the family's home. Transportation could be arranged by the school for the family member to come to the school. Child care might be provided at the school so family members can bring their children and attend meetings or observe in their child's classroom. Child care provides significant support for parents who wish to be more involved in the school.

Meetings can be held at times convenient to parents, such as during the lunch hour or in the evening. Schools also must conduct meetings efficiently. Families have severe demands upon their time, so efficient meetings are important.

## Communication Problems

Families often come from cultural or socioeconomic backgrounds different from school personnel, which can make communication more difficult. As we move into the 21st century, these differences are likely to increase. When we add educational jargon into the mix, teachers and family members can be speaking two related but different languages with different vocabularies and styles. We may believe we understand each other but in truth may have completely different understandings of the same conversation. Compounding these disparities are the differing norms for communication style within the family. Some norms represent individual differences; others are culturally defined. Some families tend to be loud and emotional in their responses to one another, whereas other families are reserved and restrained. A teacher may interpret a loud and emotional response on the part of a parent as being aggressive, but if the teacher understands the family's communication norms, he or she might interpret the mother's actions as demonstrating concern for her child. Good communication skills and hard work to develop rapport and understanding with all of the families in the school's community are invaluable.

## Lack of Understanding of Schools

Schools are complex organizations that have both overt and covert rules of operation. These rules can be formal and overt, such as the rights of parents of children with a disability, or subtle and covert, like the ways parents can influence who will be their child's teacher. If families do not understand these rules, they will be confused and can get lost in the bureaucracy. As a result, they will be unable to use the system to meet their needs or, more specifically, their child's needs, compounding their disenfranchisement. A diminished sense of control in decision making produces a feeling of inferiority and contributes to a parent's vulnerability to intimidation. Often, families of low-income or minority students, especially, experience this diminished sense of control.

If schools are to become family-focused, we must make public our rules of operation and work to ensure that families understand these rules. As a first step to becoming more family-focused, schools should examine what it is about their way of doing business that prevents parents or other family members from being full partners in the educational process. We must encourage families to be an important part of what is happening within the school. In many cases this means teaching families how to access all of the resources schools have to offer. We must create an environment and structure that empower families. When we're talking to parents about concerns and challenges their children are facing, we must recognize that parents have a sense of responsibility that can affect their interpretation of what we are communicating. Finally, we must recognize that nearly all families represent an educational resource that can enrich the school experiences of all students (Moll, Amanti, Neff, & Gonzalez, 1992).

## BARRIERS IDENTIFIED BY PROFESSIONALS

### Parental Apathy

Although some parents are apathetic or indifferent about their involvement in schools, this apathy often is overstated by teachers, particularly with respect to families of cultures different than the majority culture. Lack of involvement can occur for many reasons. Some to consider are as follows:

1. The experiences parents have had with schools may not have been positive, so parents may avoid future interactions because they think they will be equally negative.
2. Parents may believe they have little influence or power over what is going happen to their children and can experience learned helplessness (Seligman, 1975). They believe that no matter what they do, it won't make a difference, so why bother.
3. Cultural norms may dictate that the teacher is to be respected above all and that teachers know what is best. Therefore, what

could families have to say about school?

4. Perhaps what we are interpreting as apathy on the part of parents is really exhaustion from the many demands placed on the family besides school.

To combat what is perceived as apathy, we first must try to get our own biases under control and not use stereotypes about parental apathy as an excuse to avoid finding ways to include parents. It is easy to say, "Families don't care" when, in fact, we are scheduling meetings that are unresponsive to demands on families for child care, time away from work, and transportation to attend meetings. Instead, in promoting the development of collaborative schools, we must try to make schools family-centered so the activities associated with the schools generate positive feelings and positive outcomes. If parents see schools as positive places, where positive things happen, they are more likely to participate actively.

Finally, and most important, lack of involvement can be overcome by making families real decision makers within the schools. Giving families the appearance of being involved through representation on committees and attendance at key meetings is not enough. Rather, we must do everything we can to empower them to be vital decision makers within our schools. As families see that their participation is taken seriously, they will be less likely to feel apathetic and uncomfortable participating in the schools.

## Professional Time Constraints

Like parents, professionals also have limited time to meet during the school day. As a result, schools have to consider alternative meeting times, such as after school and on weekends. An often overlooked concern surrounding these meetings is the burden placed on teachers to be away from their families to devote time during evenings and weekends for meetings with members of other families. To meet the needs of both the teachers and the families they serve, more creative ways of getting teachers and parents together need to be developed. In addition, as previously mentioned, running meetings efficiently maximizes the limited time professionals have for meetings.

We also must check and be honest about our real attitudes about family participation. We have not always valued the input that families can offer. When we schedule meeting times that are inconvenient to families, we communicate that they are not important. How meetings are conducted can also communicate to families that they have lower status than the other people attending such a meeting. In this case, the damaging message that can all too easily be communicated is: my professional time is more valuable than the time you are giving as a parent.

For example, in a typical individualized education program (IEP) meeting everybody except the parents brings formal information about the child to share in the meeting. This information includes test scores, observation data, work samples, and the like. All the participants at the meeting then make a formal presentation of this information to the other group members. Family members, however, often are not asked to bring any formal information or asked if they have anything to add after other team members have presented their information. This clearly communicates that family members are not full participants since they have a different role on the committee than the rest of the participants.

Although we have always claimed that families are important members of a school, our actions have communicated a different picture. Often, when families make suggestions that are contrary to the school's views or are critical of the school, they are characterized as troublemakers. This is true particularly if the families are from a different culture or are assertive in their input. Thus, our actions and words are incongruent. Our actions suggest that families aren't equal members, while our words suggest to them that they are equal members. To ensure that our actions and words are consistent, professionals need to view the time they spend with families as an essential element in improving their students' education. If families really are equal members of the team, they should be treated as equals.

**Professional Expertise**

Collaborating with colleagues is difficult work that requires a special set of skills to facilitate communication. Working with and supporting families is equally difficult and also requires specific skills. Unfortunately, these skills have not always been part of our teacher preparation programs. Becoming proficient in the communication skills delineated in this book will give you the foundational skills necessary to be an active partner with parents.

Families are essential in providing professionals with the knowledge and information required to work effectively. Until schools become truly family-centered, any reform effort is likely to fall far short of its potential. Although we have a long way to go, some notable examples can guide us.

---

*The James E. Biggs Early Childhood Education Center is located in Covington, Kentucky, across the Ohio River from and essentially part of the Cincinnati, Ohio, Metropolitan Area. This is an urban neighborhood populated largely by families of low socioeconomic status and of diverse backgrounds. The two largest groups are from Afro-American or urban Appalachian cultures. People in the community have many problems and concerns, but, like all people, they care a great deal about their children and have many hopes and dreams for their futures.*

*Traditional approaches to involving families in their child's program typically have not resulted in long-term positive effects in this community. As a result, the administration at the James E. Biggs Center decided to try a different approach to involving families and began to take steps to conceptualize and implement a family-centered program. Rather than being child-centered, the center decided that its activities must be directed at the whole family. As the staff began thinking about the family as its responsibility, the nature of the center began to change. It developed a program for medical and dental care support and a family room to which parents and their children could come.*

*The center provides child care and transportation for parents who want to volunteer or participate in an educational program. A whole series of programs and activities has emerged, including make-up classes, Dad's night out, weight control classes, GED classes, a clothing exchange, and parent-teacher training. As a result of these efforts, families are heavily involved in the program. On any given day one can find parents in the classroom, children receiving day care, and parents dropping by the center just to sit a while in the parent room. Clearly, families are actively involved in the program, and the program is responsive to their needs.*

> *The school has become more than a school. It is thought of as a central component within the community. Where many others have failed, the James E. Biggs Center has been successful by letting go of old approaches and embracing new thinking. Rather than attempting to get families more involved, it focuses on meeting the needs of families in the community and, as a result, more families got involved.*

In this example, an early childhood center has made the transition successfully from being student-centered to family-centered. The dominant theme at this school is the mutual respect and partnership between family and school. The center was able to make this transition by working to meet the needs of families in their school and it avoided the trap of doing only "traditional school things." The strategies in the next section will help you establish and nurture an environment that encourages mutual respect and cooperation.

## ■ DEVELOPING FAMILY-ORIENTED TEACHERS

Some teachers easily overcome barriers to family collaboration, while others will need to work hard to make families the full partners they need to be. We believe it is essential that those who work in collaborative schools make family participation a central goal. However, merely setting this goal does not ensure that families will be treated as full members of the collaborative team.

Why is it that some teachers do not feel committed to making all families welcome in schools? Given the discussion thus far, one reasonable explanation is that family members who are less welcome probably interact according to a different set of norms and expectations from those of their child's teacher. These differences may stem from socioeconomic, ethnic, race, or religious factors. Given that such differences exist and that they are often likely to interfere with making families feel unequivocally welcome in schools, what can teachers do to overcome these biases?

First, and foremost, the role of families needs to be a regular topic of discussion among staff members. In this way, the subject is public and staff deliberations become an expected place for these issues to be raised. If a collaborative staff environment is developed in a particular school, its presence can support a self-reflective stance on the part of the teachers. Given the public nature of the dialogue, whole school activities can be constructed to maximize the interaction between school staff members and families. Next, individual teachers who are skeptical about the commitment that low SES parents may seem to have toward their children's education need to be encouraged to identify one or two families of their students, families who defy the stereotype itself. Then they need to be encouraged to talk with these family members about their participation in school-related activities.

And finally, teachers who are uncomfortable regarding family involvement in schools ought to be seen as the leading candidates for inviting students' parents or relatives to come into their classrooms. The purpose of these visits ought not to be just "helping out." Instead, teachers need to be looking for the kinds of skills each family member has to offer and figure out how that particular skill can make a significant contribution to the class. Skeptical teachers need to come face-to-face with their beliefs and work with families directly as a means of overcoming possible stereotyping.

Further, at the preservice level students who aspire to teach need to interact with family members as a regular part of their preparation—and not just when they are having a problem or during formal conferences. From the outset, those who wish to teach need to begin working with families to demonstrate the valuable contributions families make to the successful school experiences of their children.

## ■ FAMILY CONFERENCES

Probably the most commonly used vehicle for interacting with parents is the parent-teacher conference. In virtually all schools in America, these conferences are the primary forum for communicating with parents. Because they are frequent points of communication, conferences are an opportunity to solidify collaborative relationships with families. Turnbull and Turnbull (1990) asserted that there are four basic reasons for having family conferences:

- To exchange information about the home and school environments.

- To work together to help the child develop and to share information on the child's progress.
- To develop rapport and mutual commitment to the child's optimal development.
- To cooperate in alleviating problems and concerns.

Planning and carrying out a conference entails three phases or steps: (a) preconference planning, (b) conference implementation, and (c) postconference follow-up (Turnbull & Turnbull, 1990).

## PRECONFERENCE PLANNING

Good preconference planning can help ensure a successful conference. Kroth (1995) described four basic steps in preconference planning: (a) notify, (b) prepare, (c) plan agenda, and (d) arrange environments. We have combined two of his steps and believe that there are three basic steps: (a) notify, (b) prepare, and (c) arrange.

### Notify

The first step in preconference planning is to notify key family members that the conference is to take place. Sometimes schools have predetermined conference procedures, including scheduling conference time and space and notifying parents, through school calendars and reminders, that the conference is going to occur. In this process, however, each parent must be considered and, if needed, individual strategies developed to assure that parents are aware of the conference and are able to attend. The notification should be as nonthreatening as possible. Further, in schools with large populations of students whose families' first language is not English, all materials must be translated into the appropriate languages.

If parents feel threatened, they may find a convenient reason for not attending the conference. You can alleviate this by being as clear as possible about the purpose of the conference and who will be attending from the school.

### Prepare

In preparing for the conference, you have to be knowledgeable about the items to be addressed. Consider the following suggestions:

1. Review the child's cumulative folder and any other indicators of progress, such as portfolios, before the visit.

2. Have a clear assessment of the child's current progress or the issue to be addressed.
3. Have examples of the child's work.
4. Make an outline of topics to be addressed.
5. When appropriate, meet with other professionals to gain additional information about the child. See Turnbull & Turnbull (1990) for additional suggestions.

## Arrange

The final step in preconference planning is to prepare the physical setting. Consider the following:

1. Identify a quiet, private room. If no one will be in your classroom, that may be a good place to meet. If you have only small chairs in the classroom, however, you may want to bring in adult-size chairs and a table you can sit around, or meet in another room. Sitting on small chairs may be uncomfortable and distracting.
2. Gather all the relevant information before the meeting so you are ready to go when the parents arrive.
3. Try to schedule a time or place where you are unlikely to be interrupted. Interruptions can be quite distracting and inappropriate.
4. Make sure the room is comfortable. Uncomfortable settings can inhibit communication. Everybody should be able to concentrate on the task at hand.
5. Have tissues available in case someone becomes emotional during the meeting. This is a small detail that can make a big difference.
6. Provide for an interpreter if the family does not speak English fluently. See Turnbull & Turnbull (1990) for additional suggestions.

## Implementation: Conducting the Conference

The communication skills articulated in previous chapters are the basis of a successful conference. Begin with broad opening statements and do not get into the essence of the information too quickly; rely on active listening to help clarify parents' concerns. In general you should try to stick to the agenda, but critical new information may be raised at the conference and you will have to judge the merit of changing the planned agenda and addressing the new information. At the same time, don't be easily distracted, because it will prevent you from addressing the task at hand adequately. At the end of the conference, a good summarization will allow attendees to know what was said and decided in the conference.

## POSTCONFERENCE FOLLOW-UP

Summarizing the notes of the conference and providing a written copy to participants facilitates understanding because the participants will all have the same interpretation of the meeting. Depending on the outcomes of the conference, you might want to make a follow-up phone call to the family to see how implementation is progressing. You also may need to follow up with other team members to see if any new information is required or new actions have to be developed.

As you read about strategies to collaborate with families, ask yourself how you can incorporate these into your practice. Have you already implemented some of these strategies? Do any aspects of your approach have to be modified? Can you do anything else that we failed to discuss? Most important, how can these and other strategies help you nurture an environment that encourages mutual respect and cooperation by you, the school, and the families that your school serves?

## UNPLANNED CONFERENCES

As Turnbull and Turnbull (1990) asserted, it is a "given" that you will have unplanned conferences with family members. You need to accept the possibility of unplanned conferences and think through some ways to handle them. Even though you will be caught off guard at times, you can do some things to ready yourself when an unexpected conference comes up. First, you always should keep good data on the students in your classes. If your files are well organized, you can go to the file quickly and get the information needed to answer a parent's question. Despite the best record keeping, however, you sometimes will be asked a specific question for which you do not have the information. You will be better off to tell parents you don't have the information but will get it and get back to them as soon as possible than to bluff a response. You might even want to anticipate being caught off guard and come up with a standard response such as, "I'm really glad you took the time to talk to me. Let me make sure I get the right information for you and get back to you as soon as I can."

At times a parent will come to you, upset about something his or her child has said or something that has happened in your class or the school. This parent may be extremely angry, and you must not do anything to escalate the situation. In this circumstance, you can do some things to help defuse the aggression:

1. Listen. Don't interrupt. Let the family members get off their chest whatever they came to say.
2. Don't argue, don't become defensive, and don't try to promise something you may not be able to deliver.
3. Write down the key phrases, and when the family member calms down, repeat these phrases to be sure you heard the concerns accurately. Then tell the parent you will try to get the information and schedule a meeting with the appropriate individuals to address the concern.
4. Speak softly. This often calms people down, and they, in turn, will lower their own voice.

## ∎ PRACTICAL STRATEGIES FOR COMMUNICATING WITH FAMILIES

Frequent communication with families is important. Beyond conferences, teachers rely on many additional ways to communicate to develop a real partnership with parents. Some valuable tools are: (a) handbooks, (b) announcements for specific situations, (c) newsletters, (d) regular progress messages, (e) occasional notes, and (f) telephone conferences (Turnbull & Turnbull, 1990). All written material should be translated for families who are not fluent in English.

## HANDBOOKS

A handbook—describing your rules, philosophy, major activities, a typical day in your class—enables parents to better understand what you will be doing with their child and how they can support you at home. Going over this handbook with families at the beginning of the school year is a way to give them an overview of the classroom and a concrete basis upon which they can ask questions.

## ANNOUNCEMENTS FOR SPECIFIC SITUATIONS

When you have special activities within your classroom or special events, sending home an announcement about the activity, the purpose of the activity, and how family members might expand upon the activity is a good way to communicate with them. You also might send out announcements periodically about classroom activities and items of possible interest to families, such as how to cook quick meals, how to select interesting toys for children, and other ideas that can extend school activities.

## NEWSLETTERS

One of the most time-honored ways of communicating with parents is through frequent and regular newsletters. These can be done by the teacher, the class, or the school. Newsletters can even be done by parents in the classroom. Newsletters can be a means to provide information on upcoming events and also to highlight specific accomplishments of children or a class.

## REGULAR PROGRESS REPORTS

Progress reports should be issued periodically. This has been done as frequently as once a week or as infrequently as once a month. The reports represent a channel by which parents receive information about their child's accomplishments. You may want to have students keep a log of activities for the day and have a place for family members to sign the log, or teachers can place an entry in the log and have the parents sign the log that afternoon.

## OCCASIONAL NOTES

Another way to communicate with parents is to send occasional messages home with the child. These can be happy grams, personalized commercial communications, or little stickers the child wears home. They might be brief notes relaying something that the child has done that the family might like to hear about. The important point is that such informal, frequent forms of communication contribute to building stronger school-family ties.

## TELEPHONE CONFERENCES

The telephone should be reserved for short conversations. Long conversations are better done in person. Although the telephone is convenient and can be useful in addressing family concerns quickly, it does not allow for nonverbal messages.

When calling a family member, you always should identify yourself and ask if this is a convenient time for the person to talk. You should not use the telephone to relay negative information about the child. These communications are delicate and complex and require great effort to ensure good communication. The telephone precludes any body language from being part of the communication cycle, which severely limits the ability to communicate effectively. When sending a delicate message, you need eye contact, as well as the body language of the parent, to make sure your message is understood. Telephone calls should be planned carefully. Prior to making your call, you might jot down some of the key issues you think should be discussed. Then you can check them off as they are covered. In this way you can concentrate on the conversation and still make sure you don't forget to bring up an important topic. Parents should be given time to respond or answer questions fully. Again, because of the lack of eye contact, you may be unaware of a potential response or comment a parent would like to make.

# ■ WORKING WITH FAMILIES

Our students all have families, and their families are critical to their development. Most of the basic needs our students have are met through their families. Without an active partnership with families, schools always will be limited in what they are able to accomplish. Developing partnerships with families is one of the most valuable of a schools' undertakings. A collaborative school must include an active partnership with families. As we stated early on in this chapter, our students are all members of families first and students second. Consequently, their families are going to have the most lasting and powerful influence on their development. Developing a real partnership with families is difficult and requires a set skills that often have been overlooked in teacher education programs.

## ■ REMEMBER...

1. The family is the basic unit of our society.
2. Family configurations have great diversity, and our notion of "family" must be inclusive of this diversity.
3. Families are complex systems made up of several subsystems. Anything that impacts any aspect of the system impacts all aspects of the system.
4. The tasks that families engage in to meet the needs of members within the family are called family functions. The seven family functions are: (a) economic, (b) domestic and health care, (c) recreational, (d) socialization, (e) self-definition, (f) affection, and (g) educational/vocational.
5. The degree of cohesiveness or adaptability of the family influences the interactions within family subsystems. Cohesion is defined as the emotional bonds between family members. Adaptability is the ability of a family to change in response to outside pressures.
6. Parents have logistical concerns, communication problems, and misunderstanding about schools, all of which inhibit their ability to be full partners with schools. In contrast, professionals have identified parent apathy, lack of time, and the expertise of professionals as three major concerns that inhibit their ability to be full partners with schools.
7. Conferences represent an important way to communicate with families. In planning and carrying out a conference, three phases should be followed: (a) preconference plan-

ning, (b) conference implementation, and (c) postconference follow-up.

8. In addition to conferences, more informal and frequent ways to communicate with parents must be developed. Some of these tools are: (a) handbooks, (b) announcements for specific situations, (c) newsletters, (d) regular progress reports, (e) occasional notes, and (f) telephone conferences.

9. In forming strong school-family collaboration, one of the biggest challenges is to ensure that school personnel confront their own stereotypes regarding families of students whose race, ethnicity, socioeconomic levels, or language differs from their own.

## ■ ACTIVITIES

- In groups, take one or more of the areas of family functioning and develop strategies a school might use to help the family within that area of family functioning.
- Plan and implement a mock (or real) conference with a family member. Videotape it for small-group discussion and evaluation.
- Identify a traditional, a blended, and a single-parent family with school-age children. Interview the adults in these families to get a sense of their experience with schools and how their family configuration inhibits or enhances their experiences.
- Design a brief questionnaire or a set of interview questions regarding families' perceptions of their relationship with the school. Include questions about the resources the family might represent. Work in groups, and present your findings to the class.
- If you are a practicing teacher or in a practicum course, implement and evaluate one or more of the strategies for communicating with families, other than a conference.
- Have family members of students you work with volunteer to share a skill they have. Try to construct a lesson that incorporates these skills—even if at first they don't seem relevant.

# REFERENCES

Abelson, M. A., & Woodman, R. W. (1983). Review of research on team effectiveness: Implications for teams in schools. *School Psychology Review, 12*(2), 125–136.

Ahlburg, D. A., & DeVita, C. J. (1992). New realities of the American family. *Population Bulletin, 47*(2), 1–44.

Aldinger, L. E., Warger, C. L., & Eavy, P. W. (1991). *Strategies for teacher collaboration.* Ann Arbor, MI: Exceptional Innovations.

Barth, R. S. (1990). *Improving schools from within: Teachers, parents, and principals can make the difference.* San Francisco: Jossey-Bass.

Bauwens, J., Hourcade, J., & Friend, M. (1989). Cooperative teaching: A model for general and special education integration. *Remedial and Special Education, 10*(2), 17–22.

Beane, J. A. (1990). *A middle school curriculum: From rhetoric to reality.* Columbus, OH: National Middle Schools Association.

Bennis, W. (1984). The four competencies of leadership. *Training and Development Journal, 38*(8), 14–19.

Butler, A. S., & Maher, C. A. (1981). Conflict and special service teams: Perspectives and suggestions for school psychologists. *Journal of School Psychology, 19*(1), 62–70.

Chalfant, J. C., Pysh, M. V., & Moultrie, R. (1979). Teacher assistance teams: A model for within-building problem solving. *Learning Disabilities Quarterly, 2*(3), 85–96.

Chalfant, J. C., & Pysh, M. V. (1989). Teacher assistance teams: Five descriptive studies on 96 teams. *Remedial and Special Education, 10*(6), 49–58.

Cohen, E. G. (1981). Sociology looks at team teaching. *Research in Sociology of Education and Socialization, 2*, 163–193.

Cole, A. L. (1991). Relationships in the workplace: Doing what comes naturally? *Teaching and Teacher Education, 7*(5–6), 415–426.

Combs, A., Avila, D., & Purkey, W. (1971). *Helping relationships: Basic concepts for the helping professions.* Boston: Allyn & Bacon.

Conley, S. C., & Bacharach, S. B. (1990). From school-site management to participatory school-site management. *Phi Delta Kappan, 71*(7), 539–544.

Cuban, L. (1989). The "at-risk" label and the problem of urban school reform. *Phi Delta Kappan, 70*(10), 780–784, 799–801.

Dettmer, P., Thurston, L. P., & Dyck, N. (1993). *Consultation, collaboration, and teamwork for students with special needs.* Boston: Allyn & Bacon.

Dewey, J. (1933). *How we think: A restatement of the relation of reflective thinking to the educative process.* Boston: Heath & Company.

Elliott, J. (1991). *Action research for educational change.* Philadelphia: Open University Press.

Ellis, N. E. (1990). Collaborative interaction for improvement of teaching. *Teaching and Teacher Education, 6*(3), 267–277.

Friend, M. P., & Cook, L. (1992). *Interactions: Collaboration skills for school professionals.* New York: Longman.

Fuchs, D., Fuchs, L. S., & Bahr, M. W. (1990). Mainstream assistance teams: A scientific basis for the art of consultation. *Exceptional Children, 57*(2), 128–139.

Fuchs, D., Fuchs, L. S., Bahr, M. W., Fernstrom, P., & Stecker, P. M. (1990). Prereferral intervention: A prescriptive approach. *Exceptional Children, 56*(6), 493–513.

Fullan, M., & Stiegelbauer, S. (1991). *The new meaning of educational change* (2nd ed.). New York: Teachers College Press.

Galvin, K. M., & Brommel, B. J. (1982). *Family communication: Cohesion and change* (2nd ed.). Glenview, IL: Scott, Foresman.

Goodlad, J. I. (1984). *A place called school: Prospects for the future.* New York: McGraw-Hill.

Goodlad, J. I. (1988). School-university partnerships for educational renewal: Rationale and concepts. In K. A. Sirotnik & J. I. Goodlad (Eds.), *School-university partnerships in action: Concepts, cases and concerns* (pp. 3–31). New York: Teachers College Press.

Goodlad, J. I., & Sirotnik, K. A. (1988). The future of school-university partnerships. In K. A. Sirotnik & J. I. Goodlad (Eds.), *School-university partnerships in action* (pp. 205–225). New York: Teachers College Press.

Hames, C. C., & Joseph, D. H. (1986). *Basic concepts of helping: A holistic approach* (2nd ed.). East Norwalk, CT: Appleton-Century-Crofts.

Hargreaves, A., & Dawe, R. (1990). Paths of professional development: Contrived collegiality, collaborative culture, and the case of peer coaching. *Teaching and Teacher Education, 6*(3), 227–241.

Hebert, E. A., & Miller, S. I. (1985). Role conflict and the special education supervisor: A qualitative analysis. *Journal of Special Education, 19*(2), 215–229.

Holly, P. (1991). Action research: The missing link in the creation of schools as centers of inquiry. In A. Lieberman & L. Miller (Eds.), *Staff development for education in the '90s: New demands, new realities, new perspectives* (2nd ed.) (pp. 133–157). New York: Teachers College Press.

Holmes Group. (1990). *Tomorrow's schools: Principles for the design of professional development schools: A report.* East Lansing, MI: Author.

Idol, L., Paolucci-Whitcomb, P., & Nevin, A. (1986). *Collaborative consultation.* Rockville, MD: Aspen Publishers.

Jett-Simpson, M., Pugach, M. C., & Whipp, J. (1992, April). *Portrait of an urban professional development school.* Paper presented at annual meeting of American Educational Research Association, San Francisco.

Johnson, L. J., & Bauer, A. M. (1992). *Meeting the needs of special students: Legal, ethical, and practical ramifications.* Newbury Park, CA: Corwin Press.

Johnson, L. J., & Pugach, M. C. (1991). Peer collaboration: Accommodating the needs of students with mild learning and behavior problems. *Exceptional Children, 57*(5), 454–461.

Johnson, L. J., & Pugach, M. C. (1992). Continuing the dialogue: Embracing a more expansive understanding of collaborative relationships. In W. Stainback & S. Stainback (Eds.), *Controversial issues confronting special education: Divergent perspectives* (pp. 215–222). Boston: Allyn & Bacon.

Johnson, L. J., Pugach, M. C., & Hammitte, D. (1988). Barriers to effective special education consultation. *Remedial and Special Education, 9*(6), 41–47.

Joyce, B., & Showers, B. (1988). *Student achievement through staff development.* New York: Longman.

Kolb, D. M., & Glidden, P. A. (1986). Getting to know your conflict option. *Personnel Administrator, 31*(6), 77–89.

Kohl, H. (1984). *Growing minds: On becoming a teacher.* New York: Harper & Row.

Kroth, R. L. (1985). *Communication with parents of exceptional children: Improving parent-teacher relationships* (2nd ed.). Denver: Love Publishing.

Kyle, D. W., & Hovda, R. A. (1987). Teachers as action researchers: A discussion of developmental, organizational, and policy issues. In D. W. Kyle & R. A. Hovda (Eds.), The potential and practice of action research. [Special issue.] *Peabody Journal of Education, 64*(2), 80–95.

Lane, V. W., & Molyneaux, D. (1992). *The dynamics of communicative development.* Engelwood Cliffs, NJ: Prentice Hall.

Levine, M. (Ed.). (1992). *Professional practice schools: Linking teacher education and school reform*. New York: Teachers College Press.

LeVine, R. A., Miller, P. M., & West, M. (1988). *Parental behavior in diverse societies*. San Francisco: Jossey-Bass.

Lewin, K. (1946). Action research and minority problems. *Journal of Social Issues, 2*(4), 34–36.

Lieberman, A., & Miller, L. (1984). School improvement: Themes and variations. *Teachers College Record, 86*(1), 4–19.

Lilly, M. S. (1970). Special education: A teapot in a tempest. *Exceptional Children, 37*, 43–49.

Lilly, M. S. (1971). Forum: A training based model for special education. *Exceptional Children, 37*(10), 745–749.

Little, J. W. (1982). Norms of collegiality and experimentation: Workplace conditions of school success. *American Educational Research Journal, 19*(3), 325–340.

Lortie, D. (1975). *Schoolteacher: A sociological study*. Chicago: University of Chicago Press.

Luterman, David. (1987). *Deafness in the family*. Boston: College Hill Press.

Lynch, E. W., & Stein, R. (1982). Perspectives on parent participation in special education. *Exceptional Education Quarterly, 3*(2), 56–63.

Margolis, H., & Shapiro, A. (1988). Systematically resolving parental conflict with the goal-output-process-input procedure. *High School Journal, 71*(2), 88–96.

Mason, D. A., & Good, T. L. (1993). Effects of two-group and whole-class teaching on regrouped elementary students' mathematical achievement. *American Educational Research Journal, 30*(2), 328–360.

McNiff, J. (1988). *Action research: Principles and practice*. London: Macmillan Education.

Means, B., Chelemer, C., & Knapp, M. S. (Eds.). (1991). *Teaching advanced skills to at-risk students: Views from research and practice*. San Francisco: Jossey-Bass.

Moll, L. C., Amanti, C., Neff, D., & Gonzalez, N. (1992). Funds of knowledge and teaching: Using a qualitative approach to connect homes and classrooms. *Theory Into Practice, 31*(2), 132–141.

Molyneaux, D., & Lane, V. W. (1982). *Effective interviewing: Techniques and analysis*. Boston: Allyn & Bacon.

Noddings, N. (1992). *The challenge to care in schools: An alternative approach to education*. New York: Teachers College Press.

Office of Policy and Planning. (1992). *Today's families and today's children: A snapshot. Issue Briefs*. Washington, DC: U.S. Department of Education. (ERIC Document Reproduction Service No. ED 354 426)

Oja, S. N., & Pine, G. J. (1989). Collaborative action research: Teachers' stages of development and school contexts. In D. W. Kyle & R. A.

Hovda (Eds.), The potential and practice of action research. [Special issue.] *Peabody Journal of Education, 64*(2), 96–115.

Olson, R. A. (1980). *Evaluation as interaction in support of change.* Grand Forks, ND: University of North Dakota.

Palincsar, A. S. (1986). Metacognative strategy instruction. *Exceptional Children, 53*(2), 118–124.

Pugach, M. C. (in press). Twice victims: The struggle to educate children in urban schools and the reform of special education and Chapter 1. In M. C. Wang & M. C. Reynolds (Eds.), *Making a difference for students at risk: Trends and alternatives.* Thousand Oaks, CA: Corwin Press.

Pugach, M. C., & Johnson, L. J. (1988a). Peer collaboration. *Teaching Exceptional Children, 20*(3), 75–77.

Pugach, M. C., & Johnson, L. J. (1988b). Rethinking the relationship between consultation and collaborative problem solving. *Focus on Exceptional Children, 21*(4), 1–8.

Pugach, M. C., & Johnson, L. J. (1990a). Fostering the continued democratization of consultation through action research. *Teacher Education and Special Education, 13*(3–4), 240–245.

Pugach, M. C., & Johnson, L. J. (1990b). Meeting diverse needs through professional peer collaboration. In W. Stainback & S. Stainback (Eds.), *Support networks for inclusive schooling: Interdependent integrated education* (pp. 123–137). Baltimore: Paul H. Brookes.

Pugach, M. C., & Johnson, L. J. (in press). Unlocking expertise among classroom teachers through structured dialogue: Extending research on peer collaboration. *Exceptional Children.*

Pugach, M. C., & Pasch, S. H. (1994). The challenge of creating urban professional development schools (pp. 129–156). In R. Yinger & K. Borman (Eds.), *Restructuring education: Issues and strategies for communities, schools, and universities.* Cresskill, NJ: Hampton Press.

Pugach, M. C., & Wesson, C. (in press). Teachers' and students' views of team teaching of general education and learning-disabled students in two fifth grade classes. *Elementary School Journal.*

Rosenholtz, S. J. (1989). *Teachers' workplace: The social organization of schools.* New York: Longman.

Schrage, M. (1990). *Shared minds: The new technologies of collaboration.* New York: Random House.

Schmidt, P. (1993, July 14). District wide approach enables border system to defy low expectations for IEP students. *Education Week, 12*(39), 6–7.

Seligman, M. E. (1975). *Helplessness: On depression, development, and death.* San Francisco: W. H. Freeman.

Sirotnik, K. A. (1988). The meaning and conduct of inquiry in school-university partnerships. In K. A. Sirotnik & J. I. Goodlad (Eds.), *School-university partnerships in action: Concepts, cases, and concerns* (pp. 169–190). New York: Teachers College Press.

Sizer, T. R. (1989). Diverse practice, shared ideas: The essential school. In H. J. Walberg & J. J. Lane (Eds.), *Organizing for learning: Toward the 21st century*. Reston, VA: National Association of Secondary School Principals.

Skrtic, T., Summers, J., Brotherson, M., & Turnbull, A. (1984). Severely handicapped children and their brothers and sisters. In J. Blacher (Ed.), *Severely handicapped young children and their families: Research in review* (pp. 215–246). New York: Academic Press.

Slavin, R. E. (1991). Synthesis of research on cooperative learning. *Educational Leadership, 48*(5), 71–82.

Thomas, K. (1976). Conflict and conflict management. In M. Dunnette (Ed.), *Handbook of industrial and organizational psychology*. Chicago: Rand McNally College Publishing.

Thousand, J. S., & Villa, R. A. (1990). Sharing expertise and responsibilities through teaching teams. In W. Stainback & S. Stainback (Eds.), *Support networks for inclusive schooling: Interdependent integrated education* (pp. 151–166). Baltimore: Paul H. Brookes.

Tuckman, B.W., & Jensen, M.A.C. (1977). Stages of small-group development revisited. *Group and Organization Studies, 2*(4), 419–426.

Turnbull, A. P., Summers, J. A., & Brotherson, M. J. (1984). *Working with families with disabled members: A family systems approach*. Lawrence: University of Kansas, Kansas University Affiliated Facility.

Turnbull, A. P., & Turnbull, H. R. III. (1986). *Families, professionals, and exceptionality: A special partnership*. Columbus, OH: Merrill.

Turnbull, A. P., & Turnbull, H. R. III. (1990). *Families, professionals, and exceptionality: A special partnership* (2nd ed.). Columbus, OH: Merrill.

Warger, C. L., & Pugach, M. C. (1993). A curriculum focus for collaboration. *LD Forum, 18*(9), 26–30.

Will, M. C. (1986). *Educating students with learning problems—A shared responsibility*. Washington, DC: U.S. Department of Education, Office of Special Education and Rehabilitative Services.

Witt, J. C., & Elliott, S. N. (1985). Acceptability of classroom intervention strategies. In T. R. Kratochwill (Ed.), *Advances in school psychology* (Vol. 6, pp. 251–288). Hillside, NJ: Lawrence Erlbaum.

Zander, A. F. (1971). *Motives and goals in groups*. New York: Academic Press.

Zins, J. E., Curtis, M. J., Graden, J. L., & Ponti, C. R. (1988). *Helping students succeed in the regular classroom: A guide for developing intervention assistance programs*. San Francisco: Jossey-Bass.

# INDEX

## A

Abelson, M. A., 113, 117, 119, 123
Action research
  collaboration between general and special education and, 217
  explanation of, 210–211
  outcomes of, 216
  process of, 211–216
Adaptability, of families, 233–235
Advice, 90–92
Affection, 231–232
Ahlburg, D. A., 225
Aldinger, L. E., 15, 157
Amanti, C., 238
Announcements, 248
Arbitration, 124–126
Avila, D., 110

## B

Bacharach, S. B., 159
Bahr, M. W., 32, 148, 154
Barth, R. S., 15
Bauer, A. M., 9
Bauwens, J., 174
Beane, J. A., 11
Bennis, W., 117

Brainstorming, 140, 157
Brommel, B. J., 227
Brotherson, M. J., 228, 230
Butler, A. H., 119

## C

Chalfant J. C., 32, 148, 150, 151
Chaotic families, 234–235
Chelemer, C., 165
Clarification, 76–79
Classroom-specific collaborative problem solving. See also Collaborative problem solving
  description of, 137–139
  relationship between schoolwide and, 141–143
  similarities and differences among models of, 156–158
  structures to support, 148–150
  intervention assistance teams, 155–156

mainstream assistance teams, 154–155
  peer collaboration, 151–153
  teacher assistance teams, 150–151
Classrooom-specific collaborative problem solving, achieving balance between schoolwide and, 167–168
Cliches, 99–101
Clowning, 123
Coalition for Essential Schools, 202
Cohen, E. G., 30, 173, 177, 182, 184, 187
Cohesion, 232–233
Cole, A. L., 39
Collaboration. See also School-family collaboration; School-university collaboration
  benefits of, 23–24, 178
  in contemporary educational practice, 6–11
  elements of, 11–12, 14–16, 49
  explanation of, 29, 35

facilitative dimension of, 40
historical perspective on, 30–31
inclusive approach to, 33–35
information-giving dimension of, 41
multidimensional framework for, 37–38, 43
peer, 151–153, 156, 157
prescriptive dimension of, 41–42
qualities needed for, 16–19
regarding disabled students, 10
in site-based managed schools, 7
supportive dimension of, 38–39
teacher responsibility and, 7–8
use of term, 33, 36
Collaborative consultation
explanation of, 31–32
use of term, 33, 36
Collaborative cultures
establishment of, 19–21
place of collaborative structures in fostering, 21–23
Collaborative inquiry, 201
Collaborative problem solving. *See also* Classroom-specific collaborative problem solving; Schoolwide collaborative problem

solving
achieving balance between classroom-specific and schoolwide, 167–168
categories of, 136
classroom-specific, 137–139
consideration of contributing factors in, 145
evaluation plan for, 147
explanation of, 135–136
general features of, 143–144
generation of possible solutions in, 146
implementation and monitoring of accepted solution in, 147–148
interactions between schoolwide and classroom-specific, 163–167
models for, 149–15
problem articulation in, 144–145
problem pattern statement for, 145–146
relationship between classroom-specific and schoolwide, 141–143
schoolwide, 139–141
selection of alternative solution in, 147
structures to support classroom-spe-

cific, 148–156
structures to support schoolwide, 158–163
Collaborative schools
characteristics of, 159–161
role of peer coaching in, 161–163
Combs, A., 110
Communication
of congruent and incongruent messages, 60–61
cyclical process of, 50–56, 89
during family conferences, 245–246
between family members, 235. *See also* Families
as foundation of collaboration, 62
within groups, 109, 112. *See also* Groups
nonverbal, 58–60
offering support through, 68–69
between schools and families, 237, 247–250. *See also* Families; School-family collaboration
between team teachers, 183–184
verbal, 56–58
Communication barriers
advice as, 90–92
cliches as, 99–101
false reassurances as, 92–94
interruptions as, 98–99

minimizing feelings as, 101–102
misdirected questions as, 95–96
quick fixes as, 102–103
wandering interaction as, 96–98
Communication techniques
clarification as, 76–79
general openings as, 70–71
placing events in context as, 81–82
practice of, 83–84
reflection as, 71–75
silence as, 79–81
stating the implied as, 75–76
summarization as, 82–83
Compromise, 126, 127
Conferences. See Family conferences
Conflict
interpersonal, 121–123
intrapersonal, 120–121
role, 120
types of, 119–120
Conflict resolution
arbitration as, 124–126
explanation of, 123–124
mediation as, 126–127
Congruent messages, 60–61
Conley, S. C., 159
Connotation, 57
Consensus blocking,

121–122
Consultation. See also Collaboration
classrooom-specific collaborative problem solving and, 137
collaborative, 31–32
expert model of, 31, 33
use of term, 33, 36
Context, 81–82
Continuous feedback, 52
Conversational groups, 110
Cook, L., 33, 157
Cooperative learning, 11
Cuban, L., 176
Curriculum
interdisciplinary approaches to, 11
as problem, 164–166
teacher involvement in, 7
team teaching and reform in, 176–178
Curtis, M. J., 148, 155

**D**

Dawe, R., 19, 20
Decision-making groups, 110–111
Demonstration, as element of facilitative collaboration, 40
Denotation, 57
Dettmer, P., 33
DeVita, C. J., 225
Dewey, John, 18–19
Direct feedback, 52–53
Discovery groups, 112
Divorce rate, 225
Dyck, N., 33

**E**

Eavy, P. W., 15, 157
Economic needs, 229–230
Education, collaboration between special and and general, 217
Elementary schools, team teaching in, 192
Elliott, J., 212, 213
Elliott, S. N., 157
Ellis, N. E., 183
Emotional needs, 231–232

**F**

Facilitators
within groups, 116–118
role overload in, 120
False reassurances, 92–94
Families. See also School-family collaboration
adaptability of, 233–235
apathy in, 238–239
characteristics of functional, 235–236
cohesion within, 232–233
communication between schools and, 237, 240–242
definition of, 226–227
logistical problems of, 236–237
needs of, 229–232
role of, 225–226
school rules and,

237–238
as a system, 227–229
teachers and involvement of, 242–243
time constraints in, 239–240
Family conferences. *See also* School-family collaboration
follow-up to, 246
planning for, 244–246
reasons for, 243–244
unplanned, 246–247
Feedback
continuous, 52
direct, 52–53
indirect, 53–54
Fernstrom, P., 148
Friend, M., 33, 157, 174
Fuchs, D., 32, 148, 154
Fuchs, L. S., 32, 148, 154
Fullan, M., 22, 199, 201–202

**G**

Galvin, K. M., 227
General education, collaboration between special and, 217
Glidden, P. A., 124, 126
Gonzalez, N., 238
Good, T. L., 183
Goodlad, J. I., 10, 200, 218, 219
Graden, J. L., 148, 155
Groups
conflict resolution within, 123–127
conflict within, 119–123

functioning stages of, 114–115
responsibilities of individuals in, 116–119
skills for members of, 115–116
structure of, 112–114
types of, 110–111
working effectively within, 127

**H**

Hames, C. C., 49, 110, 112, 113, 115, 121
Hammitte, D., 31
Handbooks, 248
Hargreaves, A., 19, 20
Herbert, E. A., 120
High schools, team teaching in, 193
Holly, P., 210, 212, 213
Hourcade, J., 174
Hovda, R. A., 214

**I**

Idol, L., 31
Incongruent messages, 60–61
Indirect feedback, 53–54
Individualized education program (IEP), 240
Information sharing, 41
Instruction
inclusive, 166
increased complexity of, 10–11
team teaching and responsibility for, 181–183

Instructional groups, 110
Interactions
disruptive, 121–123
wandering, 96–98
Interactive research and development. *See* Action research
Interpersonal conflict, 121–123
Interruptions, 98–99
Intervention assistance teams (IATs)
compared to MATs and TATs, 156, 157
explanation of, 155–156
Intrapersonal conflict, 120–121

**J**

Jensen, M.A.C., 114
Jett-Simpson, M., 203
Johnson, L. J., 9, 15, 31, 32, 37, 40, 144, 145, 148, 151, 153, 212, 217
Joseph, D. H., 49, 110, 112, 113, 115, 121
Joyce, B., 161–162, 185

**K**

Knapp, M. S., 165
Kohl, H., 164
Kolb, D. M., 124, 126
Kroth, R. L., 244
Kyle, D. W., 214

**L**

Lane, V. W., 56, 60
Language. *See also* Communication

components of, 56–58

Leadership
building internal, 208–209
participatory style of, 117
of principal, 159

Levine, M., 10, 202
LeVine, R. A., 226
Lewin, K., 210, 211, 213
Lieberman, A., 210
Lilly, M. S., 30
Listening skills, 67
Little, J. W., 11
Lortie, D., 30
Luterman, David, 235
Lynch, E. W., 236

**M**

Maher, C. A., 119
Mainstream assistance teams (MATs)
compared to IATs and TATs, 156, 157
explanation of, 154–155
Margolis, H., 117, 118, 120, 124
Mason, D. A., 183
McNiff, J., 213
Means, B., 165
Mediation, 126–127
Middle schools, team teaching in, 192–193
Miller, L., 210
Miller, P. M., 226
Miller, S. I., 120
Misdirected questions, 95–96
Moll, L. C., 238
Molyneaux, D., 56, 60
Moultrie, R., 32, 148, 150

**N**

Neff, D., 238
Nevin, A., 31
Newsletters, 248
Noddings, N., 34
Nonverbal communication, 58–60

**O**

Oja, S. N., 210–211, 216
Olson, R. A., 232

**P**

Palincsar, A. S., 40
Paolucci-Whitcomb, P., 31
Peer coaching
explanation of, 40, 162
role of, 161–163
team teaching and, 185
Peer collaboration
compared to other problem-solving models, 156, 157
explanation of, 151–153
Phonology, 57
Physical environment, 113–114
Pine, G. J., 211, 216
Ponti, C. R., 148, 155
Power seeking, 122
Pragmatics, 58
Prereferral intervention, 137, 150
Problem solving
collaborative. *See* Collaborative problem solving

groups specifically for, 111
steps involved in, 144–148
Professional development schools (PDSs). *See also* School-university collaboration
collaborative relationships available within, 207–209
example of day in, 203–206
explanation of, 202–203
guidelines for, 218–219
Progress reports, 248
Pugach, M. C., 15, 31, 32, 37, 40, 144, 148, 151, 153, 177, 180, 189, 203, 212, 217, 218
Purkey, W., 110
Pusch, S. H., 218
Pysh, M. V., 32, 148, 150, 151

**Q**

Questions, misdirected, 95–96

**R**

Reassurances, false, 92–94
Recognition seeking, 122–123
Recreational needs, 231
Reflection
explanation of, 71–72
use of, 72–75
Reflective teaching,

18–19
Regular education initiative (REI), 33
Research. *See* Action research; School-university collaboration
Rigid families, 234
Role ambiguity, 120, 121
Role conflict, 120, 121
Role overload, 120
Rosenholtz, S. J., 11, 159

# S

Scaffolded instruction, 40
Schmidt, P., 36
School-family collaboration. *See also* Families
   barriers identified by families to, 236–238
   barriers identified by professionals to, 238–242
   development of partnerships to institute, 249–250
   family-oriented teachers and, 242–243
   strategies for, 247–249
   use of conferences in, 243–247
Schools. *See also* Collaborative schools; Elementary schools; High schools; Middle schools
   authority structure changes in, 6–7

barriers to family participation in, 236–242
professional development school *vs.* traditional, 202
site-based managed, 6–7
socialization options for families provided by, 230–231
School-university collaboration
   action research and, 209–217. *See also* Action research
   example of, 203–206
   guidelines for, 218–219
   opportunities in, 220
   as reform strategy, 199–200
   teacher development and, 202–203
   tenets of, 200–201
   types of collaboration within, 207–209
Schoolwide collaborative problem solving. *See also* Collaborative problem solving
   achieving balance between classroom-specific and, 167–168
   description of, 139–141
   interactions between classroom-specific and, 163–167
   origins of, 142
   relationship between classroom-specific and, 141–143

structures to support, 158–163
Schrage, M., 12, 15–17
Self-identity, 231
Seligman, M. E., 234, 238
Semantics, 57
Shapiro, A., 117, 118, 120, 124
Showers, B., 161–162, 185
Silence, 79–81
Sirotnik, K. A., 200, 201
Site-based management (SBM)
   commitment to, 159
   explanation of, 6–7
Sizer, T. R., 193, 202
Skrtic, T., 230
Slavin, R. E., 11
Special education, collaboration between general and, 217
Stating the implied, 75–76
Stecker, P. M., 148
Stein, R., 236
Stiegelbauer, S., 22, 199, 201–202
Students
   diversity of, 8–9
   integration of disabled, 9–10
   as problem, 164–166
   shared responsibility for, 179–181
Summarization, 82–83
Summers, J., 228, 230
Support, method of offering, 68–69
Syntax, 57

# T

Teacher assistance teams (TATs)
  compared to other problem-solving models, 156–157
  explanation of, 150–151
Teachers
  action research and collaboration between special and general education, 217
  collaboration between prospective and experienced, 207–208
  collaboration between university faculty and beginning, 208
  environment conducive for change in, 166–167
  family-oriented, 242–243
  increased responsibilities of, 7–8
  isolation in, 30
  team teaching as challenge for, 186–188
  team teaching providing support for, 184–185
Teaching. *See also* Team teaching
  occupation of, 5–6
  reflective, 18–19
  team teaching as challenge to improve, 179
Team teaching
  approaches to setting up, 190–191
  background of, 173–174
  challenges of, 186–188
  as collaboration, 193–194
  as curriculum reform, 176–178
  elementary school, 192
  middle and high school, 192–193
  planning considerations for, 189–190
  principles of, 179–186
  resistance to, 189–190, 194
  working conditions and, 178–179
Telephone conferences, 249
Thomas, K., 121
Thousand, J. S., 178
Thurston, L. P., 33
Time dominating, 123
Tuckman, B. W., 114

Turnbull, A. P., 228, 229–233, 243–247
Turnbull, H. R.,III, 229–233, 243–247

# U

University collaboration. *See* School-university collaboration

# V

Verbal communication, 56–58
Villa, R. A., 178

# W

Wandering interactions, 96–98
Warger, C. L., 15, 145, 157
Wessen, C., 177, 180, 189
West, M., 226
Whipp, J., 203
Witt, J. C., 157
Woodman, R. W., 113, 117, 119, 123

# Z

Zander, A. F., 118
Zins, J. E., 148, 155, 157